Are We Not Men?
We Are Devo!

Jade Dellinger

and

David Giffels

Are We Not Men?
We Are Devo!

Jade Dellinger

and

David Giffels

saf publishing

saf publishing

First published in 2003
by SAF Publishing

SAF Publishing Ltd.
149 Wakeman Road,
London.
NW10 5BH
ENGLAND

email: info@safpublishing.com

www.safpublishing.com

ISBN 0 946719 49 7

Cover photographs: Front cover: Allan Tannenbaum.
                       Back cover and inside flap: Jules Bates

A CIP catalogue record for this book is available from the British Library.

Cover and book design: SAF

Printed in England by the Cromwell Press, Trowbridge, Wiltshire.

"No one can come onto my island without a mask."

Eric Mottram, *Left for California: The Slow Awakening*

KRK Ryden

Acknowledgments:

Many thanks to the following individuals who gave generously of their time for interviews, opened their archives and provided photographs or essential information:

David Allen + Artrouble, Brian Applegate, Arno, Kathy Atkinson, Ed Barger, Walt Batansky, Anita Bates (The Jules Bates Foundation), Robert Bertholf, Richard Blocher, Mykel Board, Joep Bruijnje, Chris Butler, Ralph Carney, Gerald V. Casale, Roger Casale, Buzz Clic, Jim Clinefelter, Cheetah Chrome, Patrick Cullie, Rod Firestone, Harvey Gold, Vernon L. Gowdy III, James Grauerholz, Peter Gregg, Randy Hansen, Don Harvey, Susan Schmidt Horning, Bruce Hensal, Gary Jackett, Donna Kossy, Sammy Larson, Nicky Latzoni, Robert Lewis, Justin Keiser (Kent State Univ. Special Collections/ Library), Jennifer Licitri, Tim Maglione, Susan Massaro Aylward, Alan Mothersbaugh, Jim Mothersbaugh, Robert Mothersbaugh, Sr., Alan Myers, Nick Nicholis, Scott Orsi, Ray Packard, John Petkovic, Michael Pilmer, Rod Reisman, Martin Reymann, Ebet Roberts, KRK Ryden, Rocky Schenck, Klaus Schleusener, Debbie Smith, Rev. Ivan Stang, Allan Tannenbaum, Malcolm Tent, John Thompson (aka - Johnny Dromette), Michael Watters, Fred Weber, Bobbie Watson Whitaker, Rev. Toth Wilder, Rutherford Witthus (Curator of Literary Collections/Edward Dorn Papers at the University of Connecticut's Thomas J. Dodd Research Center), the members of the MSN Spudtalk newsgroup and alt.fan.devo.

For critical feedback and editing assistance the authors would like to thank: Eric Nuzum, Mark Price, Jeff Winner and both Dave Hallbery and Mick Fish at SAF Publishing. The publishers would like to thank Nina Antonia for additional editing.

In addition, Jade would like to acknowledge his parents for their support and encouragement, and his girlfriend Cathy Sowell for her patience and understanding. David gives deepest thanks to Gina, Evan and Lia Giffels for sacrificing their husband and father while he toiled on the Island of Lost Souls.

Without participation from those listed above this effort would not have been possible.

Head:

1966-1976

KRK Ryden

Introduction

"Any false theory is half damned if stated in simple words. It is all damned
if forced to be consistent. It is twice damned when you take off its parade
uniform and make it work."

Dr. B. H. Shadduck, *Jocko-Homo Heavenbound*

This is a story about Devo. It is not *the* story about Devo, because Devo made
truth too slippery to be grasped by a single set of hands. They did that on
purpose. They accepted as a foundation point that objective truth does not
exist. And then they went forth to prove it. If it was a joke, it was meant to be
taken seriously. And if it was serious, it was meant to be laughed at.

Look at studio portraits of the band and try to pick out which member is
which. It's hard to do. Identical uniforms; the same ectomorphic frames. It's a
matter of coincidence that Devo's two leaders, Mark Mothersbaugh and Jerry
Casale, each had a brother in the band named Bob. It's a matter of design that
they became Bob 1 and Bob 2. "They've given me a number but they've taken
away my name," Bob 1 would explain as he sang new subhuman life into
Johnny Rivers' "Secret Agent Man". Look them up in the online version of
Encyclopaedia Britannica: "Biographical information on the group's members
was withheld by Devo to reinforce its mechanistic image."

They wore masks to Thanksgiving dinner. They claimed all to wear the
same size shoe. They said they devolved from a long line of brain-eating apes.

8

They called their music "the important sound of things falling apart." And yet, strangely, they were sincere.

They were five twitchy Ohio boys in yellow synthetic suits, standing on a black plastic stage, misunderstood even as they were embraced. This is the story of the reality they created, the reality they destroyed, and the reality that eventually destroyed them. It is the story of a Plastic Reality.

Take any piece of this and hold it up to the light. The light will shine through and come out a different color on the other side. Ask Jerry Casale, the man who first concocted this elaborate plan in his secret laboratory: "You ask band members the same question, you're going to get four completely different answers if they're not in the same room. You'd read something Bob1 said, something I said, something Mark said about the same concert, and you wouldn't believe that it could possibly even be the same planet. That was the idea."

※ ※ ※

On October 14, 1978, just around midnight, Devo found themselves on a soundstage in New York City, surrounded by other Not-Ready-for-Prime-Time Players, in a confusion of destiny. Lorne Michaels, the producer of *Saturday Night Live*, stood in the wings.

"Ten ... nine ... You guys, there are 10 million people watching, and they wanna be entertained ... eight ... seven ..."

Already, Iggy Pop had tried to horn in on their action. Exiled Sex Pistol Johnny Rotten had been offered as their new lead singer.

"Six ... five ... Don't fucking blow it ... four ..."

A man in Ohio, the father of two of the band members, was nervously eyeing his newly purchased Betamax recorder, ready to capture this moment in a mutated version of the family home movie. A jilted former band member, watching at home, had vowed a "reckoning". And countless young spuds were about to experience their Beatles-on-*Ed Sullivan* moment. Or to be completely freaked out.

"Three ... two ..."

Guest host Fred Willard, star of TV's *Fernwood 2-Nite*, made the slightly bewildered introduction: "Ladies and gentlemen – DEVO!"

"One."

The beginning was the end.

※ ※ ※

This was never even supposed to be a band. This was all about an idea. A highly constructed art school brainstorm that merged acute intellectualism with potty jokes. The Exploding Plastic Inevitable. The MC5 commune.

9

Are We Not Men?

Warhol's Factory. There would be films and poetry, lectures and performance art.

A band? Maybe. But only to provide the soundtrack for the Idea.

De-evolution as a concept was developed years before Devo was a band. It brewed on and around the campus of Kent State University and in basements in Akron, Ohio, as a collective of uncommonly bright, middle-class outsiders explored the notion that humans are evolving in reverse.

Their bibliography includes a bizarre book of quack anthropology called *The Beginning was the End*, written by a man who may or may not have been an ex-Nazi hiding out in South America. The author, Oscar Kiss Maerth (whose name may or may not be a pun on Oscar Kiss My Ass), posits that human intelligence came about because cannibalistic apes ate one another's brains, leading to accelerated intellectual development but also the inevitable demise of the species.

It includes a 1948 *Wonder Woman* comic that featured a De-evolution machine.

It includes an obscure religious pamphlet called *Jocko-Homo Heavenbound*.

The seminal moment came at 12:24 p.m. on May 4, 1970, when a firing line of Ohio National Guardsmen cut loose into a Kent State campus hillside full of Vietnam war protesters and curious onlookers. Four were killed; nine were injured. Two of the dead were friends of Jerry Casale. He watched them fall.

"All I can tell you is that it completely and utterly changed my life. I was white hippie boy and then I saw exit wounds from M1 rifles out of the backs of two people I knew," he later said. "That day was Devo. It might have been the most Devo day in my life."

Legend has it that a day before she was shot, Allison Krause, Jerry's friend, slipped a flower into the barrel of a National Guardsman's rifle. "Flowers are better than bullets," she said. In a way, Devo pulled the trigger on that flower. For all the jokes, there would always be a deadly seriousness to Devo.

Still – this is not what gets one on *Saturday Night Live*.

Somewhere along the way, the rotating, mutating membership of Devo clicked. Devolved Lennon met mutated McCartney.

In this case, Lennon was Gerald V. Casale, a graphic arts and literature major who shoveled the gravel into Devo's Vaseline. Casale was brilliant and abrasive, the leader of the early de-evolution think tank.

McCartney was Mark Mothersbaugh, two years younger, a sensitive, talented artist who liked to perform in a strangely frightening ape mask.

Jack Sprat could eat no fat; his wife could eat no lean. But in between the two of them, they licked the platter clean.

The chemistry between these two contrary forces was something like the chemistry being practiced in the polymer labs that dotted the landscape of Akron, the Rubber Capital of the World. In the Devo laboratory, the two elements created a strange and wonderful new plastic.

The sharp-witted, confrontational Jerry was the obvious front man. The soft-spoken, arty Mark was not. Somehow it got worked out. "They had a lot of ideas and no talent," Mark once said, laughing, "and I had a lot of talent and no ideas." They added their brothers Bob. The final piece came in the form of a kick-ass drummer, Alan Myers, "the human metronome." Suddenly, the band that had been noodling around with ideas, weird mechanical sounds, and intentionally off-putting stage shows became tight and urgent. And for a time, everybody wanted them.

With the exception of Kiss, no successful band in rock history has managed so thoroughly to be all about a concept and also to flat-out rock. Ignore for a moment the later synthetic pop albums and roll tape backward to that October night in 1978.

Devo rocked. Devo embodied and projected the image of what a postpunk, new wave band should be – quirky and frantic, tuneful and thoughtful, raw and impossible to ignore. Even now, they seem new.

Some of America that night was inspired. Neil Young, Nirvana, Soundgarden, Beck, Moby, Henry Rollins, Rage Against the Machine – all would later pay homage to Devo. But probably most of America was wondering what the hell had just happened in the middle of their Saturday night.

This was the beginning of something. But built into Devo's DNA was its own demise. The beginning was the end.

As the band wormed their way through the pop culture consciousness of the 1980s, they innovated the art of music video. They pushed limits of performance and technology. Jim Mothersbaugh, the band's one-time drummer and later engineer, built one of the first electronic drum sets from scratch and helped create the MIDI technology that made modern electronic music possible. The band inspired one of Neil Young's greatest albums and provided its title, *Rust Never Sleeps*. They conceived the first 3-D live concert as a pay-per-view event. They urged a subgroup of a generation to think about its condition in the world. They helped nerds realize they had power. Here was a great rock band that destroyed the notion of rock glamour. They made homeliness and awkwardness and even nearsightedness seem cool. And, yeah, they wore those red flowerpot hats and sang "Whip It". Devo was a lot of things. But they were not disposable.

So now it can be told. This is the first comprehensive history of a band that was often misunderstood, that sometimes shot itself in the foot, and that manipulated the System as much as the System manipulated it. Is this the truth about de-evolution? Only if you understand Plastic Reality. For Devo, the idea of truth was literally incomplete. Their spelling of the word "true" was "tru."

But, as faithfully as facts will allow, this is a story of five spuds from an industrial wasteland with big ideas. It never should have happened. But it did. And in its wake, it leaves a parable.

Eventually, the band would ease backward. The music would become less interesting. The drummer would leave. They would make bad choices, recording lyrics by John Hinckley Jr. and the theme song to *Doctor Detroit*. The industry would cast them into exile. Machines would take over. The idea would not advance.

In the end, Devo was a microcosm of their own highly defined idea. Devo devolved. Devo ate their own brain. And who could blame them? It was one of the most delicious brains in rock history.

Chapter 1

1966

Gerald Vincent Casale walks into the Commuter's Cafeteria, in a far corner of the Kent State University student union. He is wearing a clingy fabric shirt with pirate sleeves, mod trousers with a slight flare at the bottom and a Prince Valiant haircut. He seems to understand that Brian Jones was the coolest Stone. "Lady Jane" and all that. He is neat. He is composed. He is sure of himself, even as he is surrounded by fatigued and paint-splattered beatniks, artists and poets. He is one of them, and yet he seems different somehow. He appears to know the answer to a question that has not yet been asked.

There is a young man at one of the tables, tapping away at his portable typewriter. A woman smoking a cigarette. A few people talking. Down the hall, in the "Hub," are jocks and frat boys and other assorted straights eating burgers and fries. They want nothing to do with these Commuter's Cafeteria freaks. Behind this room at the farthest end of the union is a set of glass doors that overlooks the student commons, a grassy area where, four years later, history would begin and all of this end.

The Commuter's Cafeteria has become a center of intellectual activity on a campus that is quickly maturing as an unlikely Mecca of sexy intellectualism, drugs and rock and roll. LSD is cheap; street-corner hits are less than a buck. Low-grade pot is as common as college-ruled paper. There's an established beatnik culture; young people in fatigue jackets and peacoats, people who write poetry and talk about art and revolution in that *particular* way. Some wear berets. A guy named Joe Walsh is playing with a local band called the Measles, one of the many blues and rock bands growing like magic mushrooms down on Water Street, the main bar strip. Kent is in Northeast Ohio, 20 minutes from Akron, 45 minutes from Cleveland. More importantly, it lies in the pathway of east-to-west – New York to Chicago; Los Angeles to New York. Kent is, to Jerry Casale's mind, the middle of nowhere. But that's not exactly true. It is in the middle of somewhere. But nobody knows where that is yet. That's the question that has not yet been asked.

The highest compliment you can get from Jerry is a laugh. If you can make him laugh, you have hit on something. The square-cut bangs of that Prince Valiant hairdo form a lintel over a heavy brow. His eyes are dark, but when his face breaks into its smile, there is something wild and incisive. Almost immediately, and not by accident, he becomes a dominant force at the Commuter's Cafeteria. The cafeteria has five tables; two or three are informally reserved for this clique. Any time of day, they are occupied. Jerry becomes a regular.

Are We Not Men?

The young man at the typewriter has a huge mustache and thick, curly hair. He is wearing bell bottoms. His name is Bob Lewis. He is cool. He drives a Madeira red 1965 Chevy Biscayne 283 cubic inch V-8 with three-on-the-tree. He loves his car. He, too, is a leader. Like Jerry, he's remarkably smart, born and bred in this corner of Ohio, but seeming like he should have come from somewhere else. Bob is on a National Merit scholarship; Jerry is in the honors college. Bob is studying anthropology; Jerry is studying graphic design. Which seems about right. Bob watches people and tries to understand them. Jerry is clean and ordered. He understands how to distill a message. If you say something about a complex subject that seems to drive its nail, you can get Jerry to laugh.

There's something sinister behind that laugh sometimes. Maybe it's just the way he is. He was always different, always up to something.

❋ ❋ ❋

Bob Lewis probably didn't belong in Kent. He had attended Cuyahoga Falls High School, where he was an outstanding student. He had won a National Merit Scholarship and had been accepted at the University of Chicago and Princeton. His counselor, whom Bob describes as a slightly brain-damaged wrestling coach, had neglected to mention that Pepperdine, another school that had accepted him, was in Malibu. So, while he could have been learning to surf, he instead chose to go to a state university 20 minutes from home. The reason for his choice was honorable enough. He was in love. His girlfriend of three years, a girl named Buffy, had enrolled at Kent State. Bob followed, and was promptly dumped by Buffy for a frat boy halfway through the first semester. So he turned his attention to the culture around him. Bob already had a certain style. As early as ninth grade, he had accompanied his older brother to a Cleveland venue called the Jazz Temple to see John Coltrane and Cannonball Adderley.

So it seems obvious that he would become a key figure in the Commuter's Cafeteria crowd. A young woman named Bobbie Watson, a local homecoming queen on a scholarship, developed a crush on him. He had the bell-bottoms, the hair, and the youthful sophistication.

"I didn't know him really," she said, "but sensed that if I did, the world would make more sense to me. I was right – big questions about what it's all about were answered."

The group that congealed there in the bowels of the Kent student union began to discuss the world, what seemed right about it and, more importantly, what seemed wrong. Jerry Casale was especially good at pinpointing what seemed wrong.

❋ ❋ ❋

"Biology is destiny," Jerry once said. "I was born Devo." This may be true. But sticking for the moment to the literal, he was born Gerald Vincent Pizzute at 12:53 p.m. on July 28, 1948, at Robinson Memorial Hospital in Ravenna, just a few miles from the Kent State campus. The birth came almost nine months to the day from the wedding of Patrick and Catherine Pizzute. According to the family's account, his mother's labor was induced by the trauma of seeing her sister suffer a violent epileptic fit. Jerry came six weeks premature.

As will become clear, the notion of de-evolution can be applied to most things, including the family name. Jerry's father, a tool and die man at the Colonial Machine Co. in Kent, had been born Robert Edward Casale in Cleveland to unwed parents. In 1946, he had his name legally changed to Pasquale (anglicized to Patrick) Pizzute, adopting the surname of his foster parents. Then, in 1952, he changed names again, back to Robert Edward Casale. Amid the name changes came joy and tragedy for the young couple. A pair of twins was born 12 minutes apart in 1951; neither survived. The following year, on July 14, Robert Edward Casale Jr. was born. (In the family tradition of name changes, he would eventually become Bob 2.)

The family grew, with younger siblings trailing behind the two brothers. One after another, they entered the eight-classroom St. Patrick's School in the shadow of a Gothic church on Portage Street in Kent. There were nuns in the shadowy hallways, kids crying and puking. When a student threw up, the janitor followed behind, spreading a pungent green-and-orange sawdust material to soak it up. Jerry, to keep from gagging, would walk down the hall with his head tilted upward. It was through this process that he became aware of – and eventually fascinated by – the art deco light fixtures, which looked like round upside-down pyramids. These ziggurats, and the experience they recalled, made an impression that would stick.

Jerry has carefully controlled the details of his personal story through the years, and admits outright that many of the answers he's given are fictionalized to support the purpose of image manipulation. But when asked about a recurring theme in lyrics like "Break your momma's back," and "Slap your mammy," by an Australian radio interviewer, Jerry half-heartedly confessed, "You've discovered a central problem. Devo was never loved by their mothers." Following a show billed as Devo's "Homecoming Concert" at the Akron Civic Theatre on Jan. 4, 1979, he went so far as to say he wished he'd never known his mother and referred to his aunts, uncles and other attending relatives as the entire "spud gene pool."

"It's like you're born to your parents by accident," he said in a 1980 interview. "Maybe you're not the kind of person they would associate with if you didn't happen to be blood. So here they are forced to be nice to somebody that maybe they wouldn't even want to know. It goes the other way around. So there you are, stuck. I wish no one knew their parents. It's a burden."

Maybe Jerry was loved by his mother. Probably he was. But he grew into the kind of person who would say he was not.

"I don't really know what his home life was like," next-door neighbor and later (brief) bandmate Rod Reisman recalled. "I don't know how he and his mother got along. I don't know how he and his father got along, but Jerry was not a normal person. Of course, that doesn't make him a bad person or a weirdo. I just think there were certain aspects of his personality that he let come out. Somebody else might repress them, while Jerry would say, 'This is a crazy idea. Check this out.'"

At St. Patrick's, the subversive, nonconformist Jerry began to emerge. He would hide out of sight of the nuns, making faces and gesticulating to make the other kids laugh. As early as fifth grade, it was evident to classmates that Jerry was a gifted artist. As his boyhood friend Tim DeFrange recalled, "If drawing was a way of seeing, Jerry had 20-20 vision." Their favorite singing nun, Sister Ann Therese HM, organized a poster-making competition. The theme was forest fire prevention, and young Jerry's illustration of two frolicking squirrels with the caption, "Save Our Friends!" took second place. But it was the hands-down popular favorite.

Soon, this technical facility began to merge with a growing perspective on the world. Jerry began to define targets. And more targets. And more targets, saving some of them the way his woodland friends saved nuts.

"I never had a good time because of how horrible people were," he would later say. "The kids in my class, the teachers, the local scene. (You never knew) what you might get beat up for. You'd try to leave school, and the greasers would stand on the corner with a bicycle chain or something and make you pay them a nickel to pass. And you always felt uneasy." He told a story later, most probably false, about how, at age 16, he had his teeth knocked out by a "subhuman delinquent" nicknamed Baby Huey. Once again, the notion of the picked-on outsider became an important part of the Jerry Casale – and Devo – myth. What Jerry claims is often more telling than actual fact. There is a certain kind of truth in his fabrications. In a mutated version of the Kiss Army, Jerry was learning how to groom an entire class of misfits and nerds (the vast majority of most student populations) into his own cult of followers. Sure, Jerry may not have had his teeth knocked out by a bully. Most of us didn't. But we can certainly relate to the idea, and are willing to rally around an artist who seems to be speaking for all of us poor, persecuted souls.

Jerry made the switch from Catholic to public school at the beginning of the 1960s, when he entered Davey Junior High. The school was named after the prominent family that founded the Davey Tree Company. In their honor, Kent is nicknamed Tree City. (The small town even has its own arborist.) At Davey, Jerry's personality really took hold. "Jerry was punk before punk was cool," his friend and later musical collaborator Peter Gregg recalled. "Before he knew what it was going to be, he was it. I knew it from the first time I saw him in the halls of the school. Jerry was the evil good boy from Day One. Walking elderly women across the street only to find out where their daughters would be later that night. No one had their guards up. Who knew? This was Ohio, for God's sake. We grow sweet corn. Jerry was always up to badness in the Midwest, Catholic frat-boy-gone-bad way. He did pass at a glance from a distance to the unsuspecting, however; any skirt he was seriously trolling knew he was threatening. If not, her friends would quickly swoop in and set her straight. That's why predators have such a large territory."

Jerry and Peter, two years his junior, quickly became friends. Jerry, passing Peter's study hall one afternoon, spotted his pal and began gesturing through the doorway. Peter tried to contain his laughter, but finally gave in. Both boys dug the rawer edge of the British invasion, the Yardbirds and the Rolling Stones. Jerry began calling his friend "Peter Noone," after the Herman's Hermits singer. They were both wild, but in different ways. Peter would do crazy James Brown moves at school dances. They understood one another, which was good. Because, even then, they were growing away from the usual course of life in Tree City.

"Jerry knew Devo from the earliest," Peter says. "It was not a college art project for the masses, rather an attempt to save lives – his and some others. My guess for the starting point from which Jerry drove down the Devo road is St. Pat's in Kent, Ohio. (And it began) probably in the sixth grade. Somewhere in between the sisters driving nails through his palms and ankles at every chance and the girl across the row from him running up to tell the sisters what Jerry had just asked her to do in the dark and private cloak room."

❀ ❀ ❀

For a teenager in Kent, life was distilled into a series of pictures and half-understood ideas. Something was happening on Friday nights down on Water Street, but that was a distant and exotic realm. Life instead trickled from record players and TV sets. Cleveland was the region's media center, offering the usual three television networks corralled by rabbit ears and roof antennae. In 1963, a strange set of waves crossed those antennae. A Cleveland TV announcer named Ernie Anderson had been asked to host a late-night horror-movie show. He didn't want to do it. So, to preserve some modicum of dignity, he pulled a fright wig over his head, taped a cheesy Van Dyck beard to his chin, slipped into a lab coat and became Ghoulardi. He walked onto the set of Cleveland's WJW-Channel 8 and, introduced by Duane Eddy's "Desert Rat", launched into a cool beatnik spiel, sitting on a stool smoking a cigarette, with cheap lighting effects to make him look spooky.

"Hey, group," he'd begin at 11:20 p.m., in his sultry, back-alley voice. "Would ya believe, tonight we've got Vincent Price in *The House on Haunted Hill*. This movie is so bad, you cats should just go to bed."

The show was called *Shock Theater*. It debuted on January 18, 1963 and, almost overnight (and to the surprise and partial dismay of Anderson) became a regional sensation. Friday nights became Ghoulardi nights, as he wrapped his act around movies like *Attack of the 50 Foot Woman*, *The Return of Dr. X* and, most importantly to the future members of Devo, *Island of Lost Souls*, an adaptation of an H.G. Wells novel about genetic manipulation. One of the technological "innovations" Ghoulardi employed was to insert himself into the films through the use of a blank blue background, overlaying his image into the on-screen action. He would shrink in feigned horror from the 50 Foot Woman, or pretend to tickle one of the characters. In the background, he played novelty songs and surf and garage rock – things like the Baskerville Hounds' "Space Rock, Parts One and Two". He was an anarchist, using his popularity as a shield to run roughshod over station management. He lit firecrackers in the studio and rode a motorcycle through the hallways. All of these things landed directly in Devo's bag of tricks.

"The interesting aspect, I believe, was the willingness of locals to put out what *they* thought was funny or entertaining, coming up with what was really a new art form," Bob Lewis observed. "The irreverent humor of Northeast Ohio was also evidenced by... the famous Mad Daddy (Pete Myers, thrown off WHK radio in Akron for announcing 'The One-Eyed One Horned Flying Purple Peter Eater.') Myers was a radio phenomenon – who hosted shows and had a fabulous spiel – 'Let the Mellow Jello Flow!'... This all contributed to the particular kind of humor which helped form Devo's black humor."

Mad Daddy Myers had also previously hosted a B-movie program, but with nowhere near the success of Anderson. The Ghoulardi catch phrases – "stay sick," "turn blue" and "purple knif" ("fink" spelled backwards) – would become part of the native tongue among people of a certain age.

Shock Theater lasted only until 1966, when Anderson left for a successful career as a Los Angeles voice-over artist. He became the voice of ABC – that was him crooning the syllables of *The Loooove Boat*. But at the height of his Cleveland reign, an estimated 80 percent of the televisions turned on in Northeast Ohio were tuned to Ghoulardi.

Ghoulardi would have an endearing and enduring effect on this most important generation of Northeast Ohio rockers. Erick Purkhiser, who grew up in Stow, right next to Kent, would soak up the B-movie kitsch and spew it out as Lux Interior, his Cramps' alter-ego. The Cramps' album *Stay Sick!* is a direct homage to Ghoulardi. (And the song "Mad Daddy" gave props to Pete Myers.)

Lesser-known bands did the same. The Easter Monkeys, a post-punk, grave-digging garage band whose lineup included Pere Ubu's Jim Jones, snorted a big dose of the horror-show mystique, writing a song that included the lyrics, "Stay sick, turn blue, Ghoulardi's been waiting up for you." A tall, lumbering Akron scenester who went by the stage name "Orbit" moved to California and formed a band called Orbit and the Purple Knifs. A surf-rockabilly band in New York (via Akron) was called Purple Knif. And Michael Weldon, publisher of *Psychotronic* magazine and one of the foremost authorities on B-movie culture (and Ghoulardi), was also a player in three of Cleveland's most important pre-punk bands – the Mirrors, Styrenes and Ex-Blank-Ex. Filmmaker Jim Jarmusch was watching, too, from his home in Cuyahoga Falls, not far from where Mark Mothersbaugh and his brothers were growing up. Jarmusch's black-and-white vision of an otherworldly America captured on film what others were spewing onto audiotape.

"We were the Ghoulardi kids," said Pere Ubu singer David Thomas. "It's been suggested by any number of us that the Cleveland/Akron (musical) event of the early '70s was attributable in large part to his influence. I was ten in 1963 when he went on air and thirteen when he left Cleveland in 1966. After him I believe that I could only have perceived the nature of media and the possibilities of the narrative voice in particular ways. Describing how he devastated the authority of the media, and of the Great and the Good, how he turned the world upside down, would take too long and would be too hard to translate – a dumb slogan or two, some primitive blue screen technique, and a couple firecrackers for 90 minutes on the TV every Friday night, how unsafe could that be? You have no idea. He was the Flibberty Jib Man."

The Ghoulardi aesthetic seemed to capture a much broader and more significant notion: Akron and Cleveland *were* a noirish sci-fi movie. In Cleveland, it was steel. In Akron, rubber. But both places were defined by aging brick factories with round chimneys that breathed fire and smoke. In Akron, housewives went out in the morning after their tire-building husbands had departed for the first shift and swept black "snow" from the doorstep. The powder was the ubiquitous carbon black that settled from the air. Other-worldly zeppelins and blimps lolled in the gray sky, as if this were Bela Lugosi's wet dream.

In Akron, a man who wore a hat and had a job and brought home the bacon could wake up at a house in Goodyear Heights, settle into a car with Goodyear tires, drive down Goodyear Boulevard to the Goodyear factory, grab a quick haircut at the Goodyear barbershop before clocking in at the Goodyear plant, then drive home later with the Goodyear blimp watching from above.

The windows in the Akron rubber factories were painted green, giving an eerie haze to the light inside. In the labs alongside them, rubber and polymer scientists worked with beakers and test tubes to create a new synthetic America. "Polymer Love" would be one of Jerry Casale's first significant artistic statements, a treatise on sex and technology that wallowed delightfully through the symbolism of his surroundings. He had an eye for these things, tuned in part by Ghoulardi.

The industrial landscape "worked as an art-directed backdrop for this kind of music we were making," Jerry said years later. "It had this hellish, depressing patina, this kind of dirty latex layer that fills the air, and the people in Akron seemed – their spirits were depressed; they were desperate; their kids were kind of like the characters in *Island of Lost Souls* that rebelled in the pit. In other words, they were just ready to go over the edge at any moment. They were so beaten down that they were gonna freak out. And it fit in with the early-20th century art movements – Expressionism, Dada and others that were influenced by those kinds of environments in Germany and England. We had our very own backyard version of it. A rubber version."

Jerry was a sharp kid. This stuff was worming through his brain as he began attending Kent's Roosevelt High School in 1962. He became active in theater, a member of the Drama Guild and National Thespians. He was vice president of the Christian Hi-Y club and art editor for his senior yearbook, the 1966 *Rough Rider*. But he was still Jerry, dirtied up by the Yardbirds and the Rolling Stones. So, as yearbook committee members were mulling over which pictures of the track team and cheerleading squad to include, Jerry convinced them to publish a photograph of him playing harmonica, Dylanstyle.

Someone once suggested that Devo began with the 1970, Kent State shootings.

"Wrong," Peter Gregg responded. "It's true that the events of May 4, 1970 and their aftermath cemented Jerry's anger and focused his belief that human dignity is a feeble thing. But those ideas already had a strong foundation.

"The event moved Jerry more than I know," Gregg continued, "but then again, the prom moved Jerry more than I know. He and I spoke about that event at the time and (have) over the years, and the event was not the start."

Baby Huey won round one, figuratively knocking out Jerry's teeth. But

Jerry was learning how to work the body. His sense of how to infiltrate an audience was forming; his talent for mockery, manipulation and dark mischief was sharpening. He was going to mess with the spuds, and they were gonna like it. The Class of '66 gathered in the Roosevelt gymnasium for senior's day. Jerry got up on the stage and led the group in a rousing rendition of Bob Dylan's "Rainy Day Women #12 & 35", with its subversive "everybody must get stoned" chorus. Jocks sang; straight kids sang; even some of the teachers sang. There was power in this, a subversive power that Jerry was learning and teaching at the same time.

"Obviously, (high school) was a horrible and disgusting experience," Jerry reflected. "The people who were held up to you as model students – three years later they were fat and married. The teachers were either incompetents or had real personality disorders. You had to be an alien – just observing."

He put a band together and started playing Rolling Stones, Muddy Waters and John Lee Hooker covers. Jerry was becoming a hoochie-coochie man. The band was called The Satisfied Mind, a name that seems at once mod, rocker and very, very Jerry.

Chapter 2

"At first it all seemed like perfection. I traveled through space in a completely self-sufficient capsule... experiencing total satisfaction. But in only nine short months, I found out my 'beautiful capsule' was in reality a disgusting toilet through which blood water and convulsions vomited me out into the atmosphere... condemning me to decay and die... the ribbon of time flowed one direction and there was no returning... for... IN THE BEGINNING WAS THE END."

– from *My Struggle*, by Booji Boy, a.k.a. Mark Mothersbaugh

Little Mark Mothersbaugh got a Mr. Potato Head. It was his seventh birthday, and there is ancient 8-millimeter film of this event. In the jumpy home movie, Mark is holding up the kit for his father's camera while his kid brother Bobby screams in the background. Mr. Potato Head was different back then. In the 1950s, you opened up the box to find a plastic body with a spike neck to hold a real potato. You made the faces by piercing the vegetable's skin with eyes and ears and big cartoon smiles. There was a mustache and a pipe, eyeglasses and a hat. Very few toys before or since have made such significant use of root vegetables.

Hasbro offered children the opportunity to create their own postwar nuclear family from a sack of spuds. In 1953, Mr. Potato Head married Mrs. Potato Head. In the wholesome Midwestern tradition, they began producing offspring. Brother Spud and Sister Yam came along a short time later, the first baby boomers to actually be dug from the earth. Hasbro outfitted the growing family with cars and appliances, even a boat. The Potato Heads were able to live the American dream.

Hasbro claims Mr. Potato Head was the first children's toy ever advertised on television. Mattel disputes this, insisting its Mickey Mouse guitar preceded it. Such corporate squabbling aside, it seems perfect that the first two toy commercials little Mark could have seen were for a guitar and a spud.

With that early Mr. Potato Head, every face was different, because every potato is different. This made quite an impression on young Mark. There was something human about the creative process, which transformed a child into a mad scientist-cum-plastic surgeon. Mark and Bobby were fond of making their potatoes fight. Stirred by the battle, they took bites out of their characters. "I still like the taste of raw potatoes," Mark would later observe.

That year, 1957, was an important one for Mark. In addition to Mr. Potato Head, he got his first pair of eyeglasses. Until then, his severe nearsightedness led adults to believe he was an unruly child. He got in people's faces when they spoke to him. He sat directly in front of the television. He was distracted in school, never seemed to pay any attention to the chalkboard. As a result, he was often punished. Finally, it occurred to someone at the school to have Mark's eyes tested. They discovered he was legally blind; he couldn't see more than a few inches in front of him. The day he left the optometrist's office, Mark's world changed. Through those Coke-bottle lenses, suddenly, he could see trees, clouds, chimneys, birds. "Gee, dad," he said walking outside for the first time with glasses, "is that what a jet stream is?"

Until then, when Mark drew pictures, images were of what people told him things looked like. He had never had any direct sense of artistic representation. There was a filter on everything. After he got his glasses, he began to draw trees. No other child in his class could understand why this act was so precious to him. He drew them over and over. His teacher, Mrs. Avery, said, "Why, Mark, you draw trees better than me." Mark began to dream of being an artist. At the time, he thought that being a great artist meant drawing trees better than anyone else, even the teacher. What he didn't realize was that *not* being able to see the trees for seven years probably affected his artistic vision more profoundly than anything else. His later interest in surrealism had a root in his early nearsighted existence.

Ed Barger, a Devo friend, patron and sound man, later wrote and recorded a song with Mark called "Lost at Home".

"I wrote it thinking about Mark being a baby and not able to see," Barger said. "I'm lost at home / Crawled through all the rooms / I fit in none..."

Like all the best Devo music, this song blends a childlike vision with cynicism. The primal and the intelligent. It's constantly moving forward and back. "It's a beautiful world for you... not me."

❀ ❀ ❀

Mark Allen Mothersbaugh was born May 18, 1950, at Akron City Hospital. He grew up in Cuyahoga Falls, a small city of less than 50,000 that borders Akron. His father, Robert Mothersbaugh, had served in World War II and attended college after his discharge, studying electronics before switching to social science. He had a very warm personality, and loved his children dearly. So it's probably not surprising that this man who had an affinity for making home movies would later have the tables turned and become an ongoing character in the Devo films. He would don an Army uniform and helmet to become General Boy, not because he had a rock'n'roll jones, but because he believed in his children's wacky ideas and would do anything to help them.

After college, Robert Mothersbaugh spent a year vagabonding in Mexico. But there was a girl back home in Akron who he couldn't get out of his mind. Her name was Mary Margaret Ratzer, a secretary who played piano for her church Sunday school department. "It was either, 'Go home and marry her, or let her marry someone else,'" Robert recalled. "I decided I wanted to get married." He left his wandering shoes in Mexico and returned to Ohio, where he took a job as a regional sales rep for Life Savers Candy Company. Robert and Mary honeymooned in Windsor, Canada. They had planned to wait a couple of years before starting a family, but romance intervened. Mark was born nine months after the honeymoon.

The family grew. Robert Leroy Mothersbaugh Jr. (later Bob 1) was born Aug. 11, 1952. (The same year as Mr. Potato Head.) James Michael Mothersbaugh came along in January 1954, and their sisters Sue and Amy followed. While their mother was busy with diapers and baby food, their father moved through a succession of sales jobs, leaving Life Savers to work for a book company, then a fire equipment company. He had a strong work ethic and a regard for positive thinking, honed through sales seminars and common sense. While the song "Whip It" is commonly regarded as a paean to masturbation and/or sado-masochism, it is actually derived from Dad's maxims. "If a problem comes along, you must whip it." Self-reliance is the way to salvation.

The Mothersbaughs, helped out by Robert's G.I. Bill money, bought a house in Cuyahoga Falls. As they furnished it, he decided to include a keyboard and bought a Hammond Spinet organ. Mary played in the evenings with the kids, banging out church songs and old standards. As the kids grew older, a woman named Mrs. Fox was hired to come to the house once a week

23

to teach piano. One after another, the children each sat down for a half-hour lesson, with Mrs. Fox patiently positioning their fingers on the keys. It took a good two hours to get through the brood. Mark played for his parents – church hymns and "Autumn Leaves"; "Ebb Tide" and "Row, Row, Row Your Boat".

"I hated it," Mark said. "I thought music was a punishment to keep me from playing with my friends. That's how it felt until I was watching *The Ed Sullivan Show* and the Beatles came on. It was like someone took a gun and aimed an information bullet and shot it into my head."

He was 13 at the time, and had about seven years of bad organ under his belt.

"I thought, 'This is what I want to do.' So my friend Ronnie (Weizyncki) and I bought *A Hard Day's Night* music book. We sat around this tiny organ in my parents' living room. He had this accordion and we were reading sheet music: 'It's been a hard day's night and I've been working.' We thought, 'This doesn't sound right.' After a week, we came to this horrible realization that we had learned the wrong instruments all this time. We were depressed, but it all came clear about a week later.

"I hear Ed Sullivan go, 'Back by popular demand, the Beatles!' All of a sudden, there is John Lennon sitting down behind a little portable organ, a Vox Continental. They played 'Help' and 'I'm Down'. He's playing with his elbow, up and down the keys. I'm going, 'Oh my God – I finally figured it out.'"

Mrs. Fox had never mentioned any of this.

Little Mark had to get his hands on a Beatles record. So he scratched together his pennies and asked his dad to take him to the music store to buy the latest release by the insects from Liverpool. They went to the store, and there it was – the album cover with the four shadow-lit figures in black turtlenecks and shag haircuts. "I Want to Hold Your Hand," was printed in orange above the photo. "The Original Liverpool Sound" was printed below. Mark rushed home, pulled the record from the sleeve, carefully placed it on the turntable, dropped the needle and… something wasn't right. This did not sound like the band on Ed Sullivan. Mark picked up the cover.

The Beetle Beat. He read closer. This wasn't the Beatles. It was some knock-off called the Buggs, with intentionally deceiving packaging. Mark would carry the frustrating memory of this fake band; more than ten years later, he would write a song called "U Got Me Bugged".

Undaunted and still inspired, Mark began looking for people to form a band with. Of course, he already had two built-in recruits. Bobby had a general idea that he wanted to rock, but he had a little learning to do. First, he asked his parents for a sitar. So they bought him a sitar. Then he stripped all but six strings to try to make it into a guitar. His parents were kind enough to correct the mistake by giving him a real guitar. He's left-handed, but when he taught himself to play, using the bits of theory he'd learned in his organ lessons, he came out as a right-handed guitarist. Jim, recognizing the natural order in this, soon requested a drum set for his birthday.

"It just so happened that one of my best friends owned a music store in Cuyahoga Falls," their father recalled. "So that helped. I'm not talking like I had money to throw out left and right, don't get me wrong. I had to measure all these investments. All of a sudden, we had three kids in the basement that were a trio – a group, and they were kicking it around with some music, and other kids were showing up."

Bob began picking out Chuck Berry and Rolling Stones bits on his guitar. Very soon, he began putting rock swagger into his repertoire. He learned how to mimic Pete Townshend's windmill arm sweep, a far more important discovery than anything in those years of Mrs. Fox's piano theory.

"You know, I think we always just expected it was gonna happen ever since we were little kids," Jim Mothersbaugh recalled. "I don't think Mark had a real job until he started getting involved in music. So, I mean, we took it really seriously. We spent a lot of time looking at everything about music and studying different musicians. We didn't quite know what would happen with Devo, but we knew something was there and it was worth the attention."

Actually, Mark did have at least one "real" job. When he was in grade school, his father went down to the local hardware store – one of his favorite places – and cut a little deal. He told the owners that if they hired Mark, he would pay all his son's wages out of his own pocket. He wanted Mark to learn the work ethic that was so important to him.

"He would go to the hardware store, and go to work," Robert Mothersbaugh said. "He was very proud, and I was kind of bragging him up to everybody else (the younger siblings). 'You know, Mark's doing it, and you know, one of these days, you'll get a job.' They were never on an allowance. There was always work to do."

The household was taking on an increasingly eclectic tone. Rock in the rec room, pull-yourself-up-by-the-bootstraps aphorisms around the dining room table. Potato fights. And animals. The family had a menagerie of odd pets. There were crows that had their tongues split to allow them a further range of sounds. The crows tried to talk and the kids tried to understand them. There were flying squirrels. There was a monkey. All of these things were being absorbed into Mark's fertile mind – especially the monkey. He would later start wearing an ape mask as part of his everyday wardrobe, and monkeys would populate his song lyrics and artistic imagery.

As he played around with different musicians, Mark began to broaden his tastes and his chops. In high school he took some basic lessons on jazz improvisation, which further cracked open the possibilities that had begun with Ed Sullivan and the Beatles. Around this time, he hooked up with a girl from nearby Firestone High School in Akron, really pretty, but also kind of hardened despite her young age. She was way into rock and R&B stuff. She wanted to front a band, but she was so shy at the time that everyone would have to play in the next room while she sang, sitting on top of the washing machine. A few years later, as she came out of her shell, everyone who'd listen would get to hear about how she was planning to be a rock star. Well, of course, why not? They were all, in some aspect, planning to be rock stars. Otherwise, why would Bobby have learned how to strike his guitar strings as his arm swung an arc through the air? The girl's name was Chris Hynde, the younger sister of a sax player named Terry, who would soon crack into the Kent music scene. She was slender, with a brown shag haircut. She liked to hang out in downtown Akron, which she perceived as a romantic and slightly dangerous place. She loved the train station. It seemed like those trains might be going to London or Paris, and maybe one day she would board one of them. Eventually she did get out of town, settling in London, where her band the Pretenders did finally make her a star.

Mark and Chris had a band called Sat Sun Mat (after a movie theater ad for weekend matinees). It didn't last long, but it was an early star-crossing in a series of such encounters that would continue for both of them.

Meanwhile, Mark's technical skill in art was being honed. By the time he entered Woodridge High School in 1964, his teachers were encouraging him to focus on this talent. One teacher in particular, Nancy Brown Fidler, became a mentor. Mark studied painting and sculpture, commercial art, printmaking and anatomy. At his high school graduation in 1968, he was awarded a ribbon for his artistic accomplishments, and was recognized in the *Oriflame* yearbook as "Outstanding Senior in Art".

Mrs. Fidler "probably helped save my life by making me think about going to college, and by getting me nominated for a partial scholarship," Mark said. Even so, he had not yet figured out exactly what art could mean in his life. "I was really frightened that I was going to be a schoolteacher, that I was going to teach art at school. I was really worried about that. I knew, at the time, that I really didn't have enough maturity to be able to teach kids."

But he could grow hair. Boy, could he grow hair. The growing of hair became a chief pursuit for the teenager who still couldn't get that image of a wild John Lennon flailing on his little Vox keyboard out of his head.

"I'd see pictures in *Life* magazine of hippie kids," Mark recalled. "In Akron, Ohio, I was getting beat in school if my hair touched two fingers above my collar. I'd see guys with hair down to their toenails, and I'd think, 'Man, that's wild!'"

Mark was going to school with increasingly longer locks, and was trying out the fashions he was reading about and seeing on the backs of album covers. He was sent home from school one day for wearing a pair of madras trousers. He was threatened with expulsion if he didn't cut his hair. Reluctantly, he complied. But in his "Senior Last Will" printed in the May 28, 1968 issue of the Woodarian student newspaper, he bequeathed "seven years bad luck" to "any teacher who ever had a part in my compulsory haircut!" After high school, the hair grew and grew, down his back and to his bootie. There's a picture that was snapped a few years later, of Mark sitting on the Easter bunny's lap in an oversized wicker chair at one of those mall booths. Jerry Casale had dragged Mark to Chapel Hill Mall – the "friendliest mall of all" in Akron – where parents stood in line with their children to get a portrait in the Easter fantasy land built on a plywood platform over the fountain in the mall's concourse.

Mark, wearing a tight red T-shirt, pegged jeans with the cuffs rolled and an audacious pair of two-tone, black-and-white wingtips, has wavy brown locks flowing well beyond his shoulders. Through his ever-present eyeglasses, he looks happy. The Easter bunny, with big blank eyes and floppy ears, looks – well, he looks like someone who might understand this.

Independent of Jerry Casale, Mark was forming his own reaction to the ideology of Ohio, a place, he later opined, where "people grow up and become big babies." Although he was from Cuyahoga Falls, Akron, right next door, was what passed for a culture center, a magnet for Mark's sense of self-identification. It's no accident that he once observed that "Akron" sounds like the name of a planet. There was science fiction in his reality.

"The whole band's from Akron, Ohio, where the rubber meets the road," he once said. "It's the rubber capital of the world. There's a lot of potatoes in Akron. Akron's a big potato city. There's potatoes that drive cars and have families and jobs and take bad drugs and beat their wives and stuff. So I just spend most of my time dodging them. Mostly just trying to figure out what the hell was going on on the planet and trying to avoid the spuds that were driving around."

Mark enrolled at Kent State University in the fall of 1968. He was going to study art. He feared he was doomed to be a teacher.

Chapter 3

Most people who make art make it from what's around them. This seems obvious. But it's very important. Even the most intellectual of artists – seekers who consciously look for disparate ideas and elements that appeal to their aesthetic – are rooted in the foundation of their environment. You can only stand in one place at a time. The world begins from wherever you are standing. Marcel Duchamp looked at the urinal in front of him and called it art. Kurt Schwitters gathered the images at his fingertips and turned them into collage.

By early 1970, Jerry Casale had been in Kent, Ohio, for 21 years. He had already absorbed and processed the notion of "beautiful people." They didn't appeal to him. The notion of human antagonism? Didn't like that, except when it suited his purpose. The atmosphere of industry? "A hellish, depressing patina." As an art major, he was soaking in the curvy mutations of Dadaism and the jagged, heavy darkness of German Expressionism. As a music fan, he was careening between Captain Beefheart and the Yardbirds. He was scanning across the high points of the things he didn't like and the things he did like, and beginning to see how they fit into some notion of art. He had an early sketch of something, and it was pretty damned interesting.

As a human being, he was surrounded by a set of people who were interacting like cells in a petri dish, forming a new culture. The Commuter's Cafeteria in the Kent State student union had solidified into a crack unit of young spuds. Bob Lewis and Bobbie Watson had become a couple. A guy named Gary Jackett, nicknamed "the General" for the decorations on his coat, had joined the fray. A musician from Cleveland, another unusually sharp wit named Chris Butler, was on campus. He would later play in an important local band called Tin Huey, then achieve greater commercial success with his new wave brainchild, the Waitresses. And Jerry's old school friend, Peter Gregg, the wild James Brown dancer, had remained. He wasn't a Kent State student, but he hung around the crowd.

Every day, Bob drove his '65 Chevy onto campus and parked at a set of meters adjacent to the student union. Every evening, there was a parking ticket on his windshield. He would crumple it up, throw it into the back seat, and drive home.

Bob and Jerry whiled away the hours talking about the lectures of Professor Eric Mottram, a visiting scholar at Kent in the fall of 1968. Mottram was a strongly political socialist, who talked about the working class as a base for the production of all the arts. He was quite taken with Jerry and Bob, and they with him. Bob had also become a favorite of a poetry professor named Robert Bertholf, an ex-hockey player who had studied under Kingsley Weatherhead. A little later, Edward Dorn arrived, a nationally prominent poet whose "Gunslinger" series and fascination for America's westward expansion had earned him a reputation as "the Clint Eastwood of American poetry." A colorful figure willing to sip tequila and smoke pot with his protégés, Dorn would forge a friendship with these eager, off-the-beaten-path students. Bob and Dorn would remain pen pals for years.

And then there was an art historian named Charles Swanson.

"He was really intellectual," Jerry said of Swanson, "but a guy that had flipped his wig. I mean, really gone all the way. He was like Professor Erwin Corey. You'd go to his house, in any given room was a corridor (just) wide enough for a normal human to walk through. Other than that, every square inch of the house was stacked with objects, junk, magazines and clippings. He was a pack rat collector, and just liked really heavy stuff – really incredible stuff. Then he started doing drugs late in life. He decided he was tired of talking about art; he was going to make art.

"He was this big, tall, fat guy with a big long beard. He wore velvet shirts, leather vests and homemade pendants. He was really smart and really out of his mind in the most entertaining way possible.... He would find an old leather case... line it in purple velvet and then he would find some object from a thrift store that vaguely... resembled a pussy. He would mount it in there... like a precious... jewel box or something.... It might have been ceramic lips. It might have been a piece of a bronze flower that he painted red, whatever. And then he put next to it other, just bizarre objects. Like a real World War II S.S. medallion on one side, and... a color photo from Woolworth's of a smiling pussy cat on the other side. He'd get everybody stoned, and then he'd pull these things out. He'd go, 'You're gonna love this!' He'd just wait till we were really stoned and then he'd open it up. It was all just sacrilegious... politically incorrect stuff. We just thought, okay, that's great. It (was meant to) separate the men from the boys. Let's see who gets pissed off, and let's see who gets it. That became the game."

Jerry, Bob, General Jackett and others who joined these discussions were finding an education not available in the classroom. They were in the position of being able to try out their harebrained notions on adults. And not just adults, but professors. They were being encouraged. Jerry had continued playing bass, working through the standard blues scales and notions toward something that better suited his emerging *Idea*. He had begun jamming with Bob Lewis and Peter Gregg. Bob had an apartment that he shared with two roommates above a barbershop called Haircut City, just off campus. The three of them would get together and begin noodling.

Peter was an especially good guitarist with an especially sad biography. As Bob Lewis recounted, he came from a household of six rambunctious brothers. Around the time he started high school, his father died of a heart attack. About two years later, his mother, partially paralyzed from a water skiing accident, committed suicide. So, by his middle teens, he was in need of a new family. He found it on Water Street.

"The Kent music community, including Joe Walsh and people in the Measles, kind of embraced and adopted him," Bob Lewis said. "He was a real good dancer, and was at all the clubs. On guitar, Pete was kind of an idiot savant. He could play really funky or soulful guitar, and perhaps most importantly for us, Pete had an incredible knack for coming up with riveting licks."

So they would sit in the apartment, hammering on an idea. It might be a hook or a goofy lyrical phrase. They'd run through a few different things and then Jerry would laugh. That meant they were onto something. They'd keep going, for hours. Pete usually provided the musical idea, with Jerry smoothing it out, keeping it simple with his bass. Bob would play slide guitar, often smearing it into unusual places. It was purposely monotonous, the simplicity of repetition allowing form to emerge. "I need a chick / To suck my dick / I need a dog / To lick my hog / I need a cat / To stroke my bat / I need a chick, I need a dog…"

It also was often purposely stupid. In a sense, this reflected the teachings of Eric Mottram. There was intellectual depth to the process, but no desire whatsoever to keep a safe distance from the most common adolescent humor. Devo, later, would always mix up – and sometimes struggle with – the balance between high and low. Someone would inevitably ask them to justify how a silly horny blowjob song was supposed to be art. But if it had made Jerry laugh initially, there was most likely something behind it.

❀ ❀ ❀

By the spring of 1970, Jerry had entered into a casual relationship with Kent State's Students for a Democratic Society. The SDS was a national collective of campus radicals opposed to the ongoing war in Vietnam. Jerry didn't necessarily buy into the whole thing, but he was attracted to the group's general notions of revolution and subversive tactics. The local SDS chapter often held meetings in an old Victorian house on a Kent hilltop that had become known in the neighborhood as "the haunted house." This informal headquarters shared a driveway with the Casale family home. So Jerry didn't have to fall far from the nest. He used his training in graphic arts to help make posters and other propaganda for the SDS, but he was also smart enough to sort through their rhetoric. In some instances, the mindset struck him as naïve.

"They were thinking too Marxist," he said. "They didn't trust me because I wasn't a true politico. I definitely shared a lot of their sensibility about social justice, and about the corruption of the system. I knew that. All the information was there, people just didn't read.... SDS would reprint blatant admissions by the Government.... They would get internal memos and reprint them, and everybody said it was propaganda. But it was the real thing, and nobody would believe it."

To Jerry, the government seemed even more dangerous than the SDS believed. He had a lot of people on campus to discuss these notions with. Two friends, Allison Krause and Jeffrey Miller, were also opposed to the war and interested in the ideas, if not all the tactics, of the SDS. Miller, who had come to Kent from New York, had dabbled musically with Chris Butler and was especially strong in his feeling that the war was wrong.

The most hardcore element of the campus radicals, a very small segment, had produced entire treatises on how to mess with The Man. "The night is your friend," one how-to newsletter began. "Dropping into a bush or clump of trees is often better than running. Don't move to (sic) soon. Invariably a curious dog (not a police dog) will pick up your trail and track you. Wait until dog is 3 feet away (don't move). Open your mouth as if you were going to say 'out,' and move your tongue to the rear of your mouth cavity. Then make a hissing sound as loud as you can."

There was information on the use of subsonic frequency generators, supposedly developed in secret by the government, and capable of producing a sound that would cause a person to lose control of his body functions. To Jerry, immersed in the world of sound, this was especially intriguing, partly because it also seemed a little ridiculous.

The Vietnam War protestors wanted to change the world. Among the most radical of them, anarchy was a favorite tool. They embraced mischief and outright dangerous sabotage. They studied how to disable phone systems and experimented with ammonia-filled balloons. Would they put LSD in the water supply? There were plenty in the government who believed they would. But Kent was still a Midwestern state college; most of these extreme ideas remained somewhere else. In terms of student unrest, Kent wasn't even on the radar. Who needed to know the proper technique for hiding in the bushes? You could just say your piece, then go down to Water Street to see Joe Walsh play with the James Gang.

❀ ❀ ❀

On Thursday, April 30, 1970, President Richard Nixon announced that the

Are We Not Men?

United States was escalating the war by invading Cambodia. The next day, a protest was held on the Kent State campus, sponsored by The World Historians Opposed to Racism and Exploitation (WHORE). It was a relatively peaceful affair, unfolding on a sunny day that found about 500 kids in jeans and headbands chanting slogans. Some of the history majors buried a copy of the Constitution. Friday's events carried over into the warm weekend night down on the Water Street strip. JB's and the Kove, the two most popular spots for live music, were packed and talk of politics merged with the usual conversation about parties and classes, girlfriends and boyfriends. But as the beer took hold, so did the outrage about the course of Nixon's war. And soon, trouble spilled over into the street. A bonfire was set in the middle of Water Street. Students threw beer bottles at police cars and a mob moved toward the center of town, throwing rocks and bottles through the windows of banks and utility companies.

Saturday dawned with hangovers, a downtown littered with debris and an angry mayor. A dusk-to-dawn curfew was declared and students were restricted to campus. A rumor began spreading that the campus ROTC building was to be the next target of the protestors. So, late in the day, Leroy Satrom, the mayor of Kent, contacted the Ohio National Guard. Around dark, a group of about 600 students gathered on the student Commons, just outside the glass doors of the Commuter's Cafeteria. There were informal speeches, slogans and fist-pumping. The swell began to move across campus, with other students spilling out from the dorms to join in. The group that arrived at the small, wooden ROTC building on the commons numbered more than 1,000.

Around 8 p.m., students began throwing rocks. A wastebasket went through a window, then a couple of flares. Someone burned an American flag. Then someone else dipped a rag into the gas tank of a nearby motorcycle, lit it on fire and threw it into the building, which caught fire. When the fire department arrived, protesters yanked on their hoses and jabbed holes in them with knives. Police drove away the crowd with tear gas. The National Guard arrived on the scene to assist with the dispersal. Some of the soldiers were hit by rocks as the building burned to the ground.

And then came Sunday. Another demonstration. That night students blocked an intersection and, surrounded by police and Guard troops with a police helicopter hovering overhead, they presented a written list of demands. These ranged from the immediate (that the Guard withdraw from campus) to the long term (lowering of tuition for all students). After a bullhorn announcement that curfew had been tightened, from 1 a.m. to 11 p.m., anger erupted. In the scuffle that followed, two students were bayoneted. Fifty-one were arrested. That night, as police and National Guardsmen rounded up curfew violators, they stopped one of Bob Lewis' roommates, Bob Webb, on the stairs that led up to the Haircut City apartment. They arrested him.

And finally came Monday, May 4, 1970. Around 11:30 that morning, students began to gather on the Commons, some ringing the campus bell to attract a crowd. Chris Butler and Jeffrey Miller arrived together. Miller was wearing a cowboy shirt and a pair of jeans. Butler's drum set was at Miller's house.

Jerry arrived, along with other members of the group of friends. Peter Gregg was there, along with Fred Weber, Bob's other roommate, who sang with the Measles. Like most of the students, they just wanted to see what all the ruckus was about.

More arrived, upwards of 1,500. At around 11:50, the National Guard troops borrowed a bullhorn from the campus police and made an announcement to disperse. The crowd chanted, "Fuck you." Another announcement was made. The chant evolved to "Power to the people; fuck the pigs." A third call, a third response: "One, two, three, four; we don't want your fucking war."

Some of the students did move on. Gregg and Weber retreated back onto the Commons, away from the Guard's advance. Others continued taunting and throwing rocks and other objects. Like most students, Jerry was somewhere in the middle, attracted in part by curiosity and in part by a sense of outrage. He wasn't a rock-thrower, but neither was he a disinterested observer.

The Guard, a little more than 100 strong, formed a skirmish line and moved across the Commons, away from the student union, over a hill called Blanket Hill, and down to a practice football field. Tear gas canisters flew back and forth, almost in a game of catch. Guardsmen fired canisters at the students; the students threw them back. The Guard huddled at the football field for about 10 minutes, then began moving up Blanket Hill again, back in the direction from which they had come. More rocks, more taunting.

At the top of a hill, near a small pagoda, a group of the soldiers suddenly stopped, turned and began firing. In 13 seconds, at least 54 shots were fired. A crude audiotape, made from a dormitory window, sounds like a brick of firecrackers going off. For one fleeting moment, the crowd wondered what the sound was. Blanks? Warning shots?

Then the bodies began to drop. Sandra Scheuer, a student who had been walking to class, fell dead, shot in the neck. William Schroeder, an ROTC candidate who had paused to watch the commotion, was killed, shot in the back while he lay prone on the ground. Jeffrey Miller, who had earlier made an obscene gesture at the soldiers, fell dead, shot through the mouth. Allison Krause, who had cursed at the Guardsmen, fell dead, shot in the side. Nine others were wounded. All the rest were stunned, angry and sad.

Jerry ran to Allison Krause's side. "I saw the huge M-16 exit wound in Allison's back. I almost passed out."

The standard line goes that the confusion of those 13 seconds has never ended. Decades later, even in the face of a massive investigation, depositions, photographs, 8-millimeter film of the incident, interviews – a grinding quest for answers – the event remains as ambiguous as it was on that sunny May afternoon. But all those questions didn't matter to Jerry Casale. He was one of the few who found an answer that day.

Many times, Jerry has repeated the gravity of the effect. "I would not have started the idea of Devo unless this had happened. It was just the defining moment. Until then, I might've left my hair long and been a hippie. When you start to see the real way everything works, and the insidious nature of power, corruption, injustice, brute force, you realize it's just all primate behavior."

Bob Lewis' collection of unpaid parking tickets became irrelevant. A general amnesty on library and parking fines followed the shootings, saving him $700. The FBI impounded Chris Butler's drum set from Jeffrey Miller's apartment. He never got it back. That too is irrelevant. But what those things represented – casual jamming without a sense of direction; countless afternoons in the forum of the Commuter's Cafeteria – came to an end.

"The life of the cafeteria effectively ended on May 4, 1970," Bob said. "Following the dispersal of students, immediately thereafter. The new union was built, and things were never the same. It, like Camelot, flowered, shimmered, and disappeared."

Chapter 4

Almost immediately after the Kent State shootings, James Michener came to town. He was going to write a book about an American tragedy. He interviewed student after student, everyone he could find who might have something to offer. He sent researchers out among the people. Michener was on the same fact-finding mission as much of the country in that spring, summer, and beyond. Of course, many facts would be found. But the truth would not. If there ever was a "plastic reality", this was it.

And so it came to pass that James Michener, famous author, got himself invited over to Chris Butler's apartment to eat brown rice and pick some brains. But, of course, these were no ordinary brains. Jerry was there, keeping a sardonic smile from his face as the conversation began. Michener asked them about Kent, about May 4, about what they saw, how they felt. It was an engaging exchange.

Twenty minutes into the interview, there was a furious pounding at the door. Jerry jumped up and answered it. Bob Lewis was standing there with a 12-gauge shotgun. Wild-eyed, he pumped a shell into the chamber and yelled, "There's pigs all around, man! This is the revolution!" Michener nearly blew his brown rice.

This had all been planned in advance. It was not just a prank. It was a statement. It was, in fact, an artistic statement. A performance. Much of Kent was wrapped in sadness and anger and earnest reaction to the campus tragedy. This group was no different. But a specific decision was made to turn those feelings into a fairly elaborate, subversive statement about human stupidity. This was the new manifestation of the theories Jerry, Bob and their friends had been tossing around. It was a turning point.

Shortly thereafter, there was a road trip to Washington, D.C. Jerry and Bob had arranged, through Pete Gregg's connections with Joe Walsh, to have the James Gang play at a fund-raiser for the shooting victims. The event was held at Ted Kennedy's house. The Kennedy/Camelot mystique was working its way into the iconography, emerging later in Devo's song "Come Back Jonee", which was inspired by John F. Kennedy's assassination, and in the JFK hairpieces they wore in the 1980s. Bob, Bobbie Watson, Jerry and a girl named Peggy Freemon rode in Bob's tan Pontiac Tempest OHC 6, which the year before had made a pilgrimage to Woodstock.

"We drove directly to Teddy's place," Bob recalled, "but we couldn't change clothes there, so we drove into the city to change at the Kent Students' Medical Fund office. By the time we got there, it was getting late in the afternoon, and we wanted to get to the event. You know, people from Ohio think 'on time' is 15 minutes early. It was rush hour, so we had to engage in some guerrilla-style driving. At one point I remember making a U-turn in rush hour traffic by going up over the curb and across a wide grassy boulevard divider, while a traffic control officer actually tooted his whistle and waved his white gloved hands at us. 'We're from Ohio!' we shouted out the window as we peeled out, leaving a double trail of tire tracks through the grassy sod.

"So we get to the party and it's kinda cool. The James Gang plays and there's free pop and booze and wine, and plenty of pot. About 8:30 or 9:00, Teddy Kennedy, red-faced and loaded, with a brilliantly white starched shirt, tie and rolled-up sleeves comes out of the main house with a Secret Service crew and they push through the crowd. Charles Swanson later recounted how he had been virtually knocked to the ground when he didn't get out of Ted's posse's way quick enough to suit 'em. We hadn't arranged for any place to stay, and wound up going to the James Gang's hotel just across the Francis Scott Key Bridge from Georgetown. We hung out in their hotel rooms until (two members of the James Gang posse), who had just finished some lobster dinner room service, dropped a beer bottle off a balcony and put an exquisitely centered dent in the hood of a powder blue Mercedes 280 SEL. The al fresco dining ended.

"The four of us wound up crashing in a vacant room paid for by the James Gang, although not entirely without further incident. In the middle of the night, Joe Gregg (Peter's older brother) came into our room from the adjoining room, drunkenly shouting something about us not 'putting any fucking phone bills on their tab,' and proceeded to rip the phone out of the wall. On the ride home, we were wiped out and playing some kind of road trip 20 question-type game, and the killer question and answer we came up with was:

"**Q.** If Joe Gregg's asshole was an amusement park, what would it smell like?

A. Rancid cottage cheese."

Jerry, in a more earnest attempt to commemorate the shootings, designed a graphic, a silhouetted figure falling backward, with four drops of blood. The image appeared on buttons that found their way onto tattered denim jackets and tie-dyed T-shirts. But Jerry was quickly moving beyond simple memorial gestures. The elaborate ideas of his college years were coming into focus.

❀ ❀ ❀

By 1971, a significant cross-section of the established and burgeoning local music scene became concentrated in four apartments over an electronics repair shop called DayHo Electric, with an adjoining pizza place called Guido's. Jerry lived in Apartment 1 with his girlfriend Nancy Neal. Chris Butler lived with his girlfriend in Apartment 2. Apartment 3 rotated between Peter Gregg, Joe Walsh and their friend Bruce Hensal. And Apartment 4 was home to Terry Hynde, the sax player for 15-60-75, a group that came to be known as the Numbers Band and proved to be a glue for the local scene. More than 30 years later, the Numbers Band was still playing sophisticated beatnik blues. Terry's kid sister Chrissie often crashed there on weekends.

Jerry decorated his apartment with a wall-size cardboard mural from Akron Provision, the butcher shop where Bob worked. The bottom half had a red brick pattern and the top was a pastoral scene, with cows, a barn and a windmill.

"Jerry lived down the hall from Bob and I," Bobbie Watson recalled. "He would come over every night, and so they compared their days. And they would exchange information that they had gotten during the day. Most of the talks didn't begin until real late at night. Most of the talks didn't end until two o'clock or three o'clock in the morning. I would use 'rap session' to describe them. Exploration."

Invariably, the smell of baking pizza would waft up from Guido's. They ate a lot of pizza.

There was some recording equipment downstairs at DayHo Electric, and the loose collective of musicians convinced the owner, Dave Metz, to record them. Jerry and the others had been experimenting with all kinds of sounds – windshield wipers and telephone busy signals, a washing machine. So they hauled their gear down to DayHo and laid down crude recordings of "I Need a Chick", "Rope Song", "Might Not Live Forever" and others.

"Clearly the first punk recording," Peter Gregg observed. "No matter whatever some NYC band and MTV may say about them doing the first punk recording. Not true. Jerry was way first."

Bob stuck an index card on the shop's bulletin board, announcing his desire to buy a used Fender Telecaster. A sales rep from the guitar company saw the note and told Bob he could get him a brand-new one for $150. Bob gave him the cash, and a few weeks later he was the proud owner of a blonde Telecaster with a maple neck.

❋ ❋ ❋

Around the same time, Mark Mothersbaugh moved into a house on Balch Street, in a working-class neighborhood of west Akron. The house was rented by three friends – Marty Reymann, Ed Barger and Dale McGough – who had grown up together in Akron's working-class Firestone Park neighborhood. Reymann and Barger had taken an interest in this sensitive, energetic young artist, and allowed Mark to live there rent-free. They fed him and encouraged his ideas. He was writing and making music and visual art, supported by this hippie-style patronage.

Every day, Mark wrote. He filled notebook after notebook with observations, ideas, fragments of song lyrics and drawings, with ever-growing confidence. This eventually was published as *My Struggle*, a treatise of the wry, incisive and sometimes vulnerable Mark Mothersbaugh. He held nothing back. There was something to offend everybody. The early draft of the manuscript had the working title "The sad story of a very dead man … My Struggle, or life in the Rubber City." At this point, the writing was a rather secret activity. Bobbie even admitted she was afraid to see it, worried it might reveal too much about the workings of her friend's mind. This version of the book had Mark A. Mothersbaugh listed as the author, but when it was published several years later, it was under the pseudonym Booji Boy, Mark's key onstage alter-ego.

Are We Not Men?

Despite his reticence, Mark asked his friends to contribute to the book. When few complied, he attributed some of his own writing and drawings to them. Meanwhile, he was also working on silkscreen prints and decals at the Balch Street house.

"Mark was still at college when we were living together," Ed Barger recalled. "We would go out to Kent State to shoot the negatives for his decals and burn the screens. Mark was pure, entertaining and funny. I remember Mark left the decal paper out one night, and cockroaches ate the glue off the paper. I was like Andy Warhol's assistant, and even made a few of my own decals. I certainly gained an understanding of the creative process, and Mark was a great artist."

Mark had been introduced to Reymann and Barger by a drummer who lived behind them, a guy named Mike Powell. Mark and Powell had begun playing together in Flossy Bobbit, a two-man band that was sort of a cross between Emerson, Lake and Palmer and Suicide – high concept keyboard arpeggios with a raw, violent edge. Mark had become interested in the innovative compositions of Harry Partch and the electronic experimentation of John Cage and Morton Subotnick.

"I used to take my brother's Pink Floyd records and my sister's Bee Gees records," Mark said, "and I would destroy them, put scratches in them, so I could get them to skip. Because I was looking for new ways of making music."

Powell, meanwhile, had a different set of interests.

"He used to say to me, 'You know, I just sit around with my gun and say, should I blow my head off or should I go rob a gas station. Uh, I'll go rob another gas station!'" Reymann recalled. "He did six in a month or so. He had real long blonde hair at that point. He'd take any drug you gave him. You'd just hand it to him, and he'd take it! He was one heck of a drummer when he was semi-straight, but he was terrible when he was wasted. He would just go off like a damned kamikaze."

Jerry concurred: "Mike Powell was a scary, scary guy. He was about six four, thin, hyper, speed freak, blonde hair, big bugged-out kind of eyes that looked like he needed his thyroid regulated. (He was) an amazing, way too busy drummer – like if there could be one beat, he'd put in four."

This unlikely duo was getting gigs around the Akron area, often to the surprise and dismay of bar owners. They reached their peak one night in the lounge of Bowl-a-Rama Bowling Lanes. They had picked up a guitarist named Dane Griffin and, according to some accounts, had changed the name of the band for this gig to God. In the center of the stage was an old 1950s television set filled with tomato juice. The finale was a song called "Man

Vs. TV." At the climactic moment, Powell jumped from behind the drum set, picked up a sledgehammer, and smashed it into the television, spewing "blood" everywhere.

This was clearly bad form for league night in Akron, the home of the Pro Bowler's Association. The bouncer chewed out God, but Barger was inspired. He and Reymann had been interested in fostering some kind of musical project. Reymann had some money to invest and Barger knew production.

"We initially backed Dane Griffin," Reymann said. "We bought him a Les Paul. We took him up to the 16-track studio in Cleveland with three black girls who were backup singers, and Mark and Mike Powell played on the recordings. When we listened to the tapes, we knew right away that we were wasting our time with Dane, and decided to make Mark our next project. It was obvious he was far more talented than the rest. We put a bunch of bands together with Mark Mothersbaugh. I put up the money to back the whole thing."

Barger and Reymann bought Mark a Hammond BV organ that was converted to a Hammond B3, and three Leslie speaker cabinets that Barger had customized by Harrington's in Chicago. McGough, who worked at the post office, borrowed $4,000 from his credit union, enough for a $3,000 Mellotron analog synthesizer and some P.A. equipment, purchased from Staff Music in Akron. He believed, as his friends did, that this was an investment that might pay off someday. Marty also put up the cash for a Mini Moog, which Mark played with the casing removed, exposing the electronic guts in what surely was an attempt to intensify the machine's visual presence. (Perhaps not surprisingly, Mark would be the only Mellotron player listed in the 1974 Directory of the American Federation of Musicians' Akron chapter.)

"We spent close to twenty grand on this band," Barger said, "and that's not counting the sound system; a reel-to-reel video system; two cameras and a switcher which Marty and I owned."

One day, Mike Powell decided to pull a little prank on Mark. He slipped LSD into his friend's peanut butter and jelly sandwich. It freaked Mark out. He wrote about it in one of his notebooks. Someday, this might be useful information.

❀ ❀ ❀

Over in Kent, the collective above the pizza shop solidified. They were making music together, watching television together, swapping books and writing poems. Almost everything that passed through their atmosphere was captured like a small bird, inspected, tagged and allowed to fly again.

Someone spotted a November 12, 1971, headline in the *Youngstown Vindicator*: "Speeding Auto Leaves Bodies Strewn on W. Federal." The article reported: "At least three persons were killed, and at least 13 were injured shortly before noon today when a car rolled along the sidewalk on Federal Street... sending bodies flying into the air... Horrified passersby stood by helplessly as the car mowed down its victims."

Hence came one of the earliest Devo songs, "Auto Modown": "Auto Mow-down, down in Youngstown, bodies got the blues / Auto Mowdown, noon in downtown, bodies with no shoes."

"We would watch pro football," Bob Lewis recalled, "and take Ed Podolak (Raiders) and Otis Taylor (Chiefs) and turn them into (to the tune of 'Heart-break Hotel'), 'My mother was a negro/my father was a Pole/My name is Otis Podolak/Let me shove it in your hole.' (Once, we were) watching an end zone display where the receiving end scored a touchdown, flopped on his back, waving arms and legs in celebration, which became, (in 'Praying Hands'), 'Assume the position, go into doggy submission.'"

They got into the music of Bob Marley, channeling the loose concentration of simple beats, straightforward lyrics and the notion of an artist fighting for liberation. All of these things were connecting.

There was another news item that also led to a song. But this one hit closer to home. In late summer of 1971, Jerry got a job as a cashier at the Adult Physiological Studies Center in downtown Akron, a coy code name for a place most people recognized as "the porno shop." In the pre-video era, this was where men in raincoats went to watch movies with titles like *Diary of a Nymph* and *School for Sex*.

Jerry smiled his bad Catholic school-boy smile as he took the wrinkled bills from men who averted their eyes as they went to sit in the dark. He brought home pornography in which he found equal parts disgust, titillation and humor. He'd show it to Bob Lewis, and they would get the joke. Unfortunately, Jerry had bad timing. He was serving as assistant manager in the fall of an election year, when some of the local politicians decided to make a media splash by cracking down on illicit activity. So they targeted the Adult Physiological Studies Center. There was a series of busts at the shop on obscenity charges. In one instance, police went in and arrested all the employees. Later in the same afternoon, they returned to discover the film projector back up and running and they made another series of arrests.

So Jerry was in rather dangerous territory. On Sept. 8, 1971, the cops walked in during a showing of *School for Sex*. They arrested Jerry for operating a theater without a license and hauled him off to jail. One friend, Jennifer Licitri, recalls that he gave a false name at the time of his arrest to avoid being identified in the newspaper – Jerry Casanova. It didn't work. The next day, the *Akron Beacon Journal* headline announced, "*School For Sex* Is Closed" and the story included Jerry's real name and address.

The experience may have been traumatic for him, but it did not go to waste. Jerry recalled it in a song called "I Been Refused":

"Last Monday morning, minus twenty degrees; walked to unemployment, on my knees. Left without my money, tried to make my trial. Judge said you're the porno king, go to jail for awhile."

❋ ❋ ❋

In that winter of 1971, Bobbie Watson's sister Norma gave her a stack of comic books. Bobbie was a big comics fan; she had learned to read from Huey, Louie and Dewey word balloons. She began sifting through the books. Among them was the "all-girl" issue of *Adventure Comics* #416, which included a reprint of the March-April 1948 Golden Age *Wonder Woman* (issue #28). The story focused on Professor Zool's laboratory, where he was experimenting with transforming monkeys into other animals. According to Bobbie, she showed the comic to her boyfriend Bob, who was immediately drawn to page 64, to this peculiar machine invented by Professor Zool.

It was called an Evolution Machine. It was a box with a lever and some dials on the front. At the top of the lever was the word "Evolution." At the bottom, "Devolution." Zool put a monkey into the machine. When he pulled the lever downward, the monkey became a prehistoric tree fox. Devolution in action.

This was a concept that had been emerging from all those stoned, highbrow discussions, and had been supported by the life they were observing around them. Bob got very excited. That night, when Jerry stopped over as usual, Bob showed him the comic book.

"My memory is a visual one," Bobbie said. "I see their animated faces and remember the energy in the room."

Like many of the key moments in Devo's history, this one has several versions. Bobbie has said in a sworn deposition that she got the comic book from her sister. She later recalled that it might have come from a thrift-store excursion. The silliness of such an argument over a *Wonder Woman* comic (and the fact that it became part of a court record) is pure Devo – and pure plastic reality. But it became as important as the discussion that followed, as Bob and Jerry played around with the term "devolution":

Devolution.

De-evolution.

The avant garde had marched art forward, with Art Nouveau and Art Deco. What happened when all this was outdated and art retreated?

You'd have a De-evolutionary Army.

41

Art De*vo*.

Devo.

That was it. A four-letter word said it all. But exactly who first uttered that word remains disputed to this day.

Chapter 5

Jerry was depressed. His longtime girlfriend, Nancy Neal, had left him. When they had met, he was a freshman and she was a graduate student in psychology who rode a Harley. They had been together through all those important years, and now she was gone. So maybe his eye was tuned toward dark and ugly things one day when, poking around a junk store with Bobbie and Bob, he discovered an old mask. It was a leather ski mask that covered the whole head, with holes for the eyes and mouth. It was warped from being soaked with water. "Fantastically hideous," Jerry recalled. He bought it.

He loved that mask. It just seemed to capture some part of how he was feeling. He put it on and looked in the mirror. Gorj. That would be the name of the monster inside this mask. Gorj: "He who is not always thus." He wrote what Bob Lewis called a "valium prayer to the god of depression" and had a color process print made. On one side was the prayer; on the other was a picture of him wearing the mask inside his kid brother Roger's toy space helmet. He called it the Gorj card.

Jerry put together a costume to go with the mask, a butcher's jacket with an enema bag bandoleer strapped over his shoulder. It was a frightening sight, hard to look at, but hard to ignore. And he began to think about what it all meant.

"Gorj was a flawed human character that had gone through some sort of psychic torture," he explained. "It was pre-De-Evolution devolution. It was performance art, but we didn't have a name for it. Obviously, the imagery we were going for, (or) stealing from, were all monsters, mutants, psychopathic killers and, you know, the underside of society. This is what basically everybody tries to ignore.

"They're so close to it themselves. It's a condition all humans find themselves in – they're all mutants. They're mutated apes, and they're psychotic, and as a species they are destroying every other species on the planet. They are basically full of shit. They have turned the world upside-down, and (still) believe that they're at the top of the evolution chain. We saw through that, especially when they cease being honest about the fact that they have a dark side – when they cease having a conscience. They are capable of horror. So, freaks and mutants provide the mirror – what they seek to avoid, the vanity and folly of hip, straight people."

Gorj definitely had this dark side down pat. Jerry began to make appearances at the Kent State art school wearing the Gorj outfit, with his friend Jim Bubbi literally in tow. Jerry would have Bubbi on a leash, dressed in a Mexican wrestling mask, gym shorts and high-top wrestling shoes. Bubbi's character was called Pootman. Pootman wasn't allowed to stand up. He stayed on all fours as he and Gorj toured the exhibits in the art school. Gorj had his enema bag filled with milk. The pair would stop at an exhibit, give it a look, and Gorj would point at it.

"Pootman!"

Pootman would wiggle his ass and hold his nose like it stunk. Then he would get his reward, a milk feeding from the enema tube. "Teachers and critics all dance the poot." That lesson from the song "Jocko Homo" came from Pootman and Gorj.

Jerry went to see Captain Beefheart one night at a local bar called the Draft House. Jerry gave the oddball bandleader a Gorj card. When Beefheart got onstage, he promptly smashed the microphone. The sound man got him another one, which Beefheart used to announce, "This is the dirtiest place I've ever been in my life." When the time came for band member introductions, Beefheart decided the crowd wasn't cheering loudly enough for the drummer. So he ordered the drummer out of the building until he'd decided the applause warranted his return. Beefheart seemed to understand the Gorj concept.

❀ ❀ ❀

Jerry found another girl and he became infatuated with her almost immediately. She said her maiden name was Tamara Cora Landamore, but she went by Cora Hall, indicating her marriage to an Englishman named Roger Hall. She was British, though some initially doubted her accent. And she claimed to have come from some sort of aristocratic background, but that, too seemed dubious.

"When Jerry first met her she was ill and dressed in rags because all of her belongings were elsewhere," Bobbie Watson recalled. "She had outrageous stories of things that had just happened to her. Jerry was condescending to her, instructing her about clothes to wear, disbelieving her many stories. She was really sick and weak and her stories of a grander life seemed to be a fiction – until her trunks arrived and we all saw that her belongings showed more sophistication than Jerry was wishing for. She changed her straggly hair into a cut that was a trademark look for her. She sewed up some little dresses from the Vogue pattern book."

She was, apparently, for real. As Bob Lewis recalled, her father was English and her mother was Swedish; they were high-end professionals who lived at a posh address in Kensington. Then, when her mother ran off with a Swedish ballet dancer and her father died, she was left at an orphanage. She came to the United States with her husband, Roger Hall, who had been a student of Eric Mottram.

For a time, as Jerry pursued her, Cora was the beauty and Gorj was the beast. But finally, Gorj won her blue-blooded heart. He is not always thus.

❋ ❋ ❋

In May 1972, as the spring quarter ended, Jerry and Cora flew to California. Bob and Bobbie followed in the red Chevy Biscayne, making their first cross-country trip. Their professor, Eric Mottram, published a poem the following year in the magazine *Sixpack*, dedicated to Bob and Jerry, titled "Left for California: the slow awakening."

Their friend Gary Jackett – the "General" – had moved out there the year before. He was living in Laguna Beach, in a mostly Hispanic neighborhood about an hour south of Los Angeles and a short walk from a beautifully calm beach. He was doing artwork for *The Staff*, a free "hippie, drug, music, political paper." He had been sending dispatches from out West back to his friends in Kent, and they decided to join him. Jackett said he could get them jobs writing for the paper.

Well, shortly before their arrival, there was a little incident in *The Staff* newsroom. Jackett hadn't been paid for a couple of weeks. He went in to see the editor and demanded his money. The editor pulled a gun from his desk drawer and pointed it at Jackett.

"Get back to work! I'll pay you when I can," he said.

Jackett shook his head, gathered his belongings and quit. Next thing he knew, here came the Kent contingent. Jackett was renting a duplex, and he set them up with a place to stay in the garage. Although things had turned decidedly sour at *The Staff*, Jerry and Bob still managed to get in the door.

"The editor was absolutely crazy," Jerry said. "But, you know, we drove up one week to L.A. and begged this guy to let us do something. He gave us, I think, four pages."

That was all they needed. Jerry and Bob had poured all their intellectual noodlings of the past several years into music and poetry, artwork and stuff like Gorj. Now it was time to bring it into focus. Jerry wrote a piece called "Polymer Love." Bob wrote a piece called "Readers Vs. Breeders." They would be published on July 14, 1972, in what became referred to as *The Staff*'s "Devo issue."

"Readers Vs. Breeders" drew heavily from Eric Mottram's course syllabus, making references to *The Technological Society*, by Jacques Ellul, and *Laws of Form*, by G. Spencer Brown. Mottram, who had written an essay titled

"Entropy And The Choice Of Inertia" in 1970, had given a lecture at Kent State that is widely credited as one of the seminal moments in the formation of the Devo philosophy.

In "Readers Vs. Breeders", Bob wrote that technology is forcing humans to become machines, "and imperfect ones at that." Exploring the tension between technology and the organic world, he realized, "What we seek then, is that transcendent state most fully engendered by Fred Flintstone – technologically sophisticated caveman."

He continued: "The de-evolutionaries, devolutionaries, or Devo-tees, as it were, have developed as their basic premises the concepts of cathonic progress and fluid catharsis. Cathonic progress is essentially the idea of going up by going down." Fluid catharsis accepts that (quoting Brown) "foolishness, being a divine state is not a condition to be either proud or ashamed of."

(Think about the guy in the song "Mongoloid." His is as divine a state as one could hope for.)

"The concepts of Devo are aimed at two kinds of people," he wrote, "those who should know but don't, and those who don't know but should." The first group are the readers; the second are the breeders. In the face of an increasingly, artificially sanitized world, "the devolutionaries seek to remind (technocrats) of the belch, fart and belly laugh."

"If you find this explanation and presentation stimulating, or repulsive," he concluded, "contact DEVO thru the magazine. The whereabouts of the Devotees is known."

Jerry began "Polymer Love" by defining the ambiguity of the word "plastic": "On the one hand (oooh) *plastic* is a vituperative scream hurled against the straight world for its rigidity, negation of process, fear of death. Conversely, plastic connotes superiority over natural forces. It is nonbiodegradable, nearly unlimited in its capacity to be transmuted in form and function; the archetype of the New Way."

He then romped through an anecdote about a couple, "Ken" and "Barbie," who use Neet Spray Foam to remove the hair from their genitals. "They have a vision," he suggested. "She, the LEM opening her capture latches to receive him, the capsule's probing beak – floating in space, remote from the stench of human sentiment spawned in certainty of death. They are the Beautiful People. Barbie sucks Ken's smooth hard sacs, he licks her deodorized openings. It satisfies them for the moment, but the hair grows back. It must be understood that, given this scheme of anaerobic narcissism, 'love' is predicated on the selfishness of reciprocal Suck. It's a closed system, pregnancy is error. Ken coats his cock with a latex sheath, and Barbie swabs her sleeve with acrylic foam. The space age neophytes know they've got to cover up."

Are We Not Men?

He went on to establish that "fucking and loving are the same, or should be. Man loves pussy, and pussy is the essence of woman. Therefore, man loves woman. And the same is often true of woman's regard for him." He referred to Bob's "Readers" (those who should know but don't) as adopting a love lexicon that "reflects the onset of techno-sexual consciousness:
"We docked.
"I slid my gig into her sleeve.
"I fed my rod up her toy.
"We balled.
"She did a read-out on my rocket."
And so on. As humans "evolve" into machines, they'll wonder about life: "'I don't even see how that could come out of a girl,' says Barbie, looking at a fully developed foetus suspended in a Lucite tube. 'Girls used to get wet and sticky down there, it was awful,' offered Ken."
Jerry concluded: "Like they been askin' for years: 'Does it make more sense to understand man as a biological phenomenon with all that implies, or to try to fit human behavior to the prediction-generalization model of 19th-century physics?' The man who scratches his head at that question is in trouble. To explore is divine, but to ignore is Devo."
These essays, which profoundly hammered down the foundation of the Devo Idea, were written in the California sun, as the smell of the ocean carried over the rooftops. It was, potentially, an idyllic summer. Jerry and Bob were proud of their work. Jerry went so far as to mail an inscribed copy of *The Staff* to Eric Mottram in England.
As Jerry and Bob worked on the paper, Bobbie and Cora took jobs as waitresses to help with the rent, dressing in black go-go boots and miniskirts, and they all lived together in the garage. But there was plenty of tension, mostly stemming from Cora's presence. She and Jerry had frequent, bitter fights. She liked men with money, and Jerry didn't have any. Living in a garage was not something she was accustomed to. And Cora didn't necessarily endear herself to Bobbie, either.
"She kept taking my dress out of my suitcase and putting it in her suitcase, completely visible to me when I would walk to their side of the garage," Bobbie recalled. "I would retrieve it, saying nothing, and she would take it back, again and again."
That summer, as Jerry and Bob sat in the yard writing their essays, General Jackett worked alongside them, spray painting a set of letters on 17-by-24 poster board. Too big to ignore, they spelled out the word.
D-E-V-O.

Chapter 6

Although there is a variety of potato called "Early Ohio", Northeast Ohio is not known as particularly fertile spud country. It's much better known for its sweet corn. Even so, Jerry and Mark each, independently of one another, developed a fascination for the potato as an art medium. Mark's seminal Mr. Potato Head experiments help explain his side of things. But Jerry found meaning there, too. So it would only make devolved sense that one of the first interactions between these two involved potatoes.

Mark discovered some of Jerry's cut-and-paste constructions in the Kent State art department. "Jerry had blown up pictures out of his high school yearbook of especially good-looking people, and had these little potatoes hanging all over their heads, faces and stuff," he said. "(Potatoes hanging) off this kid's ear, looking like he's reading a book." Mark, meanwhile, had been doing artwork of scientists and astronauts holding potatoes, studying them. Probably not surprisingly, each of the young artists had given deep thought to the lowly spud.

"We created our own slang, partially to entertain ourselves because we were bored," Mark said. "So we made potatoes part of the Devo philosophy and called ourselves 'spuds', both pejoratively and as a compliment." Potatoes, he said are "the dirty hard workers of the earth," rather than "the aristocratic, above-ground fruits of the world." Once again, the no-nonsense work ethic of Mark's father was showing up in his own philosophy.

Jerry was equally adept at breaking down the potato ethos. "The potato is a staple that keeps us alive," he said. "It is totally unglamorous and underrated. It is also a conductor of electricity. You know that they teach you in science class how to make potato transmitters and potato radio receivers. They have all eyes around... (and) the potato is a symbol of our humble beginnings."

Mark and Jerry's paths began to cross through Kent's art and music circles in the early 1970s. They became friends around 1972. Jerry recalls that the first time Mark saw him, Jerry was doing the Gorj shtick. This certainly seems appropriate. Not only did the whole band later embrace masks and costumes, but the sheer mutated ugliness of Gorj is exactly the sort of thing Mark would latch onto. Mark had been making a lot of art from found images. He was taking pictures from medical books, drawing himself into them and manipulating holy cards. He used a lot of idealistic '50s images. There's a drawing of a peppy-looking, uniformed service station attendant filling a vaguely erotic fur-lined woman's boot with his hose. There's what appears to be a schoolbook image of a father and son gazing cheerfully toward the night sky. The father has one hand on the son's shoulder as the son points toward the starry heavens. The caption has been edited to read, "When viewing divine creation, a parent should seize." A set of three small boxing diagrams appear above the picture, so it looks as if the boy is pointing toward them.

"Look son – Uranus!!" Mark's handwritten dialogue bubble reads. "(Little lower Johnny – lower – uh – and to the right.)"

"Oh Dad – look," the son responds. "Muhammud (sic) Ali vs. Joe Frazier. (Careful pa – I'm 'nude' to this fascist jazz.)"

✳ ✳ ✳

After his return from California, Jerry enrolled in an experimental art class at Kent State. Mark, who had continued playing in Flossy Bobbit, had also enrolled, along with General Jackett (who did a lot of traveling to and from Kent), a film student named Chuck Statler and some of the art school's best graduate students. Taught by a professor named Robert Culley, the class was called M-A-T-E-R, an acronym for something like Materials, Art, Technology, Energy and Research. "Man, did it produce some great stuff," Jerry recalled. The class was held in an old warehouse in downtown Kent, about a half-mile from the university. Kent State's enrollment had boomed in the 1960s, and the art department got squeezed by more "traditional" academics.

Nevertheless, the avant-garde class thrived outside of the campus mainstream. Jerry used the opportunity to hone Gorj; M-A-T-E-R was custom-made for his burgeoning performance art. Jackett and another student named John Zabrucky got some big square glass mirrors and constructed a time/space tunnel. Viewers crawled through about 12 feet of tunnel, reflected from all sides. Shortly thereafter, Zabrucky moved to Los Angeles and started a successful movie prop house called Modern Props.

Jerry's most memorable class project was called *The American Dream*. He got a roll of artificial grass carpeting and spread it out on the floor. Then he brought in a short-wave radio, tuned it to some horrible static, and set up a barbecue grill. He stood there cooking hot dogs in a sort of living exhibit. This was the kind of imagery Mark had been working with and that would carry throughout Devo's career – a totally recognizable, yet thoroughly mutated vision of American iconography and idealism. Bob Dobbs belonged at Jerry's barbecue.

✳ ✳ ✳

The exact reason Bob Kidney decided to name his band 15-60-75 is not clear. What did happen, though, in those heady days on Water Street, is that the loose bunch of hippies and beatniks took it upon themselves to rename the band. "Going to see the Numbers tonight?" they'd ask. And so they became the Numbers Band. The group was led by the powerfully dark Kidney, who was steeped in the blues, but eventually developed his own kind of poetic take. He's tall, and casts a commanding eye over his audiences. As the Numbers Band continued playing through the seventies, eighties, nineties and into the following century, Kidney, his brother/multi-instrumentalist Jack and saxophonist Terry Hynde evolved through an intriguing river of artsy, minimalist, roots-inflected rock, dismantling the blues and reassembling them to suit Kidney's head. The low-key, sometimes sullen Kidney would contribute to the rotating membership of the Golden Palominos in the 1980s and would remain an important link in the Northeast Ohio rock scene. In 1990, local and national musicians played benefits to cover his medical expenses after he lost a kidney. The irony of the medical malady seemed too rich. It had Bob Kidney's understated laugh all over it.

Back in the early '70s, Kidney was already a discriminating band leader. Jerry's friend Rod Reisman had been playing drums, but Reisman eventually fell out of grace. It happened at closing time one night. The band was still playing, but Reisman was exhausted, so he decided to close down the set with a flourish, Keith Moon-style.

"I started kicking my drums off the stage, off my little platform! This is with a band that says they play blues and jazz, right? So, Kidney calls me over to the piano. He's playing piano in those days too. Calls me over and asks, 'Why'd you do that?'

"I said, 'Bob, I was done. I had nothing left.' I didn't want to look at him and say I really just wanted to go the fuck home. But truly, I said, 'I had nothing left. That was it, all I could do.' And he says, 'Well I don't like it. It's been done by every rock band in town.' Like a rock band was a bad thing."

So Reisman quit and his buddy Jerry got the gig. Jerry was still on the cusp between his blues upbringing and his highly developed sense of art and subversion. Jerry was a tight, extremely simple drummer who held the band together. But Kidney soon decided he liked Jerry's bass playing better, and moved him out from behind the drums.

"Everybody did exactly what (Bob Kidney) told them, where he told them, how many notes, everything. He was the General," Jerry said. "Personally, I think that was the Numbers Band that I liked the best as far as the sound went. Everybody was so good sounding in that band. It was a band I don't think ever sounded as... aggressive or edgy after that. It really got people moving back then. And Kidney, like, pulled back because he thought it was too rock and roll. I mean, I had talked him into doing a couple Hound Dog Taylor songs and things like that."

Another friend of Jerry's, a high school classmate named Tim Maglione, was playing sax with the Numbers Band at the time. He observed the push and pull between Jerry's old-school blues sensibility and his growing sense of the modern world.

"His ego often conflicted with the even larger ego of bandleader Bob Kidney," Maglione recalled. "Even at that time, Jerry's ideas about what the band should be doing musically were kind of bizarre. 15-60-75 was doing mostly 'solid' Chicago-style blues, but Jerry would frequently argue that we should be writing music that incorporated McDonald's commercials because that's what people could most identify with. We were all inundated by television commercials. He also thought the music should sound 'mechanical and industrial' because, once again, we were all in 'the industrial age' and inside we could most appreciate a sense of 'mechanical-ness', or 'robot-like' music."

This all came to a head one evening when Jerry could no longer suppress his theater of the absurd. The band was playing Bo Diddley's "Who Do You Love", always a big boogie highlight of the set. The dance floor was packed, people were really into it. Jerry pulled out a chimpanzee mask he'd been hiding. (His accounts of this have been contradictory; in some versions it's a Colonel Sanders mask. Either way, his point was about to become clear.) He pulled it over his head and continued playing. Halfway through the song, Kidney realized that people were laughing and pointing over to his left. He looked over and saw what was happening. "He... lost it. Just fucking lost it," Jerry recalled.

Jerry was kicked out of the Numbers Band, essentially, for devolving into an ape. It seemed like he could see where his future lay.

One night, Jerry went to see Mark's band at JB's. Mark was wearing a weird silver suit. He still had the long hair and the prog-rock leanings, but he was definitely headed in the same direction as Jerry. Jerry decided that this was the musician he needed. It was time for what soon would become infamous as "the important sound of things falling apart."

Chapter 7

In early 1973, Kent State professors Robert Bertholf and Edward Dorn were given the task of putting together an arts festival. They wanted poetry and music, performance and visual art. By then, both professors had become important influences on Bob Lewis and Jerry. They had been listening to the bright students' discussions of devolutionary theory for a year or more, and had been chipping in their own ideas. Dorn, especially, had been giving considerable thought to the ironies of "progress" and wondering if civilization might indeed be moving in reverse.

"Dorn," Bertholf recalled, "was going to write a play called *Crank It Back,*

A Play For The Country On Its Bicentennial, which was a review of the transportation system in 1876 as compared with 1976. And it was proposed that the 1876 transportation system, mainly built on railroads and waterways, was more efficient than a highway. Time goes forward but culture does not necessarily go forward at the same increments of progress.

"There was talk about a lot of things. There was talk about writing a poetic line that was totally boring. (The goal of the poem) was to remove all characteristics of any high rhetorical art. And the same was talked about with music.

"...Someplace I have poems by Jerry that are so awful they would have to be devolution."

Dorn and the boys had discussed a television nature program that described both the "sea mouse" and a particular species of snake that had returned from living on land to living in the sea, reversing the expected evolutionary process. He, Bertholf and a few others had become valuable sounding boards. Bertholf found both the thought and the music to be significantly unconventional.

"Originally (devolution) could be found in various ways, in various sources," Bertholf said later. "The point was that in 1971 these two people (Bob and Jerry) together brought that idea into a new contention and redefined it... made it an active medium for understanding. First, it was a socio-political situation. And then finally a whole procedure of persistently de-classical music.

"I remember in May-June of 1972, (Bob) had just bought a white electric guitar, which to me was a fairly outrageous act. Bob was playing in the evening. They were not plugged in. They were not using their amplifiers. They were just playing, but it was what I later recognized as... like Mozart. It was the same sort of driven monotonous rhythmic base that is the inverse of Mozart. Again, it was a Mozart melody that I later recognized when I heard the music that Devo was producing... the beginning of a rhythmic structure. It was distinctive enough that when I heard Devo in concert, I (could) remember the white guitar being played and that music... the determined boring chords. They were non-melodic."

Bertholf's colleague Ed Dorn was a member of the Black Mountain school, which also included Charles Olson, Robert Creeley and Robert Duncan. A native of Illinois, he arrived at Kent shortly after the campus shootings, at the invitation of Bertholf. In the 1993 preface to his *Recollection to Gran Apacheria*, a verse study of the Apache Indian tribe, he recalled his early impressions of Kent, where this Apache poem was the basis for his course in the literature of the far West.

Are We Not Men?

"The atmosphere and mood among students and townspeople were disturbingly vindictive," Dorn wrote. "Graduate students, when you encountered them in the hallway, would stay you from appointments, like ancient mariners. The checkout women at Safeway held you in thrall, like a Gestapo slowly perusing your papers.

"Two members of the percipient Devo (Bob Lewis and Jerry Casale) were in that seminar," he continued. "The atmosphere was laden with innuendo. I came to see the Apache – which was the subject I'd assigned myself – as the students, 'the irreconcilables,' and the enemy, Ravenna and Kent, as the ranks of General Miles and the Cavalry. Whatever the relevance of the metastrophe, there was a heavy charge in the environment."

Jerry was one of the conductors – and receivers – of that charge.

"Kent wasn't then like it is today," he said. "There was some just inexplicable kind of spontaneous combustion in that area that didn't make sense really. (Of course,) we didn't know that. We were taking it for granted that this was the way college should be. This is the way it always will be. At that time, Kent had a really progressive faculty.... They were responsible for bringing most of the interesting young filmmakers, sculptors and artists from the East Coast. (The faculty) brought them in as guest lecturers, poets and musicians.

"Morton Subotnick was there doing workshops in the basement. It just was incredible. You know, Mark Rudd came and spoke – Abbey Hoffman, Norman Mailer and Harlan Ellison. They would bring in the New York Film Festival winners, and show us all these films by, like, the Kuchar Brothers and all these underground films like *Babo 73*. We were just taking this kind of stuff for granted, that this was the way it was."

Whether they appreciated it or not, the members of the Devo circle were steeped in a culture that fed and nurtured their decidedly outsider notions. So when Bertholf and Dorn began planning the Creative Arts Festival in earnest, Bob asked them if it might be possible for him and his friends to play some music. They agreed. Of course, even they were probably not certain what they'd agreed to. A date was set for the concert – April 18, 1973 – and Bob and Jerry began figuring out how to pull it off. Although they and Pete Gregg had been making music together, they had never put together a full band. But it was a given that Jerry would play bass and Bob would play guitar. For the rest of the band, they began looking around them. This was the chance Jerry had been looking for to get together with Mark. They definitely wanted him to be part of it. Rod Reisman, a townie from Kent, was a great drummer. They'd ask him to play. And Jerry's brother Bob was a decent guitarist. They could probably talk him into it. But who would sing?

Bob suggested his roommate, Fred Weber. Weber was a talented vocalist, having fronted Joe Walsh's former band, the Measles, and another big local band, Lace Wing. But he was also totally traditional. He sang pop, rock and blues covers and originals that sounded like pop, rock and blues covers. He hadn't been part of all these highbrow discussions of evolutionary theory, of human absurdity, of Dadaism and Chinese computer rock'n'roll. He was a bar band guy. But he was also Bob's roommate, and a really good guy. So when they asked him, he said, yeah, he'd do it.

The next hurdle was material. The group didn't have a set, per se. They had recorded some stuff, but that was before Mark had come into the mix, and it would all change with his keyboards.

And what about a name? The word "Devo" had stuck, but they wanted to give it more intellectual punch. So they settled on Sextet Devo, a moniker that somehow seemed befitting of the academic nature of the festival and the Kent State University Recital Hall where the performance was to be staged. In that same vein, and perhaps at the expense of the more polished Fred, they listed the singer as "Chas. Frederick Weber III."

By the time all this was settled, they had three days to practice. They worked on half a dozen or so songs, and rehearsed diligently. They wanted to put on some kind of a "show" and decided, in keeping with the simplicity and monotony of the music, that each member would dress in a different, single color, kind of like the Olympic rings. For their newspaper advertisement for the show, they used a picture Bob had clipped from the September 1954 issue of *National Geographic*. The photograph, taken in semidarkness with infrared film, captured a group of schoolchildren sitting in a movie theater, literally frightened out of their seats. The actual source of their terror was a highly climactic moment in a documentary film of a bird and snake in a fight to the death. But the band replaced that caption with the line, "A typical Sextet Devo audience."

The picture seemed just right. Sextet Devo's music was calculated to both attract and repel. The group wanted to be heard, but it also wanted to challenge and provoke. One song they had worked on, "River Run", included a long segue into Mark's interpretive reworking of the fourth movement of Brahms' First Symphony. "We weren't very good musicians except for Mark at the time," Bob said, "but we were clever. In fact, maybe a little too clever. It took a long time for the audience to kind of catch up."

Meanwhile, the members of the SDS, from whom Jerry had distanced himself after the shootings, were working up some kind of a response to the Creative Arts Festival. In a communiqué to members that proposed a "Radical Arts Project," the SDS suggested, "developing a broad and coherent methodology for organizing work around the arts... maybe a critique written concerning the upcoming Creative Arts Festival." Or perhaps better, they continued, "an Action could be done around it." In the end, they seemed content to suggest, "maybe we could put out a pamphlet about 'What is Radical Arts Project, Anyway?'"

Whether such an "Action" materialized is unknown, but Sextet Devo was about to give a musical answer to the SDS question, "What is a radical arts project?"

The evening of the show arrived. The group, scheduled for 7 p.m., was billed as "Sextet Devo: six on six" and described in the program as "polyr-hythmic tone exercises in de-evolution." Bob Casale, the budding radiologist, was wearing a set of scrubs. Reisman was dressed in black to match his drum kit. Jerry was wearing a butcher's coat copped from Akron Provision. Bob Lewis had a monkey mask over his head. And Mark was dressed in a doctor's robe, a pair of Converse Chuck Taylors and an ape mask.

The audience was rather sparse. Mark walked onto the stage alone and took his place at the keyboards, stage left. At full volume, he began to play, beginning with a mutated romp through *Here Comes Peter Cottontail*, a version that would have made Mrs. Fox's skin crawl. In a twisted voice, he sang, "Here comes Peter Cottontail, hopping down the bunny trail, hippity hoppity look at Peter go. Basket full of fun and toys, joy for all the girls and boys, hip-pity hoppity look at Peter go. There's a nurse for Uncle Johnny and a boat for sister Sue, there's a douche sack for my mommy and a box of bunny poo…"

With the band still waiting to emerge, this led to what had become known as "the headache solo." Bob Lewis described it this way: "Ka-Twinnnng (downward sliding note), Ka-Twinnng, Ka-Twinnnggg, Ka-Twing… Ker-Plannng (upward sliding note), Ker-Plannng, Ker-Plannnng, Ker-Plannnnng… Ka-Twinnng, Ka-Twinnnng, Ka-Twinnngg, Ka-Twinnng …. Ker-Plannnng, Ker-Plannnnnng, Ker-Plannnnnng, Ker-Plannnng…. This went on for 15-20 minutes, while Mark scurried about the stage, seeming to be unable to control the sound, reacting every time the cycle changed, hold-ing his head with both hands as if beset by an horrific migraine."

The table was set, and the rest of the band came out, picked up their instruments, and began to build on this unsettling foundation. Their set included the songs "Private Secretary", "Wiggle Worm", "Beehive Flash", "What Comes Around Goes Around", "Subhuman Woman", "River Run" and "Sun Come Up Moon Go Down". There was a vague sense of the traditional sound of a rock band, but with Mark's keyboard squealing and squawking over the top and Jerry's sense of intentional monotony running underneath. Poor Fred Weber, dressed in a turtleneck sweater, stood sideways, holding his microphone uncertainly, as if caught between a desire to try to pick up his musical cues and a desire not to be seen in the middle of all this.

The performance was captured on primitive, black-and-white half-inch Portapak video. At one point, Mark plays the theme song to *Mr. Jingeling*, a local, low-tech television segment that resurfaced every Christmas season. Mr. Jingeling, sponsored by Halle's department store in Cleveland, was a sort of full-grown elf who was the keeper of the keys to the North Pole. Every afternoon he appeared, whipping the children of Northeast Ohio into a frenzy of commercial wonder. The band devolves from this recognizable jingle into a throbbing, monotonous, tortured blues. A single note carries the rhythm, with a thin, repetitive guitar lead over the top. Mark, adding weird keyboard noises, occasionally swings his arms, ape-like, bobbing back and forth in a decidedly un-funky groove.

In this moment, the band has captured Jerry's notion of a completely devolved blues. And in fact, this earliest musical foray reveals what would become a Devo trademark: the ability to remove "soul" from the mix of pop expectations and to replace it with something else, usually gray matter. In the liner notes to *Mashin' Potatoes*, an obscure, late-1990s ska-oriented Devo tribute album, the band Critical Mass observed, "they have to be the absolute whitest band in recent rock'n'roll." There's a real truth in that statement. Devo's landmark deconstruction of the Rolling Stones' "Satisfaction" is a pinnacle of the band's intent to strip out one kind of artifice (white artists acting like black men) and replace it with another (white artists acting like robots). Even in this earliest performance, even with a group that didn't fully mesh musically, Sextet Devo succeeded intellectually. They managed to make their postmodern statement, by giving musical "commentary" within the context of their own music. Their business cards would soon declare this "Chinese computer rock 'n' roll, scientific music + vis. arts … for beautiful mutants." This group was the opposite of, say, the Numbers Band, which fully explored the inner workings of the blues, tuning it like a supremely talented mechanic. Sextet Devo went into the same engine with a pipe wrench and sledgehammer and turned the thing into a spaceship that was bound to crash.

In his book *Fargo Rock City*, rock critic Chuck Klosterman wrote that, "Listening to (Eric) Clapton is like getting a sensual massage from a woman you've loved for the past ten years; listening to Van Halen is like having the best sex of your life with three foxy nursing students you met at a Tastee Freez." To extend that metaphor, Devo would be the equivalent of autoerotic asphyxiation, the sexual technique of partly hanging oneself during masturbation to achieve a more intense orgasm. Like Devo, the experiment is based far more on theory than any notion of soulful (or even human) lovemaking, and has profound potential for disaster. But if it works, well, it's polymer love, baby.

The Sextet Devo performance continued, with Weber being a good soldier, lending his talented pipes to songs like "River Run", the title of which comes from the first and last words of a James Joyce novel.

The crude video of this evening shows an audience, if not frightened out of its seats, at least intrigued. There had been discussion among the band of only filming the audience, training the cameras toward the seats to record, not action, but reaction. In the audience footage that does exist, a young woman appears to whisper in the ear of her companion, half-pointing toward the stage; a young man stares in almost transparent confusion. He *wants* to get it, but he seems unsure how to accomplish that goal. Finally, at least one segment of the audience decided to go with the groove. "River Run" was the last song and included Mark's long Brahms solo, leading into a bossa nova of sorts. Harvey Bialy, a poet who was one of the guests at the arts festival, was accompanied by some California-style hippie chicks with long hair, beads and fringe skirts. They got up from their seats during the instrumental interlude and began to dance, just as they might have done to the Grateful Dead.

And then it was over. Marty Reymann, who served as the band's roadie that night, helped tear down equipment and loaded the gear into his van. Reisman, who had played on the condition that he be paid, got his money and departed. He hadn't necessarily disliked the experience, but he was sure he'd had enough. Sextet Devo didn't have any more performances scheduled, and he wasn't interested in staying involved with something that didn't seem to have much future.

As for Weber: "I enjoyed goofing around with them," he said, "but after that initial performance, I knew that was it for me. It was all too strange. I don't think it necessarily had anything to do with that appearance, but I pretty much stopped performing with bands and moved to Virginia within about a month of the Sextet Devo debut."

That left the Casale brothers, Bob Lewis and Mark Mothersbaugh to consider what they had wrought. Mark, in almost painful sincerity, reflected on the experience in *My Struggle*, the journal he'd been scribbling away on in his room at Marty and Ed's house.

"I want people to be able to look at me and say, 'There goes a responsible man,' or, 'There goes a respectable guy,' or even both," he wrote. "Somehow though, I always end up being the clown at the fish pond, or the monkey on stage.

"My band finally gets a chance to perform at the Creative Arts Festival at Kent State University … a real intellectually pretentious affair!!! Virtual orgasm for the I.Q. conscious Spud; and, how do I walk out on stage? In a doctor's robe with a monkey mask on, standing at an organ playing 'Here comes Peter Cottontail' ... and all the other guys just stood there in the wings for a full five minutes, while my face turned bright red, under the mask! Not at all the way I wanted to see it!"

Chapter 8

Mark was getting sharper and sharper at taking things out of context. He had continued a search-and-destroy mission with textbook pictures, old catalog photos, happy-homemaker advertising images and the like, cutting them up and manipulating them. A father running into the kitchen, cat attached to one leg, little boy clinging happily to his side, is carrying a dismembered woman's nude torso like a side of beef. "Poppa's got the vittles," the caption begins. His startled wife drops her cups and saucers.

Mark was finding these images all around him. He rifled through the stacks at flea markets, thrift shops and used bookstores. He knew what he liked. So it was with a highly trained eye, not long after the Sextet Devo show, that he came across an old religious pamphlet with a brown cover. The title was *Jocko-Homo Heavenbound*. The cover showed a man pushing himself out of the body of an ape, with an angel standing behind, raising her finger skyward. The writer's name was B. H. Shadduck, Ph.D., author of *Puddle to Paradise* and *The Toadstool Among the Tombs*.

The pamphlet had been published in Roger, Ohio in 1924. As Mark leafed through the pages, he discovered the book's only illustration, of a devil with big wings, horns and a pitchfork, and the word "DEVOLUTION" written across his chest. The devil is standing behind a gruesome-looking ape gnawing on a bone, and gesturing toward a flight of stairs. A bat flits by for effect; bones and a skull are scattered below. Each of the steps on this stairway to hell is labeled with sins. A whole litany of them: world war; tax, usury; toil; suicide; morphine; cocain (sic), dope; orgies; cock fighting; white slavery; slavery; alcohol; insanity, idiocy; pre-natal murder; nameless crimes; nameless diseases; make your own god; and might makes right.

With the possible exception of world war and cock fighting, this could have been the backstage shenanigans at an early-'70s rock concert. The good Dr. Shadduck, of course, couldn't have made that connection as he wrote 50 years earlier. But he also, based on his commentary, would not have been surprised by how quickly such activity had become romanticized by youth culture.

Shadduck clearly had a bone to pick with the state of humanity. Mark did, too. So the young art student read on. Shadduck was a staunch opponent of

Are We Not Men?

Darwinian evolutionism; this was one of several pamphlets he wrote on the subject. Monkey-man – literally Jocko-Homo – was at the bottom of the ladder, not the top, he argued. "God made man," Shadduck wrote, "but he used a monkey to gather the dirt." His editorial-style sermon goes on for 40 pages, ending with the genteel suggestion, "Reader, if this little book seems worth while to you, why not send a copy to the boy in college?"

Mission accomplished. Mark found the little book incredibly worthwhile. Author Donna Kossy, in her book *Strange Creations*, referred to "Jocko-Homo Heavenbound" as the Devo "Old Testament". The book's title and ideas would later be applied to the group's musical manifesto, "Jocko Homo", a song that says pretty much everything one needs to know about the band's philosophy. Mark showed his discovery to his friends, and they recognized it as a significant entry to this bibliography they'd been compiling.

"It really pleased us to have that book," Jerry said in a 1995 magazine interview with Kossy. "(We were) building more of a reservoir… a storehouse of quack information."

Jerry and Mark, if they didn't share Shadduck's Calvinist views, were at least sympathetic to his notion of human corruption. Jerry, echoing his own reactions to the Kent State shootings, paraphrased Shadduck's thesis statement by asking, "…(H)ow can people who are responsible for so much pain, suffering and moral hypocrisy think that they are ascending into Heaven, when really, they're twisted and sick and what they think is 'good' is 'bad?'"

The book also gave ammunition to a growing notion of "plastic reality", the concept that truth is often contradictory and impossible to nail down. "You ask band members the same question, you're going to get four completely different answers if they're not in the same room," Jerry once explained. "You'd read something Bob 1 said, something I said, something Mark said about the same concert, and you wouldn't believe that it could possibly even be the same planet. That was the idea. In other words, it would start to become clear how each level of reality was working independent of the other one, sometimes together, sometimes causing horrible conflicts. We were into that."

"Devo," he said another time, "knows everything is based on inconsistency."

In Shadduck, they found moral affirmation of this. "In every false teaching," Shadduck wrote, "there is an element of truth."

With this important piece of information in hand, they continued their music-making, albeit at a casual pace. Although the Sextet Devo performance had been seen by some as a grand success, the group did not appear in public again until a full year later, at the second Creative Arts Festival.

Bertholf began planning the event months in advance. In a December 1973 letter to Ed Dorn, he wrote, "Talk of the spring Arts Festival has come up again. In fact, there is a lot of pressure from far corners to change the thing around, which means, now that people see it is a good thing, they want part of the action."

Devo, having dropped the "Sextet" from its name, would be part of that action. As with the 1973 festival, Bertholf invited a number of notable poets. Robert Creeley, one of the most important figures in the Black Mountain school, was to attend. Dorn, who had left the university, would be back as a featured poet, along with Holbrook Teeter and Joanne Kyger. Devo would be in heady company.

The group's lineup would require some significant retooling. The singer and drummer were gone. Jerry would at last get to move up to the microphone and handle most of the lead vocals, and Mark suggested that his brother Jim, who had been playing in bar bands with their other brother Bob, might be interested in playing. The Mothersbaugh siblings were fairly tight; Bob, in fact, shared an Akron apartment with his sister Sue, who was working as a receptionist. So Jim was an obvious choice, but also an intriguing one. Jim had been tinkering with a set of homemade electronic drums, attaching guitar pickups to rubber practice pads. But the gigs he was playing as part of groups like Sneaky Pete and The Mothersbaugh Band didn't exactly lend themselves to this kind of experimentation.

"My brother Bob and I were off doing the rock'n'roll thing, and getting tired of it," Jim recalled. "We realized that in the little bars in Akron nobody was going to walk up and say, 'Man, you write great music! We're gonna give you a record deal!' We had been coming to that realization, you know. We had figured out fifty different ways to play 'Smoke On The Water' – from polka versions to classical versions. And so, the Devo thing... I think Bob and I both didn't understand where it was coming from really. I don't even know if Mark and Jerry did back then. I think I was sort of an emergency fill-in when I was brought into Devo to be the drummer. It just sort of worked out because I was a willing participant for a long time, (and) they... put up with my electronics. It was a mutual arrangement."

The new version of Devo worked up a considerably different set of material. The group was scheduled to perform on April 23, 1974, in the brand-new Kent State University Governance Chambers, a room that looked like a miniature United Nations and would later be the setting for a significant scene in Devo's seminal film, *The Beginning Was the End: The Truth About De-Evolution*.

Somebody must have been smitten by the previous year's gig. The day of the performance, the *Daily Kent Stater*, the campus newspaper, waxed ecstatic: "Devo makes a triumphant return to the site of last year's spectacle... This is your chance. This year's performance will degenerate in the Governance Chambers (as is altogether fitting). Seats will be at a premium, so get there early. Don't miss 'Private Secretary', 'I Been Refused', 'Sub-human Woman', 'The Rope Song', 'Pigs Waddle', 'Be Stiff', 'Androgyny', 'O No' and 'All of Us' as performed by Gerald and Robert Casale, Robert Lewis and James and Mark Mothersbaugh... the incredible Devo."

At 7 o'clock that Tuesday evening, Devo took the stage. As with the previous year, the music was primitive, with weird keyboard splashes and droning robotic structures. Jim Mothersbaugh's drum kit cemented the mechanical intent, sounding more like something out of a tire factory than a music store. There were blips and beeps from Mark and staccato punches from Jerry's bass. They were continuing to deconstruct the idea of a rock band, and to construct the grand idea that had been worming its way through all the art they were making.

After the show, Bertholf hosted a party at his home to close down another successful festival. The members of the Devo crowd attended, as did Robert Creeley. Creeley's most distinctive physical characteristic was the patch that covered his missing left eye, giving him a somewhat gruesome presence. He looked like a pirate. After a night of drinking, the Devo musicians found themselves on Bertholf's front porch, engaged in an intellectual discussion with Creeley, who was also rather drunk. As Bob Lewis recalled, Jerry appeared, wearing his Gorj mask and putting on the whole act that went along with it. As Mark sat watching, Gorj sidled up to the famous poet and intoned, "I was not always thus."

Creeley, not missing a beat, turned to Gorj, flipped up his eye patch to reveal the ugly hole underneath, and responded. "No shit? Me neither."

Mark screamed in horror. Or was it delight?

※ ※ ※

A month after the second Creative Arts Festival, Bob Casale got married. The 21-year-old, who was working as an X-ray technician, was wed to a secretary named Sherry Lynn Stringer, who had been Bob's high school sweetheart.

Their lives were moving forward. Although he would not graduate, Mark was pretty much finished with college, and Jerry, having earned degrees in both 20th-century literature and drawing and design at Kent State, was ready to try his hand at teaching. In the spring semester of 1974, he got a job as a part-time art instructor at the University of Akron, hoping this might be the beginning of the course of his life. He had become friends with some of the University of Akron art faculty; Don Harvey, whose reputation was growing, invited Jerry to talk to his classes about the Devo multimedia concept and attended Devo performances in Kent. The job was going well, and Jerry liked doing it. Unfortunately, Mark unintentionally derailed his friend's teaching career.

Jerry had started his students keeping sketchbooks. The idea was to teach them that they didn't have to suddenly create a masterpiece, that the process of art was incremental, and by keeping a daily art journal, they could develop their creativity and style.

"Whatever you want to do in them, I don't care," Jerry told the class. "If you want to, cut things out of magazines, paste them in there and draw funny additions to them."

Art can be funny, he explained. There are no rules. But you still have to work at it.

The questions in response were inevitable: "What's it supposed to look like? What do you expect us to do?"

"They want to know exactly what was going to get them a grade," Jerry recalled. "Pathetic. And I go, 'No, you don't understand. No two should even be alike.' Well, that even bummed them out more."

So the diligent teacher brought in sketchbooks by his artist friends to provide examples of how others had done them. Most of the friends had been in the M-A-T-E-R class. One of those artists was Mark Mothersbaugh.

"(Mark) did these really frightening scatological drawings and tracings out of medical books... but then he would draw himself as the doctor," Jerry said. "I only showed... the kids the funny stuff like... a face just barfing on the moon, and things like that. (I presented them with) ridiculous drawings... a little baby's body... (with) an old man's head on it and he'd have him saying something. I thought, 'Well, they'll think this is funny and they'll see that they can be funny.'

"Well, other stuff in that book, you couldn't possibly show it at a state university, and I knew it. So, I had just marked the pages of everybody's books that I wanted to show the class, and I hired an AV guy with an overhead projector. Then I would just show those pages of the book. We were about halfway looking through sketchbooks when a mandatory break came up, with a bell that rings. The books were under the shelf on the overhead projector cart, and the light came on and everybody leaves the classroom. I go to the teacher's lounge.

"Pretty soon I get a teacher coming in going, 'Jerry, will you step outside?'"

"What's going on?" Jerry asked.

"Well, you know, Stacey's down with Dean so-and-so and she's still crying; she's hysterical.

"She had gone back into the classroom early before the break was over, grabbed Mark's book and started flipping through it," Jerry continued. "And (she) saw – it's like this complete medical diagram of a baby being pulled out of a woman, breech birth. Mark has drawn himself in with a phone company tool belt on and a big grin on his face. Just really, really – just nasty shock-value creepy. And that did it."

The images were from a series of 1972 cards titled "Parlour Games" that also would appear in *My Struggle*. Each illustration manipulated a medical-book drawing of the birthing process, with Mark adding chainsaws, hammers and other disturbing elements. In one picture, Dr. Mark Mothersbaugh is holding a baby that has been cut in half.

"So, I go to the Dean's office and it was just like out of a good bad movie. I walk in and the girl won't look at me. She's got all red eyes, and she stands up and leaves. (The dean) tells me to sit down and he's holding the book. And he goes, 'Well, Mr. Casale, is this your idea of an art education at Akron University?' He just turns it around, and shoves it at me open to that page. I tried to explain myself, but it didn't cut any ice. He said, 'You can finish out the semester, but you better go look for another job.'"

❋ ❋ ❋

Two months after the Creative Arts Festival, *Time* magazine published a review of an odd book that had been making waves in Europe. It was called *The Beginning Was the End* by Oscar Kiss Maerth. The red cover, with a hollow-eyed, almost skull-like image of a man's face, bore this brief explanation of what lay inside: "How man came into being through cannibalism – intelligence can be eaten."

The basic premise of the book is that the human species was an accident of evolution. That cannibalistic apes began eating brains because it increased their sexual desire and intelligence. This brain consumption led to a sort of hyper-evolution, which led to man. But that process had also led to an oversized brain too big for the human skull to accommodate, and a resultant mental illness that triggered a perverse sense of progress, bound to lead to human demise. Maerth believed the primates had been able to communicate by ESP, but that their brain-eating had destroyed this power.

"Man is a newcomer on the earth," the book begins. "He can remember neither the hour of his birth nor his origin. For a long time he fancied himself the centre of the world as he imagined it, and by God's will its appointed master. He placed himself at the apex of an imaginary self-constructed pyramid, and he has had to climb down from it step by step in the course of the last two thousand years. He stands at present on the lowest step, but he must now retreat even from there. He must learn the truth concerning his origin and himself."

The truth about de-evolution, in other words. As soon as the Devo members learned of this book, they carried the *Time* magazine review with them as proof such a book existed and became obsessed with finding a copy. Bob Lewis wrote Ed Dorn asking for help in tracking it down. They knew it would be important to them. Like "Jocko-Homo Heavenbound", this strange piece of scholarship placed Man on the final step of his downward climb.

The Beginning Was the End was rumored to be a bestseller in Europe. "Oscar Kiss Maerth" was thought to be a pseudonym, a pun on "Oscar Kiss My Ass." The author was alleged by some to be a former Nazi hiding out in South America. According to both his widow, and his close friend Klaus Schleusener, who provided editing advice, Maerth was not a Nazi or Nazi sympathizer. Even so, he clearly supported the eugenics movement for improving society, i.e. those with the best genes should be encouraged to procreate, and those with inferior genes should be prevented from breeding.

Time magazine seemed not to take the book very seriously. The reviewer, R.Z. Sheppard, wrote that it, "bears all the markings of pristine eccentricity: a big theme, a closed system of self-perpetuating logic, a disdain for accepted thought, no specific scientific references, no index, and no bibliography."

The book, impossible to find in Kent or Akron, appeared to be a masterpiece of plastic reality, not to mention a treasure trove of devolution. Although it would take more than a year before Jerry and Bob Lewis found a copy in a New York City bookstore, it would become, in Donna Kossy's words, the Devo "New Testament".

Chapter 9

"What is the law?"

Dr. Moreau, standing at the edge of the House of Pain, is trying to restore order among the half-men he has surgically created from beasts. This is his domain, the *Island of Lost Souls*, in the creepy 1932 film adaptation of H.G. Wells' novel *The Island of Dr. Moreau*. Charles Laughton, as Moreau, cracks a whip and casts a menacing eye over his throng of mutants. Bela Lugosi, face covered with hair, gives the rote response.

"Not to run on all fours – that is the law." He addresses his fellow mutants:

"Are we not men?"

"Are we not men?" they grunt in unison.

The call-and-response goes on.

Are We Not Men?

Laughton: "What is the law?"
Lugosi: "Not to eat meat – that is the law. Are we not men?"
Mutants: "Are we not men?"
Laughton: "What is the law?"
Lugosi: "Not to spill blood – that is the law. Are we not men?"
Mutants: "Are we not men?"

Seventy years later, this scene still sends shivers. "His is the hand that makes," the congregation continues. "His is the hand that heals. His is the House of Pain." When the film was first released, it was widely banned, so disturbing was the notion of a scientist twisting God's work. But *Island of Lost Souls* did eventually find an audience, and 40 years after its release, it had become a touchstone for young people in Northeast Ohio, thanks to Ghoulardi and his long-running successor and protégé, Chuck Schodowski. "Big Chuck" teamed up with a TV weatherman named Bob Wells. Patching together their nicknames, *Hoolihan and Big Chuck* continued the tradition of airing old horror movies on late-night television, amid schlocky skits and 'certain ethnic' (read: Polish) jokes. *Island of Lost Souls* was a classic staple, and it burned itself into formative brains.

"It was one of those films that just scared the shit out of me as a kid," Bob Lewis recalled. Jerry, too, held a special place in his heart for the film, which he found equally frightening but also somehow sincere. And Mark had an epiphany as he made a connection between the on-screen horror and the conditions of his own existence.

"I remember watching *Island of Lost Souls*," he said, "and there's this scene near the end where there's a revolt, where the subhumans, the failed experiments – or as they called themselves (imitating a horror-movie voice) 'Not men, not beasts – THINGS!' are rebelling. They lit the jungle on fire and you see them running – at night, the fire is reflecting their shadows on the House of Pain as they run through the jungle, and you don't really see them; you see their shadows. These hunched-over creatures, hobbling in pain and terror and chaos, just trudging by this House of Pain. And I remember at that moment feeling a camaraderie, and feeling like, 'I've been there'."

To him, Akron, with its German Expressionist landscape of smoke-stained factories, seemed to reflect the House of Pain. Akron is the nation's second-cloudiest city, after Seattle. It's not hard to dwell on darkness there. Mark and Jerry shared a certain disdain for a place where great numbers of young people had no future outside those hot, grimy rubber factories. Somewhere in the growing accumulation of Devo details was the movie's key line – "Are we not men?" – which seemed to capture so much of what Devo was about, and would become a key phrase in their vocabulary. The line evoked the darkness of evolutionary misdeeds, which had become a staple of the Big Idea. But it also captured, with odd poignancy, the feeling of being an outsider. Devo were brave nerds, and that line could just as easily be uttered in a jock-nerd confrontation. "Am I not a man?" a brave nerd might utter as the jock grabs him by the shirt-front. Of course, the jock would probably just screw up his face for a moment, trying to figure it out, before popping him one anyway. Still, the idea of the put-upon outsider rebelling against his conditions had an important resonance.

❀ ❀ ❀

Devo still didn't think of themselves as a working band, or even, necessarily, a band. The core members were making art of all sorts, and music happened to be one medium. But it was also an increasingly obvious one. Perhaps even the strange music of these art students could find a niche. If a message was to be spread, a stage in a bar was better than a highbrow 'zine or an art journal.

In Kent, that connection was especially obvious. The college town's music scene had continued to thrive. The James Gang had broken out, and Joe Walsh, former scenester, had become a bona fide rock star. When the James Gang opened for the Who in Pittsburgh in 1969, Pete Townshend called Walsh "the greatest living guitarist." Walsh, even as he grew more famous, remained a touchstone for the musicians back in Kent. Others, including Glass Harp's Phil Keaggy, had also gotten attention. Keaggy was an unusually talented guitarist. He was, in fact, reputedly one of the few guitarists Jimi Hendrix ever allowed into Electric Ladyland studios. There had been nights, not so long before, when one could go see both guitarists playing in bars next door to one another.

Back home, the Numbers Band remained a rock of the foundation, holding court at JB's, the Kove, Walter's Café and other clubs. So, after the second Creative Arts Festival, Jerry asked Bob Kidney if his group might be able to open for the Numbers Band. Kidney, despite the previous tension with Jerry, agreed.

Jerry immediately got busy designing his stage costume. He obtained a butcher's coat and spent countless hours dipping the ends of a couple hundred tampons into liquid latex primary colors – red, yellow and blue. He had a girlfriend help him sew the tampons onto the coat. When it was finished, it looked like a fringe jacket, which was the desired effect. It worked as a commentary on the whole Woodstock aesthetic: Roger Daltrey looked good in fringe. Sly Stone looked good in fringe. Jerry looked mutated in fringe.

The coat is described in Booji Boy's *My Struggle*, complete with a diagram for painting the tampons. This "simple experiment involving the phenomena of dreams" came with a warning: "This experiment should not be performed by children, without adult supervision."

The show was at the Kove. Jerry had asked his friend, Pete Gregg, to sit in with the band on a few songs – "I Need a Chick", which Pete had co-written, "Auto Modown" and "I Been Refused", the song inspired by the Adult Physiological Studies Center affair of a few years before. Jerry donned his outrageous coat of many tampons and took the stage. Jaws dropped. These were Numbers Band fans, after all. They had come to boogie. Jerry and company had come with a completely different agenda. There was a certain sense of convention even in a bohemian college town and Devo, from its very beginnings, was finding friction at nearly every turn. The experiment had succeeded in the safe haven on the Creative Arts Festival. Now it was time to carry the word out to the masses.

"Am I not a man?" the coat seemed to scream.

The band began playing, anchored by Jim Mothersbaugh's electronic drums. Jim had been working steadily on improving this kit. It was impressive not only for its innovation – one of the first of its kind – but also for its sheer visual effect. He had gone to a local Midas muffler shop and had pieces of tailpipe bent and plated with chrome. The kit, with a white noise generator for a high hat and pads triggered by humbucker guitar pickups, was hooked to a synthesizer that sometimes took on a life of its own. The operation, Jim recalled, was still very crude. "I mean, sometimes we'd be on stage and these things would just lose control and start making their own sounds and noises," he said. "We'd have to stop and get the stage quiet from vibrating, so we could get 'em fixed and get going from there."

To Jerry, the drums were the instrumental equivalent of the tampon coat. "God, those homemade electronic drums sure looked impressive," he said. "Incredible, frightening looking. Everything was made from scratch. It's like if the Little Rascals said, 'I could make some drums.' The welded base alone, it opened up into a V, it weighed something like seventy pounds. We'd set that up for a gig. People would just look and go, 'What the fuck?' They would just be horrified. And then the sound that came out was completely unmusical. It was just like amplified trashcans. Made it sound great though."

The drum machine was a rarity. Sly Stone had pioneered its use, including one on his 1971 hit, "Family Affair". But the last place one would expect to find such a kit was behind a struggling local band in Kent, Ohio.

Recollections vary on the band's lineup that night. Bob Casale probably didn't play, and Bob Lewis probably did. Regardless, everyone and everything on the stage – even Jim's drum set – took a backseat to Jerry's coat. He would turn sharply and the tampons would fly about from his sleeves and body. He would pull them off and throw them into the crowd. His effort at perform-ance art was met with bewilderment.

Midway through the set, Jerry invited Gregg to join in. This had been his main musical partner at the beginning of this experiment. Gregg was a tal-ented guitarist, but uncomfortable playing before a crowd. So, suffering from a combination of stage fright and what he later described as a "home medica-tion accident", stoned and dumbfounded, he spent his whole time on stage tuning his guitar. Confused barflies probably assumed it was part of the show. At least he wasn't pelting them with feminine products in the name of art.

❋ ❋ ❋

Bob Lewis was growing more serious about Devo's possibilities. In a letter to Ed Dorn, he wrote, "Up until now, the stuff that has been put together is a poor joke, with the punch line being that there was lacking one rather crucial factor, i.e., the sheer physical dexterity necessary for any successful assay into the world of musical performance. This, with time, has been somewhat allevi-ated, and it begins to progress more rapidly. Will send cassette when possible and congruent with ego prerequisites."

The band had continued recording sporadically. Marty Reymann and Ed Barger had been so enthusiastic about Mark's future that they decided to build a studio specifically for him. Behind a car wash Marty's brother owned in Norton, near Akron, they built a small concrete-block building. Mark came up with its name. He dubbed it Man Ray Studios, a play on Reymann's surname that also directly referenced the famous French Dada-Surrealist, Man Ray.

"Marty and I built Man Ray Studio from the ground up," Barger said. "We owned the building and equipment, while Marty's brother Dennis owned the land and car wash. I designed the studio, and it was made of cement blocks. I even had the slabs soundproofed from the walls, so when the trucks rumbled by you wouldn't hear them. The control room slab was separate from the studio. The sound from the studio was separate from the control room. This was not some converted garage, but carefully planned and built as a recording studio. I had an all-tube Ampex four-track – just like the machine with which The Beatles recorded *Sgt. Pepper.*"

The band soon began to rehearse there, which, Mark recalled, came with a rather unusual set of conditions.

"It cost us 50 cents every time we rehearsed because we had to drive through a car wash to get to our bunker," he said. "In the winter... our car would just be covered in a sheet of ice."

Even as Man Ray was emerging as a home base, Devo ventured into Audio Recording, a state-of-the-art 16-track studio in Cleveland, to cut a demo.

Playing on those sessions were Jerry and the three Mothersbaugh brothers. Their friend Bruce Hensal, who had been touring with Joe Walsh, went with them to help produce.

"We were freaking the engineer out because he was used to working with Grand Funk Railroad," Hensal said, "and we kept asking him if he could make the guitar a little smaller, a little thinner. He was like, 'What?'" Not to mention this crazy set of electronic drums. Bob Lewis remembers that the material recorded in Cleveland included "Mechanical Man" and "Smart Patrol".

Devo had also produced some tapes at an Akron studio called Krieger-Field, named after a St. Bernard. The growing archive of increasingly proficient material had yielded a respectable demo tape, and Bob decided to try to move the matter forward. A friend from the early college days, Patrick Cullie, had moved out West at the urging of Hensal. Bob and Cullie, along with Fred Weber and a few others, had gone to Woodstock together and had both been students of Bertholf's. In 1970, right after the shootings, Hensal had gotten a job working for famed promoter and rock impresario Bill Graham, running sound at the Fillmore West in San Francisco. Hensal hired Cullie who, in part through his friendship with Joe Walsh, had gotten into the record business. But he had still maintained his Kent friendships. This led to an almost sur-realistic moment on May 4, 1970. "The day of the shooting," Cullie recalled, "I was riding in a limo to Ann Arbor with Rod Stewart and the Faces, heading for a photo shoot when it came on the radio. I was freaked because all my friends, lovers and both my sisters were there."

Bob and Cullie had remained close. So in the summer of 1974, Bob and an old Commuter's Cafeteria friend named Peggy Freemon set off for California to find him.

"Bob wanted to get advice on how to market a rock group, because that is what Cullie was doing, and very successfully," Bertholf recalled. "He was trying to get information from a person who was experienced in the field. How do we approach the act of making it and how to find a studio in California that would make a master tape, or whatever the technical term is."

Bertholf, at the time, had "serious doubts" about whether Devo had any chance of succeeding. But Cullie had seen Devo during his visits back to Kent, and had been especially impressed with Mark. "I saw then the genius of this kid I had been hearing about," he said. Cullie had also seen the tampon coat, which helped lead him to believe Devo was "a performance art project, not really a commercial entity."

Bob did find Cullie in California. They talked. Cullie offered what advice he could, and agreed to accept the 16-track demos Bob had brought along.

He would see if he could open any doors. Through these same connections, Bob also managed to get the tapes into the hands of Irving Azoff, "a young self-made millionaire via the Eagles, Joe Walsh, Minnie (Ripperton), etc." Cullie shared Devo's art-school sensibilities, but he worked in the music business mainstream, and recognized these tapes might be hard on the ears of his associates. He promised to do what he could.

❄ ❄ ❄

Meanwhile, the more Devo gelled into a band, the more tension there was between the members. Jerry argued with Jim. Mark argued with Jerry. Bob Lewis, who also argued with Jerry, was being eased out. Marty Reymann and Ed Barger, Mark's patrons, didn't get along with Jerry. There was not yet a stable lineup, yet even the core group seemed unstable. At one point, everyone except Mark and Jerry had quit the band. Bob Casale stayed away through 1974 and much of 1975. "The important sound of things falling apart" – adopted as the band's slogan – was as fitting a description for the personnel as for the music.

Bobbie Watson recalled that a lot of Jerry and Bob's ongoing conversations focused on "how frustrated they were about the band moving forward and Mark not directing his energies the way Jerry would like him to. During that period there was a lot of hostility between Jerry and Mark, and Bob (Lewis) was the mediator. Mark was resistant to anything directly from Jerry."

Jim also found himself a subject of Jerry's criticism.

"Jerry realized he could run Jim off," Barger said. "He would do things that the others would scratch their heads and wonder about. Jerry was very sophisticated, and would plan years ahead. The other band members would go along with Jerry, not knowing that these deeds would come back to bite them later. I think he was also looking ahead to whoever would be the drummer. He knew whoever replaced Jim would eventually hate him too. Everyone would eventually."

Jerry was, indeed, a dominant personality. He was ambitious and confident, and these characteristics inevitably earned him some enemies. Reymann, who had invested considerable money, time and goodwill in Mark, was frustrated with the direction of Mark's career, and especially blunt about Jerry's involvement. "Since the beginning, we kept on telling (Mark) to get rid of this dud. I've disliked Jerry Casale since the moment I met him. We told Mark so many times to throw that jerk out of the band."

But Devo clearly needed Jerry. He was the engine that kept the thing driving forward.

❄ ❄ ❄

The band recorded some more material in the fall of 1974. At Krieger-Field

Studio in Akron, Devo put down versions of "Be Stiff" and "Can You Take It?" The music, in the studio anyway, was becoming more polished and coherent, even as the live shows continued to confound and occasionally inflame audiences. According to the band's official *Devo Rap Sheet*, membership at the time included all three Bobs – Lewis, Casale and Mothersbaugh.

As the Krieger-Field sessions continued, Devo was booked to play a benefit at JB's for *Shelly's*, a homespun literary magazine produced by Shelly's Book Bar in Kent. As described the following year in Kent State's *Chestnut Burr* yearbook, Shelly's was a "dingy dimly-lit bookshop where, since October 1973, a group of poets and assorted interesteds have been meeting weekly in an atmosphere both argumentative and appreciative. Shelly's is the kind of slice of life depicted in Norman Rockwell paintings. The faded green walls and the aisles are lined mostly with used paperbacks, and there is that inevitable scent of mustiness found in all bookstores worth their salt. Many of those who participated in *Shelly's* from the start were originally associated with the *Human Issue*, the university-sponsored literary magazine. In an obscure little store in a mostly obscure town, a refreshing and intense experience takes place regularly that receives no prizes and is accorded little acclaim."

The magazine's first issue, in October 1974, included song lyrics by Jerry, poetry by Bob and illustrations by Mark. Jerry's lyrics to "All of Us", which would later be reworked into the song "Going Under", include a quintessential verse about a place where "dreams are crushed" and "hopes are smashed".

"All you stupids anyway," it continues, "We're all going to die someday..."

Mark's illustrations continue his twisted-doctor motif. The magazine printed a two-panel image he'd been producing on decals. In one of the panels, a man in glasses and a lab coat stands before a man in an armchair, reading a newspaper printed with "ALL OF US". The doctor is holding a pitchfork with what look like testicles dangling from the end, aiming the tines toward the man's head. A child holding a tire appears to be falling from above, toward the seated man. These panels would later be published in *My Struggle*.

Bob Lewis wrote a poem about May 4, titled "Tree City #1". After describing the dawn, Bob writes,

"*Mid day, mid day*
the fourth day of May
a calm unreality in the airs
above the Commons,
the guard

ranged across the open …
fire in the streets!
fire on the green!
Anarchy / Revolt / Alarum
terror sweeps the velveeta people.
…gas …gas …it's a gasssss

Devo supported this literary venture by playing the JB's benefit. Bob had set up the show, which proved to further a growing trend. Audiences were repelled by the group, and Devo's response was to heap on more revulsion. As long as they were on stage, they could crack Dr. Moreau's whip. The lessons Jerry had learned goading his high school assembly to sing "everybody must get stoned" were finding a real-world application. He found a thrill in this.

"I remember playing (JB's in the fall of '74)," Jerry said. "We were doing 'Last Time I Saw St. Louis' and songs like that. 'Oh No', 'You Go Home' and all those really obnoxious kinds of things. We'd go, 'Here's one by Bad Company!' and we'd play 'Can You Take It'. People are going, 'What the fuck?' Losing it."

Although Bob Lewis had booked the show and remained dedicated to helping Devo progress, this gig proved to be a turning point. It was his last time on stage as a regular member of the band.

Maybe this was inevitable. Bob Mothersbaugh, clearly a more accomplished guitarist, was becoming a regular member of the lineup. Additionally, there was tension between Bob Lewis and Jerry. It stemmed from the proto-Devo days, right through Bob's insistence on Fred Weber as the Sextet Devo vocalist and continued through his inability to make headway with Patrick Cullie and the California music industry. So maybe Bob saw a split coming, but that didn't make him feel any better about it.

Chapter 10

In January of 1975, Bob Lewis wrote a letter to Ed Dorn and his wife Jennifer.

"With the equinox comes the spring issue of *Shelly's*, which will follow shortly, and which promises to be hot stuff. It appears that Messrs. Casale, Mothersbaugh and myself will be able to affect at least a temporary overthrow of portions of La Charity's god-son, at least long enough to get in a couple of shots, and there is talk of having various local personae 'lecture' to freshman classes, (We already have in our possession a number of grad assistant types who require the magazine for their courses), and I can just see Jerry talking to various assembled concerning potato love and the genetic imperative."

Are We Not Men?

"La Charity" is a reference to the owner of Shelly's Book Bar. The store and its literary magazine were providing a much-needed platform. Bob, as editor of the third issue of *Shelly's* magazine, had found a nonmusical venue for a philosophy that had by then been festering for years. He used the magazine to reprint Jerry's "Polymer Love", and his "Readers Vs. Breeders" from *The Staff*. He also included artwork by General Jackett – a dark illustration of a woman in bondage, bending over from behind, with a train barreling toward her bare buttocks. In a separate, inset panel, the same train is making its exit.

The issue was published shortly after the fifth anniversary of the May 4 shootings. As Bob's poem from the October issue attests, the event still resonated sharply. In the issue edited by Bob, Mark wrote his own May 4 poem. Written in four numbered stanzas, it includes a passage about Allison Krause from the perspective of her lover. "Allison – sweet Allison… We were to be wed in June," it says, going on to sketch the shootings in vivid minimalist style.

Among Jerry's contributions was a form letter for the breakup of a relationship. The letter, attributed to "Lt. Jerry Casanova", seems generic, with fill-in-the-blank spaces where the names should be. It begins, "It isn't that I've tried to avoid you but I have decided that we shouldn't see each other anymore." But it also includes the line, "I'm going to Jamaica for awhile with friends." Cora Hall, having toyed around with Jerry's heart (and filched his favorite pair of sunglasses) had, several months before, traveled to Jamaica to house-sit for friends.

Bob reported this news in a letter to Ed and Jennifer Dorn: "As you may already know, Cora is at this moment in time located in England. You see, after visiting Jerry in L.A., making $100 worth of long-distance calls around the globe, and ripping-off his most prized sunglasses, she went off to Jamaica on a little jaunt. On the way back to the Coast, she met some guy in Vegas who was flying to England the next day, so she wangled an invite, and wound up on the sceptered isle. Well, England bummed her, so she called Jerry trans-Atlantically and asked him to front the ca$h for her flying back to the Coast; well now, my man Jerry is often a turkey, but not this close to Thanksgiving, and he politely declined to get suckered that way."

So maybe the letter was real and maybe it wasn't. But Jerry Casanova was behind in the count.

❀ ❀ ❀

With the band in a state of relative confusion and near-limbo, Mark continued diligently working on his art. In February of 1975, he scored a solo show at the Packard Gallery, an edgy venue for Akron, run by an owner dedicated primarily to bringing current New York artists to the Midwest. Ray Packard had brought Peter Max to town and trotted him out in front of an elementary school class. He regularly showed works by burgeoning artists from around the country. His gallery presented significant exhibitions by Andy Warhol and Louise Nevelson, among others. An outspoken critic of the local art scene, Packard once commented that, "If all the world were like Akron, art would die for lack of support."

So he was probably especially pleased to be able to support a home-grown talent like Mark. The show, which opened in February of 1975, featured a series of hand-stamped prints and lithographed postcards. The prints had the aspect of wrapping paper, with a series of small, repeated images, some from children's rubber stamp kits and some from old engravings from grocery store ads – things like soap boxes and tomato juice jars that evoked Warhol. The postcards recreated old magazine and book illustrations.

When the show opened, Mark was featured in an *Akron Beacon Journal* story, which described him as "good-natured and somewhat shy" and made special note of his eyeglasses and their yellow, green and blue enameled frames. Perhaps to appease a mainstream audience, Mark told the reporter, "I've decided to quit being crazy and try to come up with something coherent. What I was doing before – things like silkscreens of disemboweled females – wasn't doing me any good. It was getting people mad at me." The article made no mention of Devo, and only passing reference to Mark being a "composer and performer of rock-oriented music for keyboard synthesizers."

Mark's pieces at the Packard Gallery were priced cheap – $20 or $30 – but he had trouble selling them. He was finding the same frustration Packard had been stewing in. Mark had even gone so far as to place classified ads in *Rolling Stone* to sell his artworks, but was receiving little response.

"I remember my Uncle Gene came to one show," he recalled of another exhibit, "and he was the only person who bought a painting. He felt sorry for me."

Still, Mark did find a way to make a living using his art background. He rented a space in a downtown Akron mall, Quaker Square, in the converted former Quaker Oats factory. Marty Reymann says he put up some money to help get the venture started. Surrounded by history – the place was once famed for its "cereal shot from guns!" – Mark opened a shop called Unit Services, where he sold rubber stamps and printed T-shirts. Jerry joined him working the counter. The 12-hour day was divided into two six-hour shifts, but they often spent long hours together in the store, talking.

Mark spent a good deal of time rummaging for materials. Although he made a lot of his own stamps, he also used discarded dies that he found at rummage sales, flea markets, antique stores and the like. He was especially fond of shopping in novelty shops. Ed Barger accompanied him on some of these trips.

"He would always ask the owner if we could go into the back rooms," Barger said. "We would rummage through everything. Mark has this great novelty collection. Since I knew he liked them, I bought lots for him. And things I liked, he would buy for me. Mark was a generous person."

On one of these trips, Mark ventured into a shop in nearby Canton called Marsino's. Digging through the oddball goodies, Mark came across a rubber mask of a baby's head, with orange molded hair, rosy cheeks and a round, open mouth. It was innocent-looking, but also kind of disturbing. Mark, who had been wearing his rubber ape mask on stage, was immediately drawn to this baby's head. He bought it and, as Jerry had done a few years before with the Gorj mask, he created a name and character to go with it: Boogie Boy, which would later be amended to Booji Boy, thereby distancing the character from the hippie get-down music of the Water Street bar strip.

Booji Boy represented the infantile spirit of de-evolution. When Mark wore the mask, he spoke and sang in a high-pitched tone, unburdened by the realities of the world. "Oh, Dad – we're all De-vo!" Booji Boy would later exclaim to General Boy, who, of course, was Mark's real father.

Around the same time, and most likely at the same store, Jerry discovered a pair of "Chinese specs", novelty glasses with flesh-colored lenses and slanted eyes. These immediately suggested another character – the Chinaman.

"Chinaman was a persona I took on to dispense shocking, un-liberal, un-American-style wisdom and thought," Jerry said. "Dispense it as if you're, like, this philosophical Chinaman. You know, like Chinese philosopher say, 'Ha Ha, Fuck you!' It was partly... to attack Western ideology – Western mindset, and to be a foil to the infant spirit of Booji Boy.... To be (like) Rowan and Martin from *Laugh In* – that kind of team. You know, Booji Boy and China-man would have made a good talk show.... Booji Boy had a beautiful, full-headed mask, and had universal appeal. I mean, who doesn't like a baby?"

"The Chinaman" would eventually write the introduction to *My Struggle*, and become a character in *The Truth About De-evolution*. In that introduction, he would write that Booji Boy "wears his mask not to hide from justice, but to perform it."

Mark and Jerry began wearing masks most of their waking hours. This would seem strange anywhere, but Akron, especially, was not the kind of place to embrace these performance art ideals. There were practical concerns, as well. "It was hard to eat," Jerry explained. "Mark would always ask for a straw and order a milkshake."

❄ ❄ ❄

Mark and Ed Barger had moved out of Marty's Balch Street house in 1973 and were living as roommates at the Beaven Apartments on Walnut Street, across from Harlan Hall, an apartment building Mark's father owned. But by late 1974, Ed Barger was spending most of his time at his girlfriend's place, and could no longer justify paying rent for both him and Mark. So Robert Mothersbaugh Sr. offered his son a free apartment at Harlan Hall if Mark would agree to serve as manager. Mark accepted. He became responsible for this old, 29-unit brick building with Tudor accents, known as the first fireproof building in Akron. This would seem like an ideal setup, except that Mark was required to handle basic maintenance. "Oh, boy!" the senior Mothersbaugh recalled with a wry smile.

Mark may not have been adept at basic repairs, but he was very good at securing tenants. He would put Jerry up in unoccupied units, shuffling him around like a human shell game. Barger lived in the building for a time, as did a friend named Ward Welch, who would later adopt the stage name Rod Bent (and, still later, Rod Firestone) as the singer for the Rubber City Rebels. Bobbie Watson lived there, as did Mark's younger sister Sue. As with the Kent apartments above Guido's Pizza, the place became an enclave of music and art. This was great for them, but not so great for the other, more established tenants.

"All the tenants were scared out of their minds of me," Mark said. "One night, we were up making a tape. It was a torture routine and we were getting pretty carried away, shouting things like, 'No, not the punishment cone!'... This old lady knocks at the door at two in the morning, and I answer it in a dress and a hood. Jerry had this rubber chimp mask on and his hands were tied behind his back. That poor lady..."

Mark continued working on *My Struggle* while he lived at Harlan Hall. In it, he wrote about his job as apartment manager: "I don't need no doctor, in spite of what the tenants here at my fair old Harlan Hall say. They really love me, even that witch LePera. She writes a couple letters a day about lights in the building that need fixed, or bitching about her drain. Worst part about it is, she lives across the hall from Chatty, the little nurse down in 202 who is always letting us put things in her freezer, or some other good deed only a nurse should perform."

"Chatty" was a woman named Cathy Mirwin, whom Jerry had briefly taken up with after the breakup with Cora. Bobbie recalled that he urged her to cut her hair and dress like Cora, almost as an extension of the Pygmalion myth. But he also apparently was sneaking around with Marty Reymann's girlfriend, Jennifer Licitri. "I was tip-toeing around, and being a bad girl. It was pretty serious, and he wanted me to move to California with him," Licitri later recalled. "I have old letters from Jerry calling himself Chinaboy and calling me Chinagirl. I have poetry with his Chinaman face that he gave me as a break-up letter."

Mark, meanwhile, had begun living with a woman named Marie Yakubic, who also went by the name Marina. She was married to a musician who had played in the Mothersbaugh Band. Apparently her husband didn't care. Mark and Marina's relationship blossomed under tragic circumstances. According to Bob Lewis and Bobbie Watson, Marina had been raped at gunpoint by an intruder while still living with her husband. He did not visit her in the hospital, and Mark took pity on her and went to see her. After her release, he took her in.

"Their apartment at Harlan Hall was one room basically," Bobbie recalled, "mats on the floor for bedding. Wall-to-wall bed was all Marie wanted, with a little kitchen to warm her tea. Their body heat never left the room. She said the perfect day for her (days on end) would be for them to never leave that room and spend the day touching. Mark would invite others (over) and she was willing to keep Mark happy by being the gracious hostess – but it was not her choice. She resented Mark's activity with anything that took him away but was not vocal about it – she sighed deeply. She was gifted in touch and massage."

All in all, it was a pretty good set-up, with days at Unit Services and nights at Harlan Hall. But Jerry and Mark were still convinced that something could happen in California. So they gathered up copies of their demos, the Booji Boy mask and the Chinaman glasses, and headed west.

Chapter 11

Jerry and Mark hung a tape recorder from the rearview mirror as they set out for California. As they drove, Mark wore the Booji Boy mask and Jerry wore the Chinaman glasses. For 20 hours, the routine droned on – the cassette recorded them as the Chinaman asked philosophical questions about life and Booji Boy answered them in his innocent squeak.

"Booji Boy – what is meaning of life?"

"Gee, I don't know. But that sure is a pretty sky."

There was strange chemistry between these two, and their alteregos seemed to capture it. Jerry was overtly intellectual and confrontational. Mark was in many ways pure and sincere. They needed each other – Jerry needed to be asking the questions, and Mark needed someone to ask them.

They had their demos in the car with them. The primal early recordings were becoming more sophisticated, with Mark's synthesizer emitting robotic, hypnotic (and occasionally erotic) discord. From his cartoon-drenched perspective, this was "*The Jetsons* meets *The Flintstones*." Their ultimate destination on this road trip was Joe Walsh's estate in Topanga Canyon. Despite the closer proximity of New York City, Devo was beginning to home in on California as their musical promised land, feeling the pull of the West just as Ed Dorn had. Much of the reason for that was the road paved by Walsh. By now, his solo career was in full bloom and he was on the verge of joining the Eagles. And despite the obvious chasm between every aspect of their aesthetics, he was someone who could do something for them. Bob Lewis had helped arrange the visit, again with a call to Patrick Cullie. Walsh had agreed to meet with Mark and Jerry.

Their old friend General Jackett had become an airbrush artist and was painting Walsh's stage T-shirts for him. He had been talking up Devo in the Walsh circle, telling people about this great Moog player, and this really strange but intriguing sound. When Jerry and Mark arrived in Topanga Canyon, Walsh was ready for them. They sat and talked awhile, then pulled out the tapes.

Walsh listened to this band with clanky electronic drums; a singer who sometimes sounded like an alien; the rigid, minimalist guitars; the lyrics about potatoes, monkeys becoming men, and men becoming monkeys.

"It was a nice scene," Jerry recalled. "He swung on his swing, and went to the kitchen to make popcorn, and uh, he put his arms around us out by his eucalyptus trees and told us to listen to the hoot owl, and then he kind of drew us close to him and hugged us and said, 'This is how I really feel – come back when you got something.'"

Still scratching his head, Walsh later admitted to their mutual friend Peter Gregg that he couldn't tell if the tape was running backward or forward.

Even with the disappointment of this continuing rejection, Mark and Jerry kept scheming, with a healthy sense of dadaism. While they were still in California, they caught a show called *Help Thy Neighbor* on a public-access channel – a call-to-arms to help people in need. Mexican kids were interviewed saying that they were going to resort to a life of crime if they couldn't find jobs. They wanted to become gardeners, not gangsters. So the host would say, "You heard it folks, now let's… help thy neighbor!" Calls came in to the show with donations of gardening supplies.

A woman phoned in to say that the family's father had died recently at home in bed. The kids and other family members were upset about the mattress. Soon, bed donations came in from the audience.

Mark and Jerry looked at one another. What if they went on the show in wheelchairs, claiming to be Vietnam vets? "We've got a good attitude about life," they'd say, "but it's just so hard to get folks to listen to our music." Then they'd ask for a record deal. It was one of those just-might-be-crazy-enough-to-work ideas. But they didn't go through with it.

❋ ❋ ❋

Jerry and Mark's trip included Thanksgiving dinner at the home of Peter Gregg, who, like Walsh, was living in Topanga Canyon. Mark brought a keyboard and Jerry brought his bass, and they sat around having a devolved, pre-supper hootenanny. Mark was wearing one of his masks – the Bluesman – a Sambo-like caricature with curly white hair, big earrings and big Aunt Jemima lips. As Gregg's girlfriend worked in the kitchen, the three of them sat together in a spare bedroom and Gregg played a version of a Keith Richards lick while Jerry sang, "I don't smoke, I don't drink, I don't know what I do do," over and over. They were having a good time. When dinner was ready, Gregg's girlfriend called everyone to the table. They all took their places, including Mark, now in his Booji Boy mask.

As he tried to eat through the mouth opening, Gregg's girlfriend began to get upset, thinking Mark was making fun of her carefully prepared meal. So Jerry, always the domineering force in these absurdist performances, told Mark to take off the mask, and the holiday meal proceeded.

They continued experimenting with their performance art as they explored the Los Angeles streets. With Jerry in his Chinaman get-up and Mark again as the Bluesman, they stood on the boulevard median in Hollywood. When traffic stopped for a red light, they would work their routine. Things got a little dicey when they wandered into a bad neighborhood and the locals did not appreciate these two white kids flaunting ethnic stereotypes. When they stepped into a liquor store, Jerry, sensing the tension, removed the Chinaman glasses. But the Bluesman held his ground.

Mark and Jerry made the long drive back to Ohio, playing Booji Boy and Chinaman as they drove, and wondering if they were barking up the wrong tree. Obviously, Joe Walsh, the blues-drenched, folksy rocker, wasn't going to be Devo's guy. But he was all they had.

Bob Lewis, upon hearing about how they'd been received, wrote a letter to Ed Dorn: "Jerry continues to try and push our particular load of shit on the Coast, but he says that he is meeting with sales resistance, i.e., it's too REAL, and they don't want to hear about it."

Cullie, who had continued working hard to find his own place in the music business, was torn between his friendship with Devo and his understanding of industry dynamics. He still had the demos Bob had given him, but he just wasn't sure what to do with them.

"I thought it was funny, ironic, hip, all that stuff," Cullie recalled, "but I'm the first to admit, I didn't really see the commercial possibilities. It just seemed too weird to drive mainstream revenue. And maybe part of it was that since Devo and the entourage came from my backyard, I didn't give it the credence it deserved. I was looking to step out on my own and away from Irving (Azoff, the Eagles' manager), because he was a real prick. So, if I had felt that Devo was a project that I could get signed and manage and make money on, I would have done it on the spot. I just didn't see it."

So Cullie kept the tapes mostly to himself. He did eventually play them for a Capitol Records rep, and his instinct was confirmed:

"The guy at Capitol, after hearing the demo, said, 'Patrick, I like you. You're a smart guy. And my advice, if you want a career in the music business, is don't play this for anyone else. It's terrible.'"

❋ ❋ ❋

If Devo was looking for their niche, they certainly found a toehold in April of '75. The band was booked to play following a Kent screening of John Waters' new movie, *Pink Flamingos,* arranged by Kent State film professor Richard Myers, a significant underground filmmaker. Again, the little college town was getting exposed to something that normally wouldn't be expected in Ohio. Kent continued to be the beneficiary of an enlightened faculty.

Admission was $1; the film was billed as "the most disgusting movie ever made," and Devo's name in the advertising was followed by the commentary, "How LOW can you go?" This was more like it.

Bob Lewis, recognizing the opportunity, dashed off a letter to Ed Dorn. "Devo perform Friday before a special showing of *Pink Flamingos*," he wrote, "and at last perhaps will have its proper audience. The aficionados of Miss Divine are already well along the trail toward devolving. It's a little scary."

By now, the members of the band were being billed by their characters' names. This night would feature Boogie Boy (apparently not yet evolved into "Booji"), China Man, Jungle Jim and The Clown. This almost sounded like the cast of characters in a John Waters film. It's certainly hard to imagine a significant American artist more in tune with the Devo aesthetic. Waters used low humor with allegedly high ideals; the infamous scene where Divine, an overweight transvestite, eats dog feces is the film equivalent of a song like "I Need a Chick". They loved kitsch, they loved laughing at American conventions they found stupid, and they loved to put on a show that would make audiences squirm.

"*Pink Flamingos* was our favorite film," Jerry said later. "We just couldn't believe he got it made. We thought this was incredible. We just wanted to meet John Waters, you know? Basically, he and his friends were the Devo of Baltimore. The same kind of transgressive, irreverent, kind of collage-like...

'let's rethink all this, folks.' People that are kind of blue-collar, but smart, and have no respect."

Even with what would seem a more sympathetic audience, Devo still struggled for acceptance that night. The band played two sets, after each of the film's showings. At one point, Mark walked onto the stage while the movie played and, pulling a trick from Ghoulardi's bag, used a long stick to point out various aspects of the film.

❊ ❊ ❊

The encounter with Joe Walsh had served to underscore a growing ideal in the Devo philosophy. Although they'd had no personal experience with stardom, or even acceptance, they bristled against the notion of the Rock Star. Even though punk rock didn't yet exist as a recognized genre, this notion of knocking idols off their pedestals was a cornerstone of the ethic, and Devo fully embraced it.

"What we hated about rock and roll was stars," Mark said. "We watched Roxy Music, a band we like, slowly become Bryan Ferry and Roxy Music. If you got a band that's good, you bust it up and sell three times as many records."

Devo was an odd tangent of that concept, however. The band was elitist in many ways. Although the members would generally lump themselves in with the rest of the spuds (at least rhetorically), the simple act of pointing out dullards put them in a position of superiority. There were Readers, and there were Breeders, and it's safe to assume Devo didn't consider themselves Breeders.

Still, the band clung to a certain populism, even as they distanced themselves from the populous. Some of this, no doubt, grew from the no-nonsense work ethic Mark had inherited from his father. Mark was a serious young man, and while he had not chosen anything close to his dad's career path – he vehemently resisted traditional day jobs – he did work hard on his art. He wrote in his journal; he made postcards and rubber-stamp prints; he practiced on his keyboard. He was a workman, but fully outside the traditional definition. Devo once said that artists are good-looking people who can't hold down real jobs. This seemed to be a commentary on themselves, and to capture both a sense of self-denigration and self-realization.

And so it was that Devo went shopping for clothes. The band was scheduled to play at the third Creative Arts Festival in April. The crude, but structured accessorizing of the 1973 festival, when each of the members had worn a single color, had evolved. The fascination with masks and uniforms was growing. For this performance, they chose hard hats and blue workmen's jumpsuits. They were becoming spuds, Mark's "dirty hard workers of the earth."

Completing the ensemble were matching clear plastic masks, which essentially erased the face. Mark still had his beloved long hair, but these masks were a conscious attempt to portray the anti-rock star. There would be no personalities; there would simply be personality.

By then, Kraftwerk's watershed 1974 album, *Autobahn*, had found its way to Ohio. Jerry loved this record. The early Kraftwerk recordings had been the work of two breakaway members of the progressive "kraut rock" scene, with long, ponderous jams. They played in sweaters and leather jackets, experimenting with synthesizers and traditional instruments. But a growing fascination for robots and a desire to make the music an entire, controlled package led to the *Autobahn* aesthetic. The German band had sharpened its image, accomplishing the same things Devo was trying to do halfway across the world. *Autobahn* seemed to be the work of automatons. Close-cropped hair, emotionless faces, minimalist graphics and a growing refusal to divulge any personal details. Kraftwerk was, in a sense, becoming post-human. Devo recognized the possibilities in that.

✳ ✳ ✳

Devo was trapped between two worlds, a point made even more clear when Joe Walsh came back to Ohio to play a concert with his Barnstorm Band. Although Mark, Jerry and the others still clung to a hope that they might be able to make use of his coattails, they had a growing disdain for Walsh's music, lifestyle and audience. Mark showed up at the concert wearing the Booji Boy mask, and left it on for the entire show.

Bruce Hensal remembers that the mask was especially distressing to the Barnstorm Band's piano player. "He started yelling at Mark because the mask was freaking him out," Hensal said. "The guy was shouting, 'Take that off! Take that off!'"

There was a party afterward at General Jackett's house, a place nicknamed the Headquarters, above a flower store. Walsh attended with his band and the rest of his entourage. Lots of drugs were consumed. So when Jerry and Mark – still wearing his rubber baby mask – arrived, there was some chemically enhanced confusion. Many of the partygoers thought the mask was actually Mark's face. Mark's girlfriend Marina had brought some raspberries to the party. As Booji Boy stuffed them in, red juice ran down his face, looking an awful lot like blood.

It's safe to say Walsh would never witness such behavior from Glenn Frey.

Chapter 12

If the Devo gigs were still few and far between, at least they were becoming more choice. Halloween 1975 found the band booked to open for Sun Ra at

Are We Not Men?

Cleveland's WHK Auditorium. The concert was a private Halloween party for Cleveland's top album-oriented rock station, WMMS-FM. None of this really made sense.

Sun Ra, although a nationally significant figure, fell outside the station's heavy rotation of Rolling Stones, Bad Company and Lynryd Skynryd. And Devo – well, it's pretty certain none of the station's employees had even heard of them. Probably someone had suggested that the Akron band might be good for a Halloween joke without really explaining the punch line. Sun Ra was in residence at Cleveland's Smiling Dog Saloon from October 28 to November 9. Ed Barger worked there, so it's possible he had something to do with Devo being booked. However it came to pass, though, the night proved to be a defining moment in Devo's ability to use music as a weapon of mass destruction.

The WHK Auditorium dated to the 1930s, when it was built as a radio broadcast theater. Located on a stretch of Euclid Avenue between downtown and some of the city's worst neighborhoods, the "HK" was a perfect symbol of a collapsing industrial giant. Once lovely and ornate, it had fallen into decadence; rock and rollers were gathering together the detritus of someone else's dream. Tuxedoed men and fashionable ladies had once enunciated into chromed microphones there. And now Devo had arrived to set up their gear.

Various members of the WMMS staff were milling about with their friends, dipping into a vat of tequila sunrise and inhaling nitrous oxide. WMMS was known as the "Home of the Buzzard", taking the nickname from an annual event in nearby Hinckley, where, once a year, turkey vultures came home to roost in Ohio's version of the San Juan Capistrano swallows. The station's logo, ubiquitous on T-shirts and bumper stickers, featured a cartoon buzzard, and had become a symbol of everything Devo thought was wrong about rock and roll. Mindless mass consumption of music programmed by clueless suits. There was an intensely blue-collar image to WMMS; Leo Travagliante, known by the handle "Kid Leo", closed each afternoon drive-time shift by announcing it was "time to wash up and punch out." Kid Leo would soon gain significant industry cred by championing a young New Jersey singer/ songwriter named Bruce Springsteen. WMMS and Springsteen were made for each other – all denim-and-leather, no-nonsense working-class rock. Widely credited as a key figure in breaking Springsteen, Kid Leo would eventually become a Columbia Records vice president. But before he left the station, his incessant claim that Cleveland was the "rock and roll capital of the world" would help land the Rock and Roll Hall of Fame and Museum on the shores of Lake Erie.

Back in 1975, though, Kid Leo was mostly concerned with celebrating at the big Halloween bash. Although the WHK Auditorium sat 1,500 people, the crowd was relatively small, with select invited guests from Cleveland's rock elite. Murray Saul, one of the station's best-known personalities, was tapped to be master of ceremonies. Saul was known as "the get-down man" for his trademark bellowing of the catch phrase, "Gotta, gotta, gotta... GET... DOWN!"

Devo was dressed that night in the same blue Dickies work suits and clear masks they had worn at the Creative Arts Festival. Mark wore the baby mask. Once again, they were billed under their characters' names. Mark was Booji Boy; Jerry was the Chinaman; Bob Mothersbaugh was the Clown; and his brother Jim was Jungle Jim. Their appearance didn't raise a lot of eyebrows at first. Who knew they always dressed like this? It was Halloween, and everyone was wearing a costume, although most had opted for the traditional witches, gangsters and hunchbacks.

Devo set up its gear, complete with the Halloween-ish electronic drum set, and Jerry called for Murray Saul to say a few words into the microphone, with the high-pitched Booji Boy piping in, "Murray – Murray." Saul ambled onto the stage and started spewing his husky, stoned-hipster radio spiel, stumbling through a thick-tongued commentary on Cleveland's new marijuana law.

"Aaaaahhh-ooohhh, such the easy life. It is what it is, and it is such the such," he said, making virtually no sense. He turned to the members of Devo, wishing them a happy Halloween.

"Good evening," Saul continued. "I thought you would at least come in, at least, real clothes instead of such out-rage-ous costumes."

"Tell it like it is, Murray," Booji Boy warbled.

"Dass right," Saul said. "You got da concept."

"He tells it like it is," the innocent Booji pointed out to the crowd.

Saul rambled on about the long-neglected auditorium and then broke suddenly into an almost belching, "Ooooooohhh-Aaaahhhhhhh! We have been goin' crazy, goin' nuts because IIIITTTTSSS FRIIIIDAYYYYY! FRII-IIDAYYYYY!! FRIIIIDAYYYYY!! (Unintelligible.) Yowza, howza whadda-hodda-hodda."

Then, after a couple more hee-za's and yowza's, he explained that this will be a crazy party and, "We're gonna do it, cuz we GOTTA, GOTTA, GOTTA (followed by about ten more slurred gotta's) GET DOWN!"

And finally the introduction: "Oh, we gotta go low with De-vo. What it is!"

And then Saul stumbled off as Jim started plunking out a staccato rhythm on the drums, Mark following with a series of grating, repetitive mechanical screeches from his synthesizer. Once this musical hair shirt was sufficiently spread out, Jerry, in what was now a fully mutated version of his backwater blues, began howling, "My woman's subhuman…"

It began to dawn on the audience that if this was a joke, it wasn't funny. And if it wasn't a joke, it had to end immediately. Drunken ghouls and witches began shouting at Devo. A beer can flew toward the stage. Then another, and another. The band's response was obvious. They didn't like it? Then we'll just give 'em more. They soldiered on, inspired by the confrontation.

They played "Bamboo Bimbo", an equally tortured – and torturous – blues variation. When it ended, there was an almost inaudible smattering of applause. Devo had some friends in the audience, which is probably the only reason they weren't killed that night. Marty Reymann had come with his brother, a tough, brawling Vietnam veteran, and some other guys from Akron's working-class Firestone Park neighborhood, guys who liked a good fight. They became de facto bodyguards for this bunch of skinny "performance artists" who seemed intent on ruining someone else's party.

"We're Devo – D-E-V-O – and we'll prove it right now," Jerry spat out. While a few members of the audience remained, perhaps hoping to kick some ass, the room was nearly evacuated. "You guys just can't take it," Jerry said. It was brutal. One of the band members took a bullwhip from a Halloween "dominatrix" and began cracking it at her, ordering her to submit. This had worked for Dr. Moreau, but it was having the opposite effect on the drunken audience.

Late in the set, the band debuted what would become its defining anthem, "Jocko Homo". The song went on and on and on, with the group repeating the call-and-response: "Are we not men? We are Devo."

Someone grabbed a microphone and screamed, "You're a buncha assholes!" prompting Jerry to begin taunting in a cracked voice, "Is he not a man? Is he not a man? …He is Devo …He is Devo," finally driving the offending figure from the room, with the band continuing to taunt as he left the building. "Jocko Homo" went on for six minutes, but seemed three times that long. As it ended, Mark's synthesizer emitted a wash of noise over and over as Devo played "I Need a Chick", driving the final nails before the whole mess fell apart in white noise and confusion.

"Why don't you get outta here?" someone yelled as the sound began to fade. "I'm telling you to get outta here!"

The battlefield was littered with beer cans and other debris. It wasn't clear who had won. Certainly not Sun Ra, who made his entrance to a nearly empty auditorium. As he opened his set with "25 Years to the 21st Century", the only people there to see him were Devo and their handful of friends.

This was as close as Devo would come to fulfilling one of its fantasies. Jerry, in his days with the SDS, had heard about subsonic frequency generators, which were capable of producing a noise outside the normal audible frequency, and to cause people to lose control of their body functions.

"I asked myself, 'What are the creative uses of those?'" Jerry once said. He and Mark often repeated their description of the ultimate Devo concert.

"We'd like to hand out diapers at the door at a concert of 10,000 people and then for the finale we'd turn on the subsonic frequency generators and cause spontaneous bowel movements!" they once explained in a joint interview. "And rather than being uptight about it they would love it! Like that's what they came for and they would be mad if they left without it! Rather than lighting matches for the Eagles – one mass infantile, pre-sexual eruption – all tense muscles going lax!"

In other descriptions of this hypothetical "perfect concert", Mark and Jerry envisioned these performances taking place all over the globe, with Devo controlling the music and – by virtue of subsonics – the audience, from afar. This carried another echo from Kraftwerk, who talked about having robots perform concerts around the globe simultaneously, as the members ran the show from their Düsseldorf studio.

If Devo hadn't succeeded in making the members of the WMMS Halloween audience shit themselves, they had used a wall of sound to drive them away, like the Pied Piper in reverse. This may not seem like a significant accomplishment, but it did serve to cement a piece of the Devo theory: It was open season on pinheads. The reaction of the audience, to Devo's mind, simply proved that the great masses were clueless spuds.

The night passed, with the four members of Devo and their few friends being treated to a private audience with Sun Ra.

That same night, not far away, another, equally confrontational local band made its debut. They were called Frankenstein, playing at a Cleveland bar called the Piccadilly Penthouse. The singer, Stiv Bators, got into a fight during the band's set, and Frankenstein broke up immediately. They would reform that winter, and take a new name – the Dead Boys.

❉ ❉ ❉

That Halloween of 1975 was riddled with bizarre turns for Devo. Mike Powell, the volatile, drug-addled drummer from Flossy Bobbit, had asked Jerry if he could borrow the Gorj mask for a costume party. Jerry didn't really want to part with it, but Powell was not the kind of guy you wanted to argue with. So Jerry handed it over, went off to play the WMMS gig, and Powell headed out for devil's night in Akron. Along the way, he stopped into a convenience store. Wearing that hideously twisted leather mask, he pulled out a gun and robbed the place.

He would eventually be caught and charged with four counts of aggravated robbery, for holding up beverage stores and a pizza shop. He was convicted and sent to prison. In the process, the Gorj mask was taken into evidence. Jerry never saw it again.

Gorj or no Gorj, Devo's visual image was becoming more provocative and cohesive. Even Mark fell into line with the others, allowing Marty's girlfriend (and Jerry's mistress) Jennifer Licitri to cut his beloved locks. Maybe this had something to do with the heat inside the Booji Boy mask, but now all Mark had to shake around was a set of unruly bangs.

Devo began doing some photo shoots. They gained access to Goodyear's "World of Rubber", a museum devoted to the wonderful science of tire-making. The museum contained antique tires, part of a Corsair built in one of the company's Akron factories during World War II, diagrams of the tire production process, and one of Mario Andretti's race cars, poised for racing action on a set of Goodyears. Devo posed in this setting. It was perfect for them, a place where reality was crossed with Ghoulardi-like science fiction. They romped through a forest of fake rubber trees and sat behind the wheel of Andretti's car.

In the process, they further developed their oddball photogenicity. They had, early on, discussed the idea of Devo as a multimedia project. Music was becoming a means to that end, but, in those long days at Unit Services, Jerry and Mark began to discuss the other possibilities. This was an art project. What other media could they tap into?

They began to kick around the idea of making a film.

❀ ❀ ❀

At this point, Jerry was outnumbered in Devo, three-to-one, by Mothersbaughs. His brother Bob, married and working as a radiologist, had lost interest in the project, and there was tension based on family dynamics. Several members of the Devo circle recall Jerry riding Jim Mothersbaugh hard, complaining about the technical bugs in his drum set and his inability to keep good time. And Jerry had begun lobbying his brother to rejoin the band.

By mid-1976, with the gigs continuing sporadically, Bob Casale finally decided to return and, after a show in Cleveland and another *Shelly's* magazine benefit in Kent, Jim finally decided he'd had enough.

"I think Jerry brought his brother Bob in because he was a little overwhelmed by the Mothersbaugh brothers," Gary Jackett said. "It was obvious that there were two different musical directions that Devo was trying to pursue. With Bob Casale (back) in the band, Jerry sort of had two votes. It wasn't long before Jim got sick of Jerry's routine. At a certain point, he just didn't want to do it anymore. Jerry could be a fun-loving, great guy or he could be a total jerk. One day you loved the guy and had great fun with him, and the next day he'd be totally flipping out."

Without a drummer, the band was free to focus on some of its other goals. Early in 1976, they began working on a script that would help explain what, by then, was nearly a decade of discussion about de-evolution.

Body:

1976-1979

KRK Ryden

Chapter 13

After years of false starts and frustration, 1976 was Devo's turning point. It's hard to say precisely why it took so long for the group to sort itself out. They had talent and ambition and encouragement from people they respected. But they were also kind of a mess live, and the membership was always in flux. Still, maybe there was a whiff in the air that some sort of musical revolution was brewing in New York and London, or maybe there was just a maturity to the grand Idea. Whatever it was, Devo, in late 1975, started on the project that would change their life.

Mark and Jerry had met a film student named Chuck Statler while attending Kent State. They had discussed the idea of making films to go along with their songs. This was a novel idea at the time. Sure, the Beatles had done *A Hard Day's Night,* but aside from straightforward film clips of performance, there wasn't much of a precedent. Devo wanted to do shorter conceptual pieces, art films that used their music as a beginning point. After the glorious disaster of the WMMS Halloween show, the band realized they were getting nowhere playing local clubs. It was time for this different tack.

Statler had graduated and moved to Minneapolis, where he was trying to get his film career started. Jerry and he began writing letters, trading ideas back and forth. "Although we were visually inclined, we had no knowledge of filmmaking," Jerry said. "That's where Chuck came in." Statler gave them a sense of how a film was made, what it would cost, how to write a script and the like.

The first hurdle was the budget – around $2,000. Jerry and Mark had saved a little money from Unit Services. But they would need to borrow more. Kate Myers, a friend of the band, agreed to put up some cash. The Myers family was prominent in Akron; Kate's parents, Louis and Mary Myers, were major patrons of the arts and owned the largest private collection of modern art between New York and Chicago.

Mark and Jerry knew they could save money on talent. They began enlisting their circle of friends, the "devo-tees". And they began thinking about how they might want to present the "truth about de-evolution". The concept, as it had picked up steam, had become too far-reaching to be wrapped up in a neat entertainment package. Things like "Polymer Love" and "Readers Vs. Breeders" had helped broaden the idea, and now it needed to be brought back into focus. Certain elements had emerged since then that would clearly work in a short film. Booji Boy, for instance. That face and the voice behind it would be great in a movie. So they began writing a script.

Are We Not Men?

Although Bob Lewis was no longer playing with the band, he remained close. On the back of a postcard to Ed and Jenny Dorn, postmarked April 9, 1976, he wrote, "Work on 'The Script' progresses slow. All devo-tees pinned out. Rubber fumes everywhere. Bertholf requests Devolution lecture for Honors College Freshmen."

Unit Services became the central office for the film, with friends and band members popping in and out to discuss the progress. Quaker Square was a sprawling complex, with shops, restaurants and displays about Akron history filling the former cereal factory. The old silos had been converted into a hotel, so every room had round walls. That winter, Jerry had met a young woman, Susan Massaro, who worked downstairs in Quaker Square's large restaurant. She and Jerry had their first date on Valentine's Day and quickly became a couple. Jerry wanted her to move in with him at Harlan Hall, but Susan had a six-year-old daughter and didn't think it would be a very good environment for her. But she and Jerry became close, as she dropped into Unit Services a couple times a day on her breaks.

"I remember Bob (Lewis) coming into Unit Services and saying that he had got the Governance Chambers to film a portion of the movie," she said. "I helped him and Jerry set up a sheet that was to be mimeographed with lyrics to the songs that were going to be used in the movie, that was to be handed out."

The Governance Chambers in the Kent State student center had been the site of the Sextet Devo performance four years before. The band liked its official-looking setting, with rows of seats with desktops facing a stage. They knew they wanted some sort of *Dr. Strangelove* set, where the news of human decline could be properly conveyed. Similarly, they secured the "president's room" at a McDonald's restaurant near downtown. The room had a long conference table, and its walls were lined with large, officious portraits of suit-and-tied white males. A fast-food restaurant may seem like a strange place for an executive dining room, but it made sense in Akron, where the white and blue-collar aspects of the tire industry were intertwined. This particular McDonald's was nestled between the world headquarters of the Goodyear, Firestone, Goodrich, General and Mohawk tire companies, and also the aging factories that surrounded them. So presidents and punch-clock workers alike could dine there.

The rubber industry also provided another movie set, Goodyear's World of Rubber, where the previous photo shoot had taken place. The museum included rubber chemistry equipment, large vats with pipes and gauges that gave an aspect of retro-futurism. The scenes of the band playing would be shot on the basement stage at JB's in Kent.

And they knew of a great location for an outside establishing shot. Mark's father owned Great Falls Employment Agency at the time, in a century-old building in Cuyahoga Falls. A few years before, he had undertaken a restoration project to return the façade to its original appearance as a 19th-century dry goods store. But that was the front of the building. The side boasted a decidedly 1970s mural, painted on the brick by a group of high school students as part of a city project the previous summer. Lady Liberty's arm extended in from the right, holding a torch surrounded by the sun, with beams emitting across the side of the building. Over to the left were clumsy images of great Americans. And in the center, in huge block letters, was the slogan "Shine on America".

By late spring, the group was ready to begin production. They had decided to base the film on two songs – a twisted cover of Johnny Rivers' "Secret Agent Man" and "Jocko Homo", the song that served as Devo's thesis statement. These seemed like logical bookends for the movie. "Jocko Homo" explained de-evolution, and "Secret Agent Man", which turned the original spy-rock riff around backwards, showed it in action. Johnny Rivers' heroic, cloak-and-dagger protagonist became, in Devo's hands, a victim of mind control. This would be the only notable lead vocal appearance by Bob Mothersbaugh in the band's history, but in a world of Bobs that found him billed as "Bob 1", the key line, "They've given me a number, but they've taken away my name," took on an ironic and less valiant meaning. It was devolved.

And "Jocko Homo" said it all. The lyrics drew on years of intellectualizing, and serve as a refined collage of the elements that defined the truth about de-evolution, right down to the title, lifted from B.H. Shadduck's religious pamphlet. The song, filled with the quirky mechanics that had become the group's trademark, begins: "They tell us that we lost our tails / Evolving up from little snails / I say it's all / Just wind in sails…"

This is all that highbrow discussion with poets and professors summed up in 21 words. Then comes the chorus, "Are we not men? We are Devo". This defining statement, of course, came directly from *Island of Lost Souls*, the film that entertained, frightened and helped teach de-evolution. Then the second verse: "Monkey men all in business suit / Teachers and critics all dance the poot…"

Devo's intent was to take the stuffing out of pompous humans. "We're only smart monkeys, let's not get too snotty," Bob Lewis once explained. The poot, of course, was Jerry's dance from the early Gorj days, intended to ridicule someone else's creation. But, as always, Devo included themselves in the criticism: "We're pinheads all." Devo was smart enough to recognize the foibles of mankind, but also smart enough to recognize they themselves couldn't be immune.

The key players for the film were selected. Although Devo was in a state of flux, the departed Jim had agreed to play drums with Jerry and his brothers Mark and Bob. Ed Barger, General Jackett and Jennifer Licitri were enlisted, as were the girlfriends – Marina, Susan and Bobbie Watson, who was still with Bob Lewis. One of the Harlan Hall residents, Karen Freeman, who waitressed at a mall restaurant with Bobbie, was also talked into taking a role. (She was shy, but they promised she'd be wearing a mask, just like most of the other actors.) Even Susan's young daughter Sarah would take a part. The script was nearing completion. A key role was the character of "General Boy," who would announce that it was time for the "truth about de-evolution." A lawyer friend agreed to play him.

Devo decided to wear their blue work suits, hard hats and clear masks for the live performance scenes. They gathered together their collection of masks, strange glasses and costumes to distribute among the "actors". They went shopping at an Army-Navy surplus store for the General Boy outfit, returning with a military dress uniform. The Governance Chambers shoot was scheduled for May 17, 1976. To fill out the seats not already claimed by "devo-tees", the group advertised on campus: "Mon. 12 noon – Be In A Movie!"

The pieces were coming together. Statler came to town and they began filming. With such a small budget, everything was being done simply, shot on 16 millimeter film. "Though Chuck was the director, he was mainly there for technical stuff, camera angles and lighting, and to take care of the production end of it," Jerry recalled. "The concepts, the images and ideas were all ours, we always had that together. As a director, Chuck's into the straight-ahead, no-nonsense industrial approach – no camera moves at all, just static shots and sharp cutting. That certainly influenced me a lot, and I think it's a sensible way to work: the images and the montage, the editing, should do the work themselves. You shouldn't have to resort to fancy camera moves to make it work."

The band was ready to shoot the General Boy scene at the McDonald's "president's room". They had made a large portrait of Booji Boy in a uniform to tape over the picture hanging at the end of the room, creating the look of some sort of Devo war room. But at the last minute, the lawyer slated to play General Boy backed out. With everything tightly budgeted and scheduled, they didn't have much time to spare. They had to come up with someone who could look official, and who would fit into the uniform they'd bought. Mark, Jim and Bob knew of a good candidate – their dad.

The question was put to him, and Robert Mothersbaugh Sr., upstanding businessman and local churchgoer, agreed. "When you have five kids and you love them – you do this," he later said. "I served three years during the Second World War. I'll let you in on a little secret – I didn't become a general until the boys started Devo! I wore the blue-green Army jacket, pith helmet, black trousers, white shirt and black tie. The De-Evolutionary Army dress code allowed some flexibility."

They sat him at the end of the conference table, under the Booji Boy picture. With him in the role, the scene took on a different tone. Mark, as Booji Boy, comes into the room to deliver a set of papers. In the script, Booji Boy was supposed to be General Boy's son. Now, wearing a rubber baby mask, the real-life son was interacting with his real-life father.

"I remember there was relief and excitement when Mr. Mothersbaugh became General Boy, and how it was so much better than what was planned," Bobbie Watson said.

Filming was complete, and Susan drove Jerry to Minneapolis for the editing. By then, Jerry had taken up with another woman on the side. This made the trip miserable for her.

"We stayed with Chuck Statler and his wife," she recalled, "and they were great hosts and took good care of us, but Jerry and Linda (Waddington) had started up, and she sent special mail to him, and called him, and it really pissed me off. So here I was, stuck in a strange city, among strangers, having taken my vacation and driven my car and spent my money for a person who was wooing and being wooed by another. I wanted to leave him there and just go home to Sarah, but he convinced me otherwise. Do you know about Jerry's relationships with women? Do you know about his temper and anger? Well, this was the first time I experienced it directed toward me. He is really good at turning the tables on you when he has done something wrong. Things went from bad to worse after that trip."

After the editing sessions in Minneapolis, the film was complete. It commences with the title, *In the Beginning was the End: The Truth About De-evolution*. The opening scene shows the band in their blue suits and masks, working in the World of Rubber set. It's quitting time and they all depart, Booji Boy removing his cap to wipe sweat from his brow. They pile into Mark's beat-up old blue Chevrolet, and drive off. They arrive in front of JB's. As they file into the club, no one seems to notice the sign taped to the door, which boasts the familiar numbers – (15-60-75). Then "Secret Agent Man" begins.

It's hard to believe this is the same band that, just six months before, had tortured the WMMS crowd. Devo's version of the song is tight, polished and

catchy. Behind the band (and mostly obscured by them) is a set of cut-out letters spelling "D-E-V-O," a larger version of the set General Jackett had spray-
painted in California four years before. The performance footage is intercut
with little scenes: A pair of ectomorphic band members in gym shorts and
monkey masks paddle Karen Freeman, unrecognizable as promised, in a
bathrobe and a strange china-doll mask. A few seconds later, the Chinaman
appears to be genitally stimulating a coat hangar in the shape of a woman's
spread-eagled legs. During the guitar solo, General Jackett, wearing jeans, a
decorated leather jacket and sunglasses, wails away on two strapped-together
guitars, with a space heater for an amplifier.

Then comes one of the film's most captivating moments. Mark, wearing
a John F. Kennedy mask, a pink-and-purple Latin bandleader's shirt and a
pair of padded pants, dances with Marina, dressed in some sort of tight-fit-
ting nurse or waitress uniform. Their moves are slow, almost hypnotic, and
softly twitchy. It is as clear here as anywhere that the band has achieved an
impressive visual command. The paddling and dancing continue, the song
ends with JFK waving goodbye, then the scene cuts to the "Shine on America"
mural.

Booji Boy, dressed in an orange jumpsuit, enters and runs pell-mell past
the mural and up the building's outside staircase. He enters General Boy's
inner sanctum.

"Come in, Booji Boy. You're late," the General says. He pronounces the
first name "Boogie". Jerry later explained that the spelling change (and inevitable mispronunciation) came when he was putting together the credits for
a Devo film (probably not this one), and he ran out of "g's." So he used a "j"
instead, and liked the way it looked without the "e" at the end.

Booji Boy approaches his father.

"Have you got the papers the Chinaman gave you?" General Boy asks.
Booji hands them over, the General gives them a quick glance, then turns to
face the camera.

"In the past, this information has been suppressed," he intones seriously, in
his nasal accent. "But now it can be told. Every man, woman and mutant on
this planet shall know the truth about de-evolution."

"Oh, Dad," Booji Boy responds enthusiastically. "We're all Devo!"

A series of quirky, staccato, synthesized blips follows, keeping time with a
series of still images of neon letters, spelling out "D-E-V-O." Then the scene
changes to the Governance Chambers. Mark, dressed in a white suit, bow
tie, orange rubber gloves and swimming goggles, is standing between a set of
devo-tees in matching blue surgical caps, dust masks and sunglasses. Susan
Massaro is to his right; Bobbie Watson is to his left, watching dispassionately.

Mark begins a loose-limbed, jumpy dance to the intro of "Jocko Homo", then leans over the table as if preparing to deliver a lecture. He gestures animatedly as he begins lip synching. When he asks, "Are we not men?" the scene cuts to the other three band members, in sunglasses, with colored stockings over their heads, giving the response, "We are Devo". When his audience is finally shown, the Governance Chambers is filled with people in the same surgical caps and masks, bobbing in rhythm to the music. The other three band members lie writhing on a large table, their stockinged heads poking out of yellow latex body bags.

"We're on a giant conference table, wearing these rubber costumes from the neck down, and goggles and colored stockings on our heads," Jim recalled. "So (people from the college) see us in there doing this and they're like 'What the hell?'"

As the song picks up steam, some of the audience members pump their fists in time with "We are Devo," as if they have enthusiastically accepted their fate. "O.K., let's go," Mark says, and the song ends.

This is followed by tuneless synthesizer noises and a collage of grainy, disconnected images as the backdrop to a list of "laws." Also known as the "Devo precepts," these were appropriated directly from B.H. Shadduck's *Jocko-Homo Heavenbound*:

1. Wear gaudy colors or avoid display.
2. Lay a million eggs or give birth to one.
3. The fittest shall survive & the unfit may live.
4. Be like your ancestors or be different.
5. We must repeat.

The music changes then, to an oddly soothing tune – the Beatles song "Believe", wholly unrecognizable after Mark ran it through a frequency analyzer. This is the poignant soundtrack for the film's most gripping scene. A shirtless Booji Boy is duct-taped to a chair. A man (Ed Barger) enters, pulls off the rubber baby mask to reveal Mark's face, and stabs him. The credits roll.

In the Beginning: The Truth About De-evolution was complete. But now what? The band's first step was to enter it in juried film festivals, including the Ann Arbor Film Festival in neighboring Michigan. But Mark had higher aspirations. He recognized that his band had just completed a wholly new kind of musical project, one that might have far greater value than becoming a decent bar band with record deal potential.

"We thought back in 1975 that by 1976 everybody was going to own a laser disc player," Mark said later. "At least that's what it said in *Popular Science* magazine, and I believed it. So we said, 'There's going to be a new medium – sound and vision.' We were positive that we were going to start something that was going to erase rock and roll, but rock and roll kind of co-opted it, which erased the idea of it being artistic."

Chapter 14

Bob Mothersbaugh didn't want to quit playing with his brother Jim. But after the film was in the can, Jim's stint in Devo was over. Bob and Jim put together another band called the Jitters, playing much more traditional, Bo Diddley and Rolling Stones-influenced rock. But Bob was smart enough to know this wasn't his future. The Jitters were a bar band. They played for beers. Devo, even for all its problems, held much more promise. So he took Jim's departure pretty hard. One night, he went out to an Akron bar called the Bucket Shop to drown his sorrows.

The Bucket Shop was a rowdy place. Girls danced on the bar; the floor was always sticky with spilled beer. It was in Akron's Highland Square neighborhood, which cross-pollinated blue-collar homeowners and the city's bohemian crowd. Harlan Hall wasn't far away, and a lot of the Akron-Kent musicians had found apartments nearby. Chris Butler, who had played with the Numbers Band and would soon be playing with Tin Huey, eventually wrote a song about the Bucket Shop girls who liked to flirt with all the boys. The song became the hit that propelled his later band, the Waitresses, out of Akron – "I Know What Boys Like".

But on this night, Bob wasn't interested in having fun. He was sitting at the bar, nursing a beer, when his friend Alan Myers walked in. Alan lived a couple of blocks away, on Dodge Avenue. He had lived there since he was 15, when his liberal-minded parents had allowed him to move out of their house and take up the lifestyle of a free spirit. The Dodge Avenue house was kind of a commune for musicians, and although Alan was only in his early 20s, he had been jamming on a wide variety of instruments, with a wide variety of players, in a wide variety of styles for an unusually long time. He and Bob had played together in yet another of Bob's straight-ahead, blues-based rock bands. That gig had been pretty much a matter of chance.

"One day, I was sitting out on the front porch of my house at 117 Dodge Avenue, and this guy I knew named Crazy Dave was walking down the street," Alan recalled. "In typical small-town fashion, he informed me that the cover band he fronted had just split over artistic differences! Although he stuttered a lot, Crazy Dave was a very nice, warm person, and as it turned out, he was trying to put together another group. He still had a steady gig at a local bar, and it was hard to get a gig in those days, much less anything steady.

"He said, 'Hey Alan. Do you want to join a group and play at this club?'

Above: Mark Allen
Mothersbaugh, Class of 1968
Senior yearbook photo.

Above: Devo on the jobsite in construction helmets.
Photo © 1977 Ebet Roberts

**JOCKO-HOMO
HEAVENBOUND**
SCIENCE? RELIGION? FOLLY!

Before you bring "railing accusation" against this picture-parable of "modernism," consider that it portrays what passes for both science and religion with many people.

There was recently unveiled with solemn ceremony, in a New York "church," a "graven image" called "The Chrysalis." Since satan initiates sacred things, it might better be called "The Modernist Madonna." It is the image of a youth coming forth from a gorilla. Since these "worshippers" profess faith in some sort of heaven, the artist has added what is presumed to be the next stage of evolution, and BEHOLD THE FOLLY OF IT ALL!

Copyright 1924 by B. H. Shadduck

Above: *Jocko Homo: Heavenbound*

HEAVEN
AFTER
2,000,000 YEARS
OF HELL

WORLD WAR
TAX, USURY
TOIL
SUICIDE
MORPHINE
COCAIN, DOPE
ORGIES
COCK FIGHTING
WHITE SLAVERY
SLAVERY
ALCOHOL
INSANITY, IDIOCY
PRE-NATAL MURDER
NAMELESS CRIMES
NAMELESS DISEASES
MAKE YOUR OWN GOD
MIGHT MAKES RIGHT

D-EVOLU-TION

EVOLVO-SPOOF-US
BEFORE THE PARADE STARTED

This squat "ancestor" with doubtful table manners, is presumed to be the dam or sire of the race. When we found "it" in a magazine, this crude poem of our pedigree was only about three drops of ink removed from glorious manhood. They called it "Scientific Symbolism." Elsewhere, this hairy poem is called all sorts of names ending in "-pus." When "Mother Goose" scientists fix up a positure like this they OMIT the prose DETAILS. I have asked the artist to add the brutal facts that put a "D" before evolution. The Bible says, "He that sitteth in the heavens will laugh." No Wonder!

4

4TH EDITION   PRICE 20 CENTS

**JOCKO-HOMO
HEAVENBOUND**

BY B. H. SHADDUCK, PH. D.

AUTHOR OF

"PUDDLE TO PARADISE"

"THE TOADSTOOL AMONG THE TOMBS"

Above: The cover of Dr. B.H. Shadduck's scarce pamphlet *Jocko-Homo: Heavenbound* (Rogers, Ohio 1924).

Left: Alden's illustration with the "D" before evolution on page 4 of B.H. Shadduck's *Jocko-Homo: Heavenbound*.

Above: Fred Weber fronts the Sextet Devo at the 1973 K.S.U. Creative Arts Festival. *Photo © 1973 Bobbie Watson*

Left: Photo-booth images of Bobbie Watson and Bob Lewis, 1975. *Collection of Bobbie Watson*

Below right: A typical Sextet Devo audience.

Above: Mark Mothersbaugh & Dead Boys Cheetah Chrome in a stand-off at The Crypt, Akron. *Photo © 1976 Bobbie Watson*

Right: Devo in diapers at The Crypt, Akron. *Photo © 1977 Bobbie Watson*

Top left and right: The mysterious Oscar Kiss
Maerth meditating at home in Italy.
Photos © 1971 Klaus Schleusener

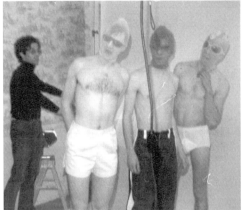

Left: Bob Lewis behind the scenes during the
"Jocko Homo" filming for "In The Beginning Was
The End: The Truth About De-Evolution".
Photo © 1976 Bobbie Watson

Below: Devo cheered by the hometown crowd
at The Crypt, Akron.
Photo © 1977 Bobbie Watson

Above: Devo at Goodyear World of Rubber. *Photo © 1976 Bobbie Watson*

Above: General Jackett plugged into a space-heater for "In The Beginning Was The End: The Truth About De-Evolution."
Photo © 1976 Bobbie Watson

Above: The backdoor at Devo Headquarters, 103 S. Portage Path, Akron, OH.
Photo © 1977 Bobbie Watson

Left: Mark and Jerry in mongoloid masks consulting with Bob Lewis.
Photo © 1977 Bobbie Watson

Above: Saluting. *Photo © 1977 Eric Blum*

Right: Booji Boy wins over the crowd. *Photo © 1977 Bobbie Watson*

Below right: Devo arrives in New York - backstage with their debut CBGB's poster. *Photo © 1977 Ebet Roberts*

Below left: Mark Mothersbaugh in neck-brace with modified Fender Telecaster guitar at Max's Kansas City. *Photo © 1977 Ebet Roberts*

Above: Devo's New York City debut at CBGB's.
Photo © 1977 Bobbie Watson

Left: Devo at Max's Kansas City for the first time on May 25, 1977. *Photo © 1977 Bobbie Watson*

Above: With a nylon stocking on Bob1's head and Gherka military pants, Devo performs at Max's Kansas City
Photo © 1977 Nicky Latzoni

Left: Alan Myers, Bob Lewis and Bobbie Watson on the NYC subway.
Photo © 1977 Bobbie Watson

Right: Devo at Max's Kansas City
Photo © 1977 Nicky Latzoni

Above left: Bob Mothersbaugh and Susan Massaro on the NYC subway.
Photo © 1977 Bobbie Watson

Above: Booji Boy's encore in "Reverse Evolution" t-shirt at Max's Kansas City.
Photo © 1977 Mykel Board

Left: Performing at Max's Kansas City in pinhead masks.
Photo © 1977 Bobbie Watson

Above left: Gig poster for Devo's debut at The Starwood, West Hollywood in 1977.
Above right: David Bowie introduces Devo as "the band of the future" at Max's Kansas City.
Photo © 1977 Bobbie Watson
Below: The Chart with record company offers. *Photo © 1977 Bobbie Watson*

Above: Director Chuck Statler crosses the stage during the "Satisfaction" shoot.
Photo © 1978 Bobbie Watson

Right: Mark Mothersbaugh rests during the filming of "Satisfaction".
Photo © 1978 Bobbie Watson

Below left: Chuck Statler gets up close with Mark Mothersbaugh during "Satisfaction".
Photo © 1978 Bobbie Watson

Below right: Mark Mothersbaugh and Ed Barger during the filming of "Satisfaction".
Photo © 1978 Bobbie Watson

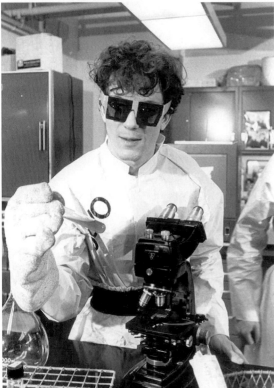

Above: Booji Boy learns an important lesson in the film "Satisfaction".
Photo © 1978 Bobbie Watson

Left: Punk scientist Mark Mothersbaugh celebrates a discovery in the laboratories of Lifeforms Unlimited.
Photo © 1979 Ebet Roberts

Below: Chi Chi Rodriguez illustration on Kent Sales & Manufacturing, Co. packaging.

RECOMMENDED BY
CHI CHI RODRIGUEZ
International Golf Star

U.S.A.

6 EACH
KENT
Practice
GOLF BALLS

PFG-6

KENT SALES and MFG. CO. Kent, Ohio 44240

Above: Devo plays the WHK Auditorium in Cleveland. *Photo © 1977 Bobbie Watson*
Below: Bob1 gets airborne at the same gig. *Photo © 1977 Bobbie Watson*

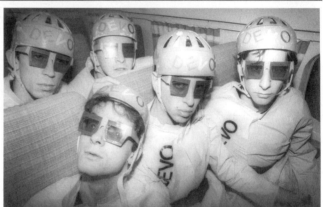

Opposite page:
Devo in the Netherlands

Top: Bob 1 times two.

Middle left: Huddle.

Middle right: Arriving from France on the tram from Schiphol airport.

Bottom: Devo acclimatizing to the Dutch surroundings.

All photos © Joep Bruijnje

This page:
Above: Mark and Bob 2 at the Bayfront Theatre in St. Petersburg, Florida on the *Freedom of Choice* Tour.
Photo © 1980 Walt Batansky

Right: Mark Mothersbaugh in Florida.
Photo © 1980 Walt Batansky

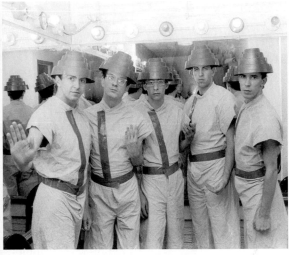

Above left: Mark at the Agora Theatre in Dallas, Texas.
Photo © 1980 Vernon L. Gowdy III

Above right: Backstage at the Agora Theatre in Dallas, Texas. *Photo © 1980 Vernon L. Gowdy III*

Left: Energy Domes down.
Photo © 1980 Jules Bates/Artrouble

Below: Posing in New Traditionalists Pomps backstage at the Tampa Jai Alai Fronton.
Photo © 1981 Walt Batansky

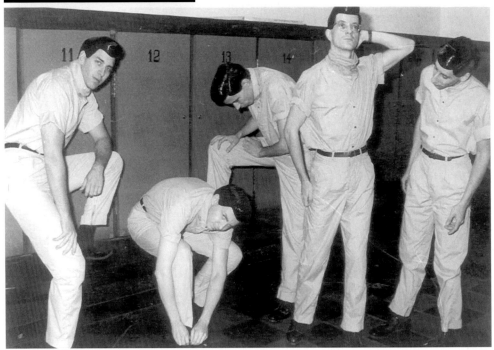

Above: Oh, No! It's Devo
– Night of the Living Dead.
Photo © 1982 Ebet Roberts

Right: A Booji Boy dons the
Mark Mothersbaugh mask.
*Illustration from Beautiful
World, No. 1 © 1985 Debbie
David/ST.EVE*

Below: All Access backstage
passes for the Oh, No! It's
Devo tour.

Devo

Top left: Bob 1

Top right: Jerry Casale

Right: Alan Myers

Bottom left: Bob 2

Bottom right: Mark Mothersbaugh

Photos © 1980 Jules Bates/Artrouble

"I said, 'Sure.'

"So he got a bass player, and enlisted his acquaintance Bob Mothersbaugh. It was the first time I met Bob, although we didn't talk much or anything. I don't remember the name of our band, but we did Chuck Berry and the Rolling Stones for $50 a week."

But by mid-1976, Alan was on a self-imposed musical hiatus. He was working as a cook, going out to see the Numbers Band occasionally, but pretty much keeping to himself. The music scene seemed dead to him; there were no interesting original acts to see, and no one he was interested in playing with. Rock and roll had lost much of its appeal, and he was listening only to jazz. Although he'd only been in the Bucket Shop a handful of times, Alan was feeling bored and lonely that night, and walked up to the bar. That's when he saw Bob sitting on a stool.

"I recall Bob was visibly distraught – maybe even to the point of being in tears," Alan said. "We talked about it, and he said his brother Jim was quitting. He didn't know what to do about the band, and was bummed out because things weren't happening."

He sat there consoling his friend over beers, and as the conversation progressed, Bob asked Alan if he might be interested in joining Devo. Alan hadn't even heard of Devo, but he said, yeah, he might give it a try. He didn't have anything else going on, after all.

"It seems fateful in retrospect," Alan said. "I suppose I provided something of a catalyst when they asked me to join the band. At that particular moment, we had just the right mixture."

Devo changed almost immediately. Not only were the odd, temperamental electronic drums replaced with a more solid foundation, but Alan Myers was special. Jerry was succinct in his praise: "Alan was one of the most amazing drummers I've ever heard." Much of that stemmed from his unusual musical education. The five years Alan had spent in the Dodge Avenue house had exposed him to a great depth of influences. And, like the rest of his Devo bandmates, he was extremely intelligent, able to process the information he'd fallen into.

"The house on Dodge Avenue became like this enclave," he recalled. "Instead of a living room, we had this collection of musical instruments. It was whatever anybody could get their hands on or borrow. There might have been an electric guitar, but I don't remember it ever being plugged in. We had all this stuff, and there was almost never a song played. We always just used to make sounds. We might get a rhythm or a key going and everybody would trade instruments. That was what happened at the house basically."

At Litchfield Junior High and Firestone High School, Alan had a classmate named Ralph Carney. In eighth grade, they were both drummers in the school band. But Alan quit when they got to high school; he wanted to play in the orchestra, but that would also require him to be in the Firestone marching band, which he had no desire to do. Still, he remained friends with Carney. They shared a similar taste in beatnik jazz and experimental rock, and Carney was also interested in playing music outside the marching band environment. So he began hanging out on Dodge Avenue.

"I (played) with Alan starting about 1970, when I first started to jam with people on harmonica, fiddle and banjo," Carney said. "He and I, plus some older musicians would play and listen to tons of records. They would smoke tons of pot. (I didn't back then.) We didn't really have a 'band,' but we would play at parties sometimes.

"Alan gave me my first saxophone lesson, sort of. He somehow was borrowing a cheap alto around 1972, and would walk around his house playing badly. There was a dog at Dodge Avenue that would howl when he played! I rented a saxophone from the local music store, and he would say, 'Just push the buttons and make patterns.' I mean, it was pretty excruciating to hear him play, but I think some hallucinogens were making their way to his bloodstream on a regular basis back then. I seem to remember a set of vibes in the huge bathroom. I think they were in the john because of the good acoustics!"

Alan continued the story: "I had just picked up a saxophone for like $125, and it was right at the beginning of us knowing each other. If you don't play sax, you really can't last for more than about five or ten minutes because your lips just give out. You haven't developed an embouchure. So, me and Ralph spent five or six hours handing the saxophone back and forth trying to make noises with it. I was giving him some jazz and classical recordings, and he already kind of knew some of this stuff. He had an interest in outside, zany stuff. I hesitate to use a word like that. Then the next day, he went out and rented his own alto sax."

Alan learned to play many instruments, but focused on drums, alto sax, upright bass and keyboards. His sophistication grew to the point where mainstream music didn't interest him anymore. His tastes gravitated toward early 20th century classical, ethnic music and experimental jazz. Along the way, he picked up Frank Zappa's *Freak Out*. The record didn't do much for him, but Zappa's liner notes did. The record sleeve included a list of influences, preceded by the disclaimer, "These people have contributed materially in many ways to make our music what it is. Please do not hold it against them."

"So, in the summer before tenth grade," Alan said, "I went out and picked up some music from this list, and that was the end of my Led Zeppelin collection. I went totally off the deep end... for John Coltrane, Edgar Varese, Arnold Schoenberg and the rest."

Around 1975, Carney and Alan hooked up with a quintet called Jazz Death, with Carney on sax and Alan on drums. The group – three horns, bass and drums – played a mix of originals and tunes by Ornette Coleman, Charles Mingus and Art Ensemble of Chicago.

"We used to play four or five gigs a year," Alan said, "but always like somebody's party. I remember playing the benediction at a Unitarian Church. Somebody would have a club. They would have an open night, and we would go in there – kind of set up and get going. The reaction would always be fifty percent out the door immediately, and twenty-five percent of them were kind of interested. The other twenty-five percent would stick around for some other reason altogether."

Carney continued: "Alan and I would drive up to Cleveland to rehearse, and we mostly gigged up there at coffeehouse-type places. (It was) kinda cold, intellectual jazz. I did most of the scream solos, and I was just 19 years old!"

By the time Alan joined Devo, Carney had begun playing with Tin Huey, along with Harvey Gold, Mark Price, Michael Aylward and Stuart Austin. The band was perfect for Carney, a left-of-the-dial mix of jazz, experimental, Captain Beefheart-style rock and quirky pop. The band had recorded an EP called *Breakfast with the Hueys*, and had become about the best band an egg-head rock fan could hope for, with Carney squawking and squealing on his sax, Gold and Price singing wry songs about human politics, and the whole band of eccentric savants purposely pushing the sound toward the surreal. Chris Butler would join in 1978, bringing a new element of stability and professionalism. After receiving fawning praise from one of the country's most influential rock critics, Robert Christgau of the *Village Voice*, Tin Huey was signed to Warner Bros Records in 1978. But the band soon imploded, plagued by a label that had no idea what to do with it. Butler would go on to form the Waitresses, and Carney would sit in with the likes of the B-52's before becoming one of Tom Waits' main sidemen.

Although they had both joined promising rock bands playing in a similar vein, Alan and Carney drifted apart. "Devo was like a cult," Carney said. "Alan cut his hair and it wasn't the same."

Alan's entry into Devo propelled them forward exponentially. Over the following few months, with Bob Casale back on guitar, the band became tight and polished, almost completely removed from their former sound. There would be no more messing around in the studio with windshield wipers and washing machine sounds as rhythm tracks. Alan was technically solid – they nicknamed him "the human metronome." He didn't overplay, but he was capable of complicated parts, like the jerky rhythm of the band's "Satisfaction" cover. He was also on the same intellectual plane as his new bandmates. Not just anyone could fit into the Devo picture, but he did. He even had the same geeky demeanor and skinny physique.

❁ ❁ ❁

With Alan's new bounce behind them, Devo began rehearsing more earnestly and writing new material. Although Jerry had been handling most of the lead vocals through the early years, Mark's vocal turn on "Jocko Homo" – and the corresponding performance in *The Truth About De-evolution* – had proved to be a turning point. Jerry had been the perfect front man for the band Devo was before. Mark was the perfect front man for the band it was becoming. Jerry was psychically durable. As a front man, he could take a punch, and considering the audience reaction of those earlier gigs, Devo needed his sharp tongue and glare at the front of the stage. Mark, on the other hand, was the guy who had performed red-faced under the monkey mask back at the first Creative Arts Festival show, and who had been hiding, nearly voiceless, behind Booji Boy for the past couple of years.

In the early days, Bob Lewis said, "Mark always liked being the scientist in the laboratory. He wasn't uncomfortable about playing music in front of people, but I think he had to kind of force himself to be the front man."

There had been tension about the lead vocalist position from the very start, when Bob Lewis had pushed for his roommate, Fred Weber, to be the Sextet Devo singer. "In the end, Fred wasn't right for Devo," Bob said, "but nobody had any idea Mark would become such a compelling stage presence. Jerry thought he should be the lead singer for our Sextet, but I was convinced it never would have worked. He was clearly offended by my insistence that we ask Fred Weber to sing at the Creative Arts Festival. In retrospect, that decision probably spawned some of the ill will and ongoing conflict that has plagued my relationship with Jerry."

Mark's hiccuppy tenor was carrying the new songs. He could croon like a sentient robot and, while his voice didn't have the range of, say, a Fred Weber, it had personality. It sounded like Devo. He had his masks to hide his shyness, but he was becoming a better performer, with a quirky way of shaking his shoulders and a growing confidence in dealing with hecklers and spuds.

Devo had finally settled on the members who would carry the band through the next decade. Internally, they had solidified, but externally, they were still a band that had yet to make much of an impact, even locally. A trip to an Akron janitorial supply shop would help change that.

Unit Services had folded halfway through 1976. Mark sold off many of his rubber stamps and Jerry went looking for another job. Through a friend, he found work doing catalog graphics for an industrial supply company called Portage Broom & Brush. Flipping through the company's catalog one day, Jerry spotted a two-piece yellow industrial suit. His discriminating eyes popped out. That suit was so Devo!

Jerry found out where the outfits came from – M.F. Murdock Company, a few blocks from Quaker Square. The band went shopping.

"We grew up as spuds in Akron, Ohio, surrounded by janitorial supply houses, rubber factories, catalogues of industrial gear, rubber gloves," Jerry said later. "Instead of being ashamed of it or trying to deny it, we used it. The band went into a janitorial supply house in Akron, saw the yellow suits, tried 'em on and said: 'We'll take 'em; they're hideous!'"

Mark, too, saw the potential. "We were looking for something that made us look glamorous. We kind of looked like giant cheeseburgers in those yellow outfits."

Where Kiss had settled on spandex and painted faces, Devo knew they had found their look. The suits were bright and riveting, vaguely futuristic working-class uniforms. The faceless, lockstep animation the band had been grooming could be achieved with each of the members in these suits. And though they were not made of rubber (they're actually more like paper), they seemed to reflect the rubber factory atmosphere that had so influenced the group. Plus, they were cheap – about $4 apiece.

Those suits were Akron, in a way that only an Akron spud could truly appreciate. The band used black electrical tape to spell its name across the front. Devo had found its new skin.

Chapter 15

The summer of 1976 had proved to be a boom time for Devo. But the rest of Akron was in a deep hurt. The United Rubber Workers, a powerful union with international headquarters in downtown Akron, had called a historic strike in late April. Eleven thousand local workers were walking picket lines, with another 13,000, not eligible to strike, watching nervously. The entire city was in a chokehold. As April dragged into May and June into July, President Gerald Ford had sent his labor secretary to town to try to break the stalemate, and tire builders were scraping at the bottom of their savings accounts. Proud workers were applying for food stamps and government aid. Grocery stores, gas stations and restaurants began to suffer, because, aside from maybe those yellow suits at M.F. Murdock, nobody was buying anything.

Akron, since the turn of the 20th century, had been an industrial center, proudly boasting the title "Rubber Capital of the World." The executive headquarters of the world's largest tire companies were there, along with a great bulk of manufacturing and research, plus the international union. Everywhere, the town carried signs of this legacy, from the Firestone Bank to Goodyear Metropolitan Park; from Goodrich Middle School to General Street. Through the World War II boom and the gravy years that followed, all of these connected forces had coexisted, and all had profited. The union had grown unusually strong; as the automobile had become a staple of American life, there had been plenty of money to go around. But by the 1970s, foreign competition from the likes of Michelin and Bridgestone had begun to cut into the market share. The Akron companies were bloated and, after strikes in 1967, 1970 and 1973 had become known as the "triennial passion plays", everyone expected the 1976 contract negotiations to be an epic standoff. They were.

By then, Devo was practicing in the basement of "Devo house", a rented home on Greenwood Avenue, a pleasant tree-lined street not far from High-land Square. The owner was a lawyer named Chris Barron, a friend of the band. Susan Massaro and Jerry were living there, as were Bobbie Watson and Bob Mothersbaugh. Bobbie and Bob Lewis had broken up after 10 years, and she had taken up with the young man known – for increasing purposes of practicality – as Bob 1. The band was peaking creatively, with new songs coming out of the basement, one after another. Susan was upstairs in the kitchen one night, listening to a song she had first heard the band tinker with at Harlan Hall.

"Mark would originally sing 'Blue Balls'. One time, I think it was the night I was baking chocolate chip cookies, and took the bowl of dough downstairs to practice, I teased him about writing a song for me, and he started calling it 'Soo Bawlz'."

The song would become a fixture in the growing set list. The band had also written a song called "Penetration in the Centerfold", inspired by the new level of graphic erotica in *Hustler* magazine, and "Clockout", with a title straight from the factory. This last entry had an ironic ring that summer. Striking rubber workers roamed around aimlessly, wearing orange T-shirts with the slogan, "URW – Catch up in '76." The pickets decorated Christmas trees at their posts, meant to deliver the message that they were prepared to stay out until winter, if that's what it took. There were fixtures of the strike everywhere. A big black man in a cowboy hat sat every day outside the gate of his Goodyear plant, playing a saxophone. The working-class watering holes, where shots and beers used to be set up along the bar to await three shift changes a day, became places both to grumble and rally around the cause.

One of those bars was a place called the Crypt, a block away from the sprawling Goodyear complex on East Market Street. It was co-owned by a

Goodyear production worker named Bill Carpenter, who had taken the place on as kind of a hobby, a rec room away from home. Beer was cheap; it was a place for him and his buddies to hang out. By mid-summer, with everyone hurting, he had slashed the price of beer to a quarter a glass – just enough to pay for the kegs.

Amid all this turmoil among Akron's established culture, an underground music scene was beginning to find some sort of order. Tin Huey was playing when it could get gigs, mostly at JB's in Kent. A young Akron songwriter named Nick Nicholis had put together a band called the Bizarros after hearing New York rock poets like Patti Smith and Tom Verlaine. A heavy metal cover band called King Cobra, led by Harlan Hall resident Ward Welch, had discovered *Creem* magazine and was starting to write songs in the vein of the "street rock" that was taking hold in New York's Bowery district, where the Ramones, Television and Blondie were beginning to follow the earlier path of the Patti Smith Group and Suicide. There was no good reason why Akron, Ohio, was becoming an outpost of a revolution whose first volleys had only just then been fired. But it was.

In Cleveland, a rock critic named David Thomas – pen name Crocus Behemoth – had formed Rocket from the Tombs and played some gigs in 1974 and '75 at the Viking Saloon. The band had spit out some members, who formed Frankenstein and had, by summer 1976, regrouped and changed their name to the Dead Boys, taken from a Rocket from the Tombs lyric. Behemoth, his musical partner (and fellow writer at Cleveland's *Scene* magazine, a weekly music paper) Peter Laughner, and a few others had evolved into Pere Ubu and by late 1975 were gigging around Cleveland with like-minded, hard-art bands the Mirrors and the Electric Eels. Laughner, who approached music as a poet, had an intrinsic, black-sunglasses sense of cool. He soon emerged as one of the scene's most talented songwriters, but also as one of its worst chemical abusers. He did a lot of drugs, and he drank even more.

Devo, it seemed, was finally finished trying to open for the Numbers Band or getting hired as a party joke. The new version of the band played a show in 1976 with King Cobra at the Bombay Bicycle Club, better known as the BBC, in the Portage Lakes area. It was a rough bar that attracted bikers and ex-cons. King Cobra was the de facto house band, and Mark had run sound and done a remote recording for them, wearing a monkey mask, of course.

King Cobra was getting a message, indirectly, from the New York bands. The group was starting to focus more on raw originals, with sometimes playful, sometimes violent lyrics, taking their hard-rock approach in a different direction. And, either consciously or not, they picked up a vital lesson from New York's CBGB's scene: find your own place to play. This had already happened in Cleveland. Pere Ubu had begun to inhabit the Pirate's Cove, in Cleveland's then-bleak, industrial Flats district. Welch wanted to do the same thing. But there was no way the BBC would put up with much of Mark Mothersbaugh in a monkey mask, nor would the biker crowds have much patience for songs they'd never heard played by a bunch of musicians who considered themselves "artists". So Welch and his buddies started casting about for a bar that might allow them to book local, original bands.

By then, the rubber workers' strike had ended, without a clear winner. In late August, the union had negotiated a good contract for its workers, but many of them felt it had not been worth the price of admission. And the skies were darkening over Akron. Michelin had opened its first American plant while the domestic industry was hamstrung by the strike, and the cornerstone was laid for a quickly growing foreign domination of the tire market. Plants in Akron would soon start closing in harrowing succession, and Asian and European companies would begin snapping up Akron's venerable tire companies. In the immediate sense, Akron felt whipped by a summer of discontent. One young rubber worker's orange T-shirt summed it up. He wore it on the late summer day when the new contract was ratified, modified to read: "URW – Beat Up in '76."

So the pieces were in haphazard place when Ward Welch and his lead guitarist, Buzz Clic, walked into the Crypt that fall. The place had a stage, and the pair asked Carpenter if they might be able to bring in some bands to play. Carpenter, who had spent the summer on strike and had lost interest in keeping his little playhouse, did them one better. If they would run the bar themselves and make the lease payment, they could do whatever the hell they wanted in there. He was finished. The Crypt was theirs. He handed over the keys.

King Cobra was in the midst of a reinvention. Welch started going by "Rod Bent" and the now-mostly original band would soon change its name to the Rubber City Rebels. Welch and Clic earnestly took on their new roles as "barkeeps", but they quickly discovered the reality of running an old rubber worker's bar. They had to serve all three Goodyear shifts, which meant they started serving shots and cheap draft at 6 a.m. But they didn't care. Their reason for doing this was to carve out a stage in Akron. Word was out that Akron had a counterpart to Cleveland's Pirate's Cove and, by winter of 1976, the Crypt was booking a formidable lineup – Devo, Pere Ubu, the Dead Boys, the Bizarros and, of course, the Rubber City Rebels. But it was hardly as glamorous as it might seem. Welch and Clic spent all day jawing with drunken rubber workers before the bands came in.

"It was, like, old guys named Leftie and Blackie and Louie," Welch said.

"And on Friday nights, they'd still be hanging out, and we'd be bringing in the bands – Devo and Pere Ubu – and here's Lefty and Blackie and Louie, and they would hear Devo warm up and – 'What the hell is this?' You had to clear out one world and bring in another one."

On December 10, 1976, Devo, now with Mark and Jerry, the two brothers Bob, and Alan Myers, played at the Crypt. Then they played again the next night. That week's issue of *Scene* magazine reported the news that the Crypt was in business: "Akron's King Cobra has found the ultimate solution to the problem of having to play what the bar-owner wants – they bought a bar. The Crypt (in Akron) now belongs to the Cobra boys, and they are reserving the stage of their new acquisition for 'bands with original music.' The Crypt will feature area 'underground' bands such as Pere Ubu, Tin Huey, and The Dead Boys, and hopes to bring in an occasional national act as well. The club's offering December 10 and 11 will be Akron's Devo, and on weeknights King Cobra (not surprisingly) will provide the music."

The following weekend, Devo played the Crypt on two consecutive nights, with Pere Ubu opening. Although Devo was considerably shinier, the two bands shared a similar aesthetic and a similar collection of egghead rockers. Both groups augmented the traditional guitars-drums lineup with a synthesizer. As front men, Thomas/Behemoth and Mark had a lot in common; although they expressed it in different ways, each drew heavily from the darkness of the industrial landscape around them. Both singers had an idiosyncratic presence – Mark in his eyeglasses and factory costumes and throaty yodel, Thomas in his emotive yelping and understated but studious theatrics. Thomas, somewhere in the 300-pound range, with impossibly thick, frizzy hair, would often perform in a trench coat, eyes fluttering as he beat his breast with a pudgy fist. He used found objects as rhythm instruments, striking a steel window weight with a hammer, for example, with at least as much visual as musical effect. Both Devo and Pere Ubu had a strong, early sense of "performance art" and would sometimes suffer for this, viewed as joke bands by fans and critics who expected convention in their rock. Nevertheless, both expanded the palette, in their own way .

Thomas, in retrospect, said Pere Ubu and Devo spoke two different languages. He was, and remains, an iconoclastic and humanistic artist, emotional, yet spare in his emotion; nostalgic, yet spare in his nostalgia. He downplays any artistic connection the two bands may have shared.

"I remember a couple songs they did then that had emotion." he said. "They soon dropped those from the set. I find their 'philosophy', i.e. what lies underneath the surface devolution material, to be vacuous, populist and cynical to a repulsive and unnecessary degree. Devo wanted a career more than anything else. We wanted anything else more than a career. They had a strategy. We found the idea of having a strategy to be really small town and hick. They were a pop band. We were a folk band."

Scott Krauss, Pere Ubu's drummer, recalled the night he first encountered the spud boys: "This one friend of mine was telling me that there's this really weird band down in Akron. He said, 'You're not going to believe this but they all wear these uniforms and sing about the de-evolution of the human race.' So we go down to check this out and it was at a little club called the Crypt. It was definitely one of the weirdest bands I've ever seen. I kept wondering, 'Aren't these guys afraid of getting beat up?' I don't know how it all got worked out, but sometimes they'd come up to Cleveland, and we'd take turns headlining. They got into a bunch of philosophical discussions, Jerry Casale and Mark Mothersbaugh versus David (Thomas) and Allen (Ravenstine, Pere Ubu's synthesizer player), and it was pretty interesting. I think they got the impression that Pere Ubu was never going to make it because we didn't care whether we made it or not. And we thought they were going to the other extreme."

Very quickly, Devo went from a band that had gigged only sporadically in its first three-and-a-half years of existence to a regular working outfit. Through the winter of 1976, the band was playing two shows a week, going back and forth between the Crypt and the Pirate's Cove, usually sharing bills with Pere Ubu or the Rubber City Rebels. Jerry described one of those shows in the liner notes to *Devo Live: The Mongoloid Years*.

"Swept up in the energy of England's punk scene, we are learning to deliver live on stage," he wrote. "Jim Mothersbaugh and his homemade electronic drums are gone. Instead, Alan Myers, the human metronome, pounds out primal beats on a 'real' drum kit. Bob Casale (Bob #2) has joined the Devolutionary Army, adding precise staccato guitar rhythms plus occasional keyboard duties so we can let Mark loose for the rapidly increasing bouts of crowd confrontation. With Bob #1 and myself, this new five member version of DEVO has only played twice before this night. But, the line-up works and will remain this way for the next ten years. Wearing black wrestling shorts and nylons over our heads, we still look like a 'weird art band.' As our tempos have gone nuclear, so have the crowd tempers. Our new precision-machine rock sound polarizes the audience into Pros & Cons. The crowd at The Crypt proves no exception."

Mark's commanding stage presence had come as something of a surprise. But it was working. He was jumping around, walking into the audience, tossing sharp-witted word bombs back at hecklers. And his songwriting had developed to the point that Jerry was no longer the focal point. The band had stopped playing some of his early, twisted sex-and-love songs, written from the perspective of Lt. Casanova.

"Jerry made a big mistake when he threw out all his 'old' Devo songs," Ed Barger observed. "It would have been more Lennon/McCartney had he not given up the early stuff that provided contrast to Mark's talents. Just like his song 'The Death of Lt. Casanova' – Lt. Casanova died one night at the Crypt! I saw it with my own two eyes.

"Devo did 'Jocko Homo', and Jerry knew it was better than anything he or Bob Lewis were capable of doing. Jerry realized Mark was going to be the star. So, he quit writing the type of songs that added a different dimension and another side to Devo, and began to concentrate on propaganda. Up until this time Jerry was the so-called 'star' of Devo."

That December, amid the flurry of club shows, Devo went into a Cleveland studio and recorded the song "Mongoloid" on a Revox four-track, touching it up afterward at Krieger-Field. The band turned out a version that showed Devo's growing technical and artistic assurance. The song and its sound would change very little in the hands of Brian Eno when recorded later for Devo's debut album.

The 1976 "Mongoloid" is a thumping, fairly straightforward rock song, with nasal, robotic vocals and droning, fuzzed-out guitars. Written by Jerry, it's a classic of this era, capturing both the new sound and the trademark double-entendre. To a casual listener, the song seems politically incorrect in its use of a "mongoloid" as its subject. But there is a sense of empathy, which, in a span of three-and-a-half minutes, grows to a message of anti-elitism. The mongoloid functions just fine in a supposedly advanced culture. He wears a hat, has a job, brings home the bacon – just like the fellow drones with college degrees. In fact, he's "happier than you and me."

Plus, "mongoloid" just sounded like a Devo word – somehow alien, but also familiar and direct, mirroring the music that propelled the lyric.

With a good version of "Jocko Homo" already in the can, the band started to talk about pressing the two songs as a single.

Chapter 16

On New Year's Eve, 1976, Devo was booked to open for King Cobra and headliners the Dead Boys at the Crypt. The ads for the show, decorated with the Grim Reaper, proclaimed: "Start the New Year with a New Attitude." By then, the Dead Boys had begun driving to New York City to play CBGB's, and had endeared themselves to Hilly Kristal, the club's owner. Kristal had become their manager, and had made plans to release a Dead Boys record on the house label he was forming. That project never bore fruit – emerging, punk-oriented major label Sire Records intervened – but the buzz was enough to for the ad to bill them as "CBGB-OMFUG Recording Artists."

The Dead Boys were, as the title of their debut album would announce, "young, loud and snotty." They decorated themselves with Nazi paraphernalia and sang songs about being juvenile delinquents and delivering "flamethrower love." A good chunk of their set was dredged from old Rocket from the Tombs material, including their signature song, "Sonic Reducer", and the dark Peter Laughner ballad, "Ain't it Fun". Laughner wrote the song when he was just 21, bringing an eerie mix of innocence and cynicism to the lyric, "Ain't it fun when you know that you're gonna die young".

Dead Boys' singer Stiv Bators was a short, scrawny, tangle-haired self-abuser, with a lot of Iggy in his shimmy. The entire band was bent on destruction, as they ravaged their way through a new version of old blues aggression. They were hungry junkyard dogs. Except for Stiv Bators, whose parents had the foresight to provide him with a stage-ready moniker, the band all took on violent noms de rock: guitarists Jimmy Zero and Cheetah Chrome, bassist Jeff Magnum and drummer Johnny Blitz.

As with the Dead Boys, Devo and Pere Ubu had a knack for crowd confrontation, but from a very different perspective. With the latter two, the message was, "This is our art, and we're gonna make you deal with it." With the Dead Boys, it was – to borrow from their second album title – "We have come for your children."

Jerry, writing in the *Mongoloid Years* liner notes, observed, "Like (the Dead Boys and Rubber City Rebels), DEVO is more than paying its dues within the confines of the psychic barbed-wire. Also, like them, DEVO is fueled by anger and frustration over The Captain and Tennille on local radio and bar bands paid to do covers of 3 Dog Night. That is about where the similarities between us stop. The Dead Boys hate DEVO. Still, we agree to open for them at The Crypt…"

It was freezing that night, but the Crypt – and Devo especially – had quickly developed a following, and the club was full. This was probably vital to Mark's emergence as the front man. He got enough positive feedback to encourage him to keep trying more. Maybe the audiences weren't saying, "There goes a respectable man," as he had hoped in *My Struggle*, but they seemed to think he was cool. This was no small achievement for a bespectacled nerd in satin gym shorts.

But it also led to a clash of egos. Devo's crowd had grown to the point that the band thought they should play last, in the headlining slot. But the Dead Boys had a crowd of their own, many of whom had driven the 35 miles from Cleveland. There was a minor argument, but Devo agreed to go on before the Dead Boys. After King Cobra played, Devo took the stage and dove into the new set of material. They had a driving sound, fully rounded with Mark's keyboards, two biting guitarists and Alan's powerful drumming. Chanted choruses and a harsh tunefulness made this version of the band seem vital – evolved. The weirdness of all those preceding years was fully evident, but so was a new punk force, as Devo made its way through "Clockout", "Soo Bawls", "Space Junk" and "Blockhead".

The Dead Boys were watching the set, celebrating New Year's Eve with Thunderbird wine, which the Crypt sold by the bottle. A drunken Cheetah Chrome and the Dead Boys' roadie, Fuji, made their way to the middle of the crowd to check out the band. Devo had stripped out of their yellow suits and, by late in the set, were wearing black wrestling shorts and t-shirts.

"The little clique from Kent were all hopping around like bunnies while we stood there getting knocked into," Chrome recalled, "and we pushed back when pushed, all in what we assumed to be good fun."

But the action was perceived differently from the stage. Devo, no stranger to confrontation, but also unaccustomed to having a roomful of fans to defend, focused on Chrome as the aggressor. During "Jocko Homo" (or "Mongoloid", depending on who's telling the story), Mark began taunting Chrome.

"Cheetah is a mongoloid!" he chanted, pointing at the red-haired Dead Boy with the dog collar around his neck.

Fuji nudged his buddy. "Why don't you pull down his shorts?" Chrome grinned devilishly, sneaked up to the stage and gave the boxers a good yank. Down they went, just like in the high school locker room. Marty Reymann happened to be standing right behind Fuji and Chrome when this happened, with Ed Barger a few feet beyond. So when Chrome returned to Fuji's side, Reymann gave him a hard shove. Fuji took a swing at Reymann. Barger lunged forward and took a swing at Fuji. The bodies went down in a pile, with others joining in. The Crypt was having its first real brawl.

In the confusion, Chrome and Fuji dropped to their hands and knees and crawled back to the bar, without anyone realizing they were gone. They picked up their unfinished bottles of Thunderbird and resumed drinking, sharing a good laugh as they watched the Devo fans fight each other.

"After it was over," Reymann said, "Ed told me he had thrown some punches, but didn't even know who he hit. Well, the next week, I had a guy come up to me all pissed off, claiming somebody hit his girlfriend two times! In all the stir, Ed had unknowingly punched out this girl! I was just laughing."

With the Dead Boys already gaining national notoriety for this sort of bad-boy hijinks, the story of the fight was immediately tacked onto into their legend.

"Exaggerated reports of the incident spread fast, causing DEVO to be linked to the U.S. punk music scene," Jerry wrote. "Commercially, it would turn out to be another case of the right thing for the wrong reasons."

The participants, especially the Dead Boys, later downplayed the scuffle. As fisticuffs were a regular part of their repertoire, they probably didn't see this as any big deal – a friendly punch in the arm. In fact, the band would soon use its influence to help Devo crack CBGB's.

"We beat 'em up, but we understood each other," Stiv Bators explained a year later.

Adds Chrome: "I'm kinda surprised to find out that this incident has gained such infamy; I always thought it was kind of a minor thing.... I'm also surprised to read what the Devos have to say about it, as I have run into them several times since then and we've always been friendly."

Even so, Chrome would repeat his pants-pulling trick at CBGB's a few months later, proving a Dead Boy could never get too much of a good thing. "Oh yeah, if memory serves me correctly, I got him *both* times," Chrome said. "You'd think a smart guy like that would learn to watch his back."

※ ※ ※

The shows continued through January. Devo had found its oasis in the Crypt, but there was still only a small group of people who got it. Bob Lewis, Ed Barger, Marty Reymann and Gary Jackett had remained loyal members at the core of a slowly widening circle. Two friends, Sue Schmidt and Debbie Smith, went to check Devo out one night that winter, and immediately struck up a conversation after being wowed by the first set. The girls, who had played with Peter Laughner in a pre-Pere Ubu band, had been trying to form a group of their own, and it was Alan Myers who introduced them to a drummer friend, Rich Roberts. The trio would soon begin playing as Chi Pig – the name copped from a chicken-and-ribs barbecue joint.

But even as this Akron-Kent-Cleveland musical movement was gaining momentum, there was tension whenever the outside world peeked in. Gary Jackett recalled one of those early Crypt shows, on a January night with the temperature near zero.

"A couple of bikers came in and sat at the bar," he said. "The Chosen Few, I think, was their club. Ten minutes later, and Devo starts playing to the small crowd. In ten more minutes, three more bikers come in. About three-quarters of the way into Devo's set, you look around and there are like twenty Chosen Few in this downstairs bar with all these nerdy, geek Devotees. Rod (Bent) just flipped. They were getting drunk, looking at the band and going, 'What the fuck is this?' You could just feel the room going cold. We quickly realized that everyone was going to get their asses kicked big time. We could all see the Devo girls getting raped, everybody stabbed. So Rod sneaked out and called the Akron police.

"Suddenly, two cops walked in and said, 'All you guys in the Chosen Few – Out!' Of course, the police walked in about two minutes after the biker guys were drunk enough to be going, 'This is pretty funny! You know, I kind of like these guys.' When the cops came in, it was like, 'We're going to burn this place down. You're all going to die!' They ran them out just when we had won them over."

When the trouble wasn't coming from the outside, Devo's wry sense of humor sometimes invited it in. As the band walked onstage for one of its first Cleveland shows with Pere Ubu, Jerry had his coveralls stuffed full of newspaper, imitating Thomas' portly physique. He ripped out the newspaper and began throwing it around. Thomas was so upset, his bandmates had to plead with him not to cancel the show.

❊ ❊ ❊

By March 1977, punk was breaking. Akron and Cleveland were unusually locked into what was happening in the centers of New York and London, but also remained isolated. Devo, Pere Ubu and the others had to make extra noise to be noticed. Devo, after struggling through all those years of gestation, accomplished this with perfect timing. That month, both their debut single and their self-produced film were released.

The band put out the 45 of "Jocko Homo"/"Mongoloid" on its own Booji Boy label. Bob Lewis said he arranged financing, borrowing about $2,000 from a friend of the band named Sandy Cohen, who was married to Kate Myers (no relation to Alan), the daughter of wealthy art collectors. Sandy Cohen's parents owned Portage Broom & Brush – Jerry's employer. Sandy was something of an intellectual, and appreciated what Devo was trying to do. But even with his backing, the single was still very much do-it-yourself. The band made all the arrangements with the pressing plant, and made the record sleeves themselves.

"It was amazing how they sold," Bob Lewis said. "All of a sudden, music stores from France were calling for a hundred copies. Every one of those covers was hand-folded, and we put the little dots on too! It was like the *Little Rascals* for a while."

Mark's recollection was somewhat different, at least as far as local sales were concerned: "I was driving around Ohio, going to record stores going, 'Hey, you guys need another Devo record here?' and the guy would go down to the last bin where it said 'Miscellaneous' and finger through and go, 'Nope, still got the one you brought in last week!' And I'd drive thirty miles back to Akron – 'O.K., well, didn't sell any today. But there's always tomorrow!'"

But by mid-summer, with influential punk/garage label Bomp handling distribution, the band had sold 3,000 copies. More importantly, the single was doing especially well in New York City.

Virtually simultaneous with the arrival of the records from the pressing plant, *In the Beginning: The Truth About De-evolution* made its premiere, on March 12, with a screening at the Akron Art Institute, followed by a free Devo concert. The art museum was a center of activity for Akron's small but enlightened cultural elite. The Myers family, with their formidable private collection, were leaders of this faction, and in fact Kate Myers and her husband, Sandy Cohen, hosted a private screening and premiere party at their home before the public opening. It seems logical that Akron's arts community would embrace this event. Mark and Jerry had already endeared themselves to professors in Kent and Akron, and had shown themselves to be worthy artists before – and beyond – their current incarnation as a working rock band. The emergence of the film at the same time as Devo's emergence as a live act solidified that impression.

But, of course, the 3 p.m. concert after the art institute screening did not go without incident. Jennifer Licitri recalled the moment that made everyone cringe: "When Devo played in the basement of the Akron Art Museum, the 'Mongoloid' song came up, and in the audience there was a child that was a mongoloid or badly retarded. It ended up being a huge problem. They just were offending everybody."

Mark got into a conversation with Robert Bertholf that afternoon. He had been working on *My Struggle* for years, and he was looking for advice on getting it published. He had brought along the lengthy manuscript, the nearly 300 pages of his photocopied manifesto laid out with his artwork of monkeys, mutated babies, potatoes and medical diagrams. The book, written by Booji Boy and "compiled by noted contemporary social scientist Mark Mothersbaugh," had an introduction by Jerry in his Chinaman guise. The illustrations included the smiling Chi Chi Rodriguez image that would become the cover of Devo's first album, and the text contained ideas that would define the band's past and future as it careened wildly through surrealistic reveries, prose poetry, sick but hilarious humor and doctored-up autobiography.

"Everything's in there," Jerry said in a 1995 magazine interview. "The philosophy is pretty well articulated in my introduction. The kind of irreverence and attack visually, the collage thing we were both doing, Mark kind of really locked into (it) in *My Struggle*, and he produced so much of it. We saw each other every day while he was doing that book and it all came from the art projects we were doing. *My Struggle*, today just about covers every offensive and politically incorrect subject you can imagine. I think the pictures kind of tell the story. All the scatology and the conscious satirization of racist and sexist stereotypes and stupid low puns and pop cultural twists and political attacks. It's all there."

This project Mark had been working on for years was mocked up and ready for the world. Bertholf gave him some guidance, and Mark showed his book to the editors at *Scene* magazine. A month later, in the April 14 issue, the music paper previewed the book: "Not to leave any medium untouched, Devo have also put together a book, *My Struggle*, to be on sale soon. Devo keyboardist Mark Mothersbaugh explained that the book's author is 'Booji Boy' (one of Mothersbaugh's on-stage characters) and that it's 'about life in Akron and life in general'."

Mark soon made contact with a mysterious character named rjs, (a.k.a. Robert J. Sigmund or Robert John Sigmond), a friend of the late Cleveland beat-era poet d.a. levy, now a legendary figure, at least in Ohio literary circles. Bob Lewis recalled driving up to Cleveland with Mark to meet with this potential publisher, "R.J. was part of that pre-post-industrial arts climate in Cleveland that self-congratulatorily worshipped levy, Peter (Rocket from the Tombs) Laughner, etc.," he said.

On the back of a postcard, "rjs," after explaining a certain amount of para-noia at having been contacted by a stranger 25 years after the fact, described his involvement. "Mark and I were once of a similar spirit," he wrote. "We agreed that I would produce his book when he promised to bring 77 bouncy booby virgin bimbos to help with the manual labor. But when he sold his soul to the devil + moved to lost angeles, I became discouraged + disconnected from him. When he sent me $200, I turned over the unfinished materials to his father, at their estate west of Akron (as per his directions). That was the last inneraction I had with him."

A few copies of *My Struggle* were produced by rjs, and Mark later released it himself. In both cases, the book was credited to the vanity imprint Neo Rubber Band Publications. It was a small, 5½-by-4-inch handbook, bound in red vinyl, although some copies exist with yellow covers. Mark's later editions would have the title embossed in gold. Its appearance was reminiscent of Mao Tse-tung's "little red book." In this sense, Mark was on the same page as Andy Warhol, who, after President Richard Nixon went behind the Communist veil to visit China in 1972, created a series of paintings from the frontispiece of *The Quotations of Chairman Mao*. Mao's status as a revolutionary icon had sexy overtones for pop artists.

Everything seemed to be happening at once for Devo. After the film's premiere at the art institute, a teenager named Michael Hurray interviewed the band for *Heavy Metal*, a local fanzine. The group announced that its first single had arrived and was available for sale. Hurray started asking questions about the band's history.

"Who started the original idea of Devo?" he asked.

Mark quickly pointed at the fellow seated beside him and without hesitation replied, "Him. Bob Lewis." He continued, "then Jerry…" Another member of the band interjected, "And then Mark – (Mark) was the next person."

That seemingly innocuous exchange would later come back to haunt them.

※ ※ ※

Three days after *The Truth about De-evolution* premiered in Akron, it was screened at the Ann Arbor Film Festival. The 10-minute Chuck Statler-directed movie won the prize (reportedly $25) for Best Short Film. A buzz was beginning. But Devo was still a local band, with gigs to play. The film added a new wrinkle to their club shows. Less than a week after the art institute screening, Devo was back at the Crypt, this time with a film projector in addition to their usual gear. They played the movie at midnight, then followed with their set. They showed the movie again the next night, in what would become a staple of their live performances.

"We would play (our film, *The Truth About De-Evolution*) onstage before we would come out," Mark recalled. "There was no such thing as MTV in the mid-'70s. There was no way to show the stuff, so we would just string a sheet up and then show the film in front of us. Then we'd pull it down and play a set. It seemed to work every time. It seemed to program people perfectly to enjoy an evening of celebrating the downward spiral."

Chapter 17

Less than two weeks after the movie premiere and the release of the "Jocko Homo" single, Iggy Pop's *Idiot* tour was scheduled to hit Cleveland on March 21 and 22. This was expected to be an especially hot show, because David Bowie was playing keyboards in Iggy's band, and some cool group from New York called Blondie was opening.

Susan Massaro was especially excited about this. Working as a waitress at the Quaker Square restaurant, Tavern in the Square, she'd had one of the busboys get tickets for her. She'd never seen Iggy before, and she watched the calendar, eagerly awaiting the show. As the concert approached, she decided she was sure she could get a Devo demo tape into the hands of Bowie and Iggy. She and Jerry had broken up six months before, and she was then dating

Bob Mothersbaugh. So she asked Bob if he wanted to go along to try to deliver a cassette. He was game. They could give it a shot.

The following account of what happened next is Susan's. It is flatly rejected by Jerry, and in fact is one of the most disputed of all Devo's stories.

Susan said she asked Mark if he wanted to accompany them to Cleveland, but he and Marina had other plans. She asked Jerry to go, but he thought it was a stupid idea. So she and Bob put together a package with a demo, a photo and promo materials. She left her daughter in Bobbie's care at their Greenwood Avenue house, and she and Bob headed off to Cleveland. The Agora was a midsize venue downtown, by far the best place to catch up-and-coming acts. An impressive procession of rock royalty passed through there in the 1970s; the Agora was the site of some of Bruce Springsteen's seminal shows with Kid Leo acting as cheerleader and emcee. The main room had a stage and a wide expanse of wooden floor, with tables and stools around the outside.

Bob and Susan arrived a little late and had to push their way through the crowd to get to the front of the stage. Blondie came on, and they both liked them. Susan thought the bass player, Gary Valentine, was cute. After the opening set, Susan and Bob went to the bar for beers, still toting the promo kit, then returned to the front of the stage, positioning themselves so they might be able to make the hand off if the opportunity presented itself.

Iggy and his band came out, Bowie dressed in a flannel shirt, and began playing. Susan was loving the show, but she was also scheming. She got a scrap of paper and scribbled a note indicating she had a package for them, and reached over the monitors with it. The hyperkinetic Iggy snatched it up, immediately shredded it, and threw it into the audience.

The show ended. Susan and Bob went to the backstage entrance and tried repeatedly to get through the door, only to be turned away by the club's security. There was growing disappointment. The plan was not going well, but she had another idea. Everyone knew that rock bands, when they played Cleveland, stayed at a place called Swingos Keg & Quarter Hotel, a short hop from the Agora. She asked Bob if he was up for hanging out there, and he said, "Sure."

Debbie Harry and Chris Stein described the hotel in the 1982 biography *Making Tracks: The Rise of Blondie*: "Swingos is famous. It may be the most music-oriented hotel in North America. The rooms are decorated in a tacky bachelor-pad chrome, with black and red rugs, subdued lights, and peeling paint. We heard screams in the night, howls in the halls, and saw festivity, coke dealers in Cadillacs, life in the middle of decay. Perhaps every soul band and half the rock bands in the world have stayed here. Here Cheetah Chrome pushed a soda machine through a wall onto a screwing couple.... Alice's snakes got lost in the lobby. Swingos has seen them all."

(Chrome disputes this story. He says it was Johnny Blitz. He was busy disabling the elevator with a fire hose at the time.)

Bob and Susan entered the lobby of this decadent rock haven. A big crowd of beautiful people were milling about. This might make things difficult. How would they be able to get these two rock stars' attention? They waited around for awhile, then, finally, Bowie and Iggy entered with their entourage. They passed through the lobby quickly and slipped into the bar.

"In retrospect," Susan said, "it's incredible that the fans did not follow. Maybe it was some Swingos protocol, unknown to us at the time. Anyway, Bob and I looked at each other, and just walked into the bar. No one tried to stop us. The room was only moderately busy, so we had full access. It only took a second to find Bowie's booth. I just walked up and started talking. It's hard for me to remember exactly what we said. Iggy wanted to know why I was helping my boyfriend. Bowie asked what kind of music it was, and I don't remember what we said. I think Bob handled that one. The meeting lasted only a minute or two, but I remember Bowie being quite polite and thanking us for the tape, and Iggy, of course, was hyper and cruder. When we left their table, we kind of floated into another booth."

They had done it. Devo's demo was in the hands of two of the most influential musicians imaginable. Bob and Susan tried to be cool as they celebrated their good fortune. Three members of Blondie – Gary Valentine, Clem Burke and Jimmy Destri – were sitting in the next booth. Valentine leaned over and asked how they knew David Bowie. Bob and Susan slid into their booth and explained what had happened, and the Blondie guys teased them for not bringing an extra tape for them. So Susan, with typical Akron politeness, said she'd be happy to bring one to the next night's show. Blondie invited them to their hotel the following night, and said they'd put them on the guest list for the concert. (Being the opening band, they were staying at a Howard Johnson's. A little seasoning was necessary before one could ease into the Swingos groove.) So they all sat and talked about music for awhile. Bob and Gary gabbed about guitars; Blondie told them about Seymour Stein, the president of Sire Records who had signed Talking Heads and was a key proponent of the emerging crop of CBGB's bands.

And then Bob Mothersbaugh and Susan Massaro – former nobodies – floated back to Akron on the cloud of one of those nights that can only happen to the young, when the theory that everything is possible seems like a proven fact.

Susan crept into her daughter Sarah's room to tuck her in, then hurried downstairs to tell her best friend Bobbie what had happened.

"Next day we called Jerry," Susan said, "and of course, he decided *he* had to go up with us, so he could say and do the right things to impress Bowie and Iggy. We hung out with Blondie at Howard Johnson's for a short while, I think we may have eaten somewhere, and went to the Agora. The show was great, although it could not match the thrill of the night before. I think we got backstage that night, but I don't remember much about it. Gary (Valentine) tried to get us an audience with Bowie, but, unfortunately, he and Iggy had to go into the studio above the Agora and mix the show, as it was to be aired on radio on Sunday. We waited for a very long time, late into the night, and finally decided to go home. Jerry berated us for wasting his time, and that was that."

Jerry's account is considerably different.

"It was me, nobody else in the band," he said. "It was me and I think one of the girls that ended up being in a band called Chi Pig. We wanted to see Blondie.... Iggy's *Idiot* tour, and Bowie was faithfully playing the keyboards. And Blondie (was the opening act). I don't know if Bob1 was along. All I know is I got in backstage with Blondie. Then we got to Iggy and we gave him a tape, an early demo tape."

Alan Myers' version of the story mirrors Susan Massaro's: "I remember Bob Mothersbaugh took the tape and went up to Cleveland. Susan might have been with him because I think they were an item at the time. They found out what hotel Bowie and Iggy were staying at, and hung around the lobby. I think it was Swingos Keg & Quarter. As I recall from his story, they were just about ready to give up and go home then in walked Bowie. I believe Bob approached him with the tape, but it might have been Susan."

In Mark's version, "We had a pretty girl take him a demo tape backstage and hand it to him."

There is general agreement on what happened next. Iggy and Bowie threw the tape into a box with countless other tapes they'd been handed on the tour, and left for the next town, where they'd be given still more tapes.

❀ ❀ ❀

Part of the spoils of winning the Ann Arbor Film Festival prize was that *The Truth About De-evolution* went on a tour of colleges and art houses. It was being seen, and audiences were taken with this quirky band that seemed to have something to say and an intriguing way of saying it. One of the people who caught the film was Kip Cohen, an A&M Records rep. Immediately after seeing Devo, he was smitten. "I want this de-evolution band! We've gotta find them."

Are We Not Men?

In April, Jerry's phone rang. It was Cohen. He wanted to fly Devo out to Los Angeles right away for some showcases. Jerry stalled. There was no way they were ready for something like this. They'd only been playing regularly for four months. There was still a lot of screwing around with the set. But Jerry was smooth. He told Cohen no, they couldn't possibly break away from their busy schedule right then. Devo was booked until June, a hot item on the club circuit there in Northeast Ohio – you know how it is. He managed to buy time until July. Cohen said he'd be waiting anxiously. Jerry hung up the phone.

This was some information. A guy in Los Angeles? The same place that less than two years before had found him and Mark scheming to get on a local access charity show to beg for a record contract? He wants us to showcase for a major?

There would be a lot of work ahead. The band had to get ready. There were weak spots in the material; there was lots of tightening to do. The band that had screwed around for years needed to get polished, and quick. They did have some shows scheduled, a couple of gigs a week through the end of the month. But Jerry realized that maybe – and quicker than anyone thought – the band had outgrown bopping between the Crypt and the Pirate's Cove. So he hatched a plan.

Jerry packed a suitcase with some Devo tapes and promo kits, a pair of corduroys and a snazzy sweater, got in a car, and drove to New York. While Devo had always, for reasons of parochial logic, focused on Los Angeles as its musical mecca, New York City was becoming an equally obvious, and far more accessible destination. When Jerry reached the city, he put on his straight clothes and walked into CBGB's and Max's Kansas City, the other club that was focused on the burgeoning punk scene. With his hair combed, he looked nothing like the guys in baggy yellow suits and 3-D glasses in the band pictures. Jerry, no stranger to performance, reached out his hand to Hilly Kristal and introduced himself as Devo's manager.

He went to the office of *New York Rocker*, one of the premier magazines of the new rock scene, and showed around some pictures and played the single. He talked to Alan Betrock – influential journalist of the underground, founder and editor of *New York Rocker* – about doing a story on Devo. Then he sat back and waited. Jerry was pretty smart. He already understood how the business worked, even though he'd operated outside it for his entire career. Based on the promise of a *New York Rocker* feature, CBGB's and Max's agreed to book Devo. And based on the promise of bookings at CB's and Max's, *New York Rocker* agreed to do a feature.

Now it was time to get busy. Devo had a series of Cleveland gigs booked at the Pirate's Cove and a new place, the Eagle Street Saloon. These would be the warm-ups for three New York shows in late May, two at CBGB's and one at Max's Kansas City. Buoyed by the sudden attention, they returned almost immediately to the reality of life in Ohio.

The Eagle Street Saloon had been taken over by a guy named Clockwork Eddie, who had previously run a club called Clockwork Orange, until it was shut down by the city.

"I don't know how they got into Eagle Street, " Gary Jackett said. "It was like Berlin 1929 in the middle of the German depression. It was a hellhole. It was great, in a horrible way."

Eagle Street was populated by rowdy, straight-rock loving, Bud-drinking bikers. It made the Bombay Bicycle Club look like an ice cream social. Devo got up to play, all focused on grooming itself for the important gigs ahead in New York and Los Angeles. They were honing the set, working on the bits they knew went over well – Booji Boy, the "Satisfaction" cover, the whole "Jocko Homo" opus. But there was one problem. Several problems, actually, but one in particular.

This one guy just kept screaming, "Aerosmith! Play some Aerosmith!"

They ignored him. Taunting Cheetah Chrome was one thing; messing with these guys in leather vests would be another.

"Aerosmith!"

"Aerosmith!"

The Booji Boy segment of the night arrived. Mark pulled on the mask and started his sweet, squeaky-voiced routine. Pretty much the antithesis of Aerosmith. Finally, the guy rushed the stage and grabbed the mask with both hands, clenching his teeth.

"I SAID AEROSMITH, GODDAMN IT!!!!!"

And he ripped the mask from Mark's face.

Fortunately, Mark had two spares.

Chapter 18

One of the highlights in Devo's set was the cover of the Rolling Stones' classic, "Satisfaction (I Can't Get No)". The band had been rehearsing in Man Ray Studios, and had been kicking around the idea of giving a Stones song the same kind of devolved treatment they had already given "Secret Agent Man". Part of this stemmed from a growing ambition. Devo had heard that a Rolling Stones tribute album was in the works, and thought that if they could come up with something, maybe they could be included. They started messing around with things at Man Ray. Bob Casale came up with a lick – a choppy, repetitive guitar pattern – and the rest of the band followed his lead. Mark caught onto the groove and started singing the words to "Paint it Black". But it wasn't working. As the band continued playing, Mark changed tack.

"I can't get no…" The rhythm was starting to fit. "…Satisfaction… I can't get me no… satisfaction." The words began to mesh with the jerky rhythm the band was cranking out. They kept at it. Alan worked out a deceptively simple drum pattern. Bouncing from snare to toms to a sharp little ring-a-ding on the bell of the ride cymbal, his foot working the high-hat at an odd interval in the time signature, it almost seemed as though he was playing backwards on the beat. The guitars were clipped and restrained; Jerry's bass pushed forward and pulled back, pushed forward and pulled back. Even as Mark's monotone vocals climaxed with that impossibly breathless stream of babybabybabybabybabybabybabybaby…, there was no break at the end as he went into the next line, "Better come back later next week, cuz you see I'm on a losin' streak." The song was all tension and no release, and added an entirely different layer of meaning to the title. When Mick Jagger claimed he couldn't get no satisfaction, there was an unspoken understanding that eventually he would, probably with a couple of hookers in New Orleans. But when Mark Mothersbaugh made the same claim, wearing glasses and a protective yellow suit, you believed him. There was no way that guy would get any satisfaction.

Without hitting the listener over the head, this delivery of "Satisfaction" applied the theory of "Polymer Love", that in an increasingly devolved world, human sex was anachronistic and human love was irrelevant. Plus, it had a beat and you could dance to it. The "Satisfaction" cover captured, as well as anything the band had ever done, the spirit of Devo. The soul of the Stones' original was replaced with the funny robotics of Devo. The song was catchy, and it made you want to move, but it wasn't funky, at least not in the traditional sense. It seemed at once familiar and completely new.

"People didn't understand Devo and we thought it would be easier to show them how to devolve a standard, a classic," Jerry said. "It was kind of like a musical faction of the deconstructivist movement in architecture."

De-evolution in action. Given Mark's seminal moment seeing the Beatles on *Ed Sullivan*, it's a little surprising he didn't tackle a Beatles cover. On the other hand, another new entry in the set, the frantic, driving "Uncontrollable Urge", took one of the Fab Four's early conventions to the Devo extreme. Where "She Loves You" had used the "yeah, yeah, yeah" harmony as a primal hook, Mark advanced the notion during the anxious build-up to "Uncontrollable Urge" – "Yeah, yeah, yeah, yeah, yeah-yeah-yeah-yeah-yeah-yeah-yeah-yeah!" He trumped the Beatles by a full nine "yeahs".

Devo had found its sound. Now it was time to see how it would play in the big city. After a final warm-up show with Pere Ubu at the Pirate's Cove on May 19, the band and their friends set off for New York. They wouldn't all fit in the van, so Bobbie and Susan, who had matching Datsun 510s, drove. Ed Barger was along to run sound and act as "the designated heavy... the rest of the spuds were small and skinny and not much help in battle." Bob Lewis accompanied them with his girlfriend Mary King, and Bob Casale's wife, Sherry, came, too. As they drove all night through Ohio and Pennsylvania, they talked about the possibilities. In those two little tin-cup Datsuns, the friends who had been together for years recognized that those days above the pizza shop and those nights picking brains with Bob Bertholf and his poetic cronies might be reaching the unlikeliest conclusion. Devo was going somewhere. Nobody knew exactly where yet, but they were definitely going to New York, to the suddenly legendary CBGB's. They had all listened to that first, groundbreaking Ramones album back in Akron, and they knew they were approaching the headwaters.

In retrospect, it seems like everyone who played CBGB's in the mid-1970s became a rock star. Talking Heads, Blondie, the Ramones, Patti Smith and Television would all be written into rock and roll history after rocking and rolling on the club's ratty, duct-taped stage. Even lesser lights like Mink DeVille and the Dictators benefited, receiving some heightened level of royalty for having been on that particular scene. None of this was completely clear in 1977, but enough of it was.

The band had shows booked on May 23 and 24 at CBGB's, and another on the 25th at Max's Kansas City – a Monday, Tuesday and Wednesday. They arrived bright and early for their sound check; Ohio kids are raised to be punctual, after all. Devo was no stranger to raunchy bars, so Hilly Kristal's claustrophobic, 167- by 25-foot club with the stage at the far end of the tunnel didn't raise any particular eyebrows, even as it was tucked in among the Bowery district's soup kitchens and flophouses. The bathrooms were about the worst they'd ever seen, but it didn't matter. The Crypt wasn't much better. And the Crypt was in Akron.

As they checked out the city, Devo and its entourage went shopping in Greenwich Village, hitting Fiorucci and the Capezio store and a bunch of vintage clothing stores. Mark and Jerry, naturally, were mask-hunting. At a shop called Unique Boutique, they discovered gherka pants, the baggy white shorts worn by soldiers in India. The band members each bought a pair to wear onstage. By then, no member of Devo could choose stage clothes without the others, upon approval, buying identical items. The uniforms were part of the ideal – Devo was a collective. There was an echo of the Ramones in this, albeit with a sophisticated edge. The Ramones all wore ripped blue jeans and leather jackets and took "Ramone" as a surname; Devo, even if they changed outfits, had a cohesive front. Kraftwerk, by then, was doing the same thing, and Devo seemed like a cross between the two. Despite the strong personalities, the band intended to present itself as unified, faceless workers, with guitars and synthesizers in their toolbox.

Bob Lewis and Jerry also went scrounging around Manhattan's bookstores. They happened into Samuel Weiser's Books on Broadway. It had been a couple of years since they'd read about Oscar Kiss Maerth's book *The Beginning Was the End*, and they'd never been able to find a copy. Maybe this would be the place. Jerry asked the clerk if they had it.

"And they acted like, 'Why do you want this book?'" he recalled. "The guys that ran the store were all Orthodox Jews, and they thought that Oscar Kiss Maerth was definitely a Nazi. They hated anything that had to do with genetics, eugenics, perfection, or any kind of social anthropology. They were so pissed, but they went in the back and got it. Of course they'd sell it to me, but it was like, 'Get out of here'."

❋ ❋ ❋

The band found places to crash. Bob Mothersbaugh and his girlfriend Susan stayed at a loft near CBGB's with Bob and Sherry Casale. Bobbie slept in her car in front of the Ramones' apartment building. Mark and Jerry stayed with an old friend from Kent. One night, to soak in the romance of New York City, some of the group stayed in the Chelsea Hotel, which had given lodging to everyone from Mark Twain to Bob Dylan to Jimi Hendrix. (In the Chelsea's version of de-evolution, Sid Vicious' girlfriend Nancy Spungeon would eventually die there.)

They also found places to eat, with mixed results. After a meal at Umberto's Clam House on Mulberry Street in Little Italy – infamous site of the 1972 gangland shooting of Mafia Boss "Crazy Joe" Gallo, and immortalized in the Bob Dylan song "Joey" – Jerry took ill. Really ill. His stomach was killing him, and Bob Lewis drove him to the Bellvue Hospital emergency room, fearing his appendix had burst. The two old friends sat together for two hours next to a gunshot victim on a gurney with his brain matter exposed. Finally, Jerry was admitted. It turned out to be a bad case of gas; when it subsided, Jerry escaped from the hospital. The show must go on.

And the shows, indeed, went well. Back in Ohio, it had been hard to comprehend exactly what a "buzz" meant. The band was sure something was happening, but it had only been a matter of days since Mark's mask had been torn from his face by a clueless, leather-clad spud. Even when Devo won a crowd over, it was mostly with friends in attendance. But now, for three nights, the band was discovering what it meant to be pursued. People had heard the record. They had seen the film. There were music industry talent scouts in the audiences. At one of the shows, a group of high school kids from New Jersey showed up with a black Ford LTD that they had christened the "DEVOmobile." The car had a huge Booji Boy painted on the hood, along with D-E-V-O. Even when the petulant Cheetah Chrome repeated his de-pantsing of Mark at CBGB's, there was a sense of importance in the air. It was hard to figure out how to deal with this.

When the band played at Max's, opening for a straight, Rod Stewart-ish band called Allen Turner and Rocks, they hung a big Booji Boy poster behind the stage. They left it up after they were finished, and Turner performed under Booji's watchful eye. After the show, he asked if he could keep the poster. There was something vaguely troubling to this. Even as Devo was being accepted, there was a gnawing suspicion that people weren't really "getting" it. They were becoming musically accessible, even as they maintained their deeply groomed philosophy. The more they rocked, the more people listened. But the less, it seemed, they thought about what the band was saying. Some of this was their own fault. Devo's mix of the high and the low invited fans of the low into the party. Take, for instance, the song "Sloppy (I Saw My Baby Gettin')." The song, co-written with Gary Jackett, comes across in a bar as a frantic porn-fest. The chorus, after all, goes, "She said sloppy, she said sloppy, she said sloppy, I think I missed the hole." But it was intended as a commentary on sexual frustration; Jackett said he wrote it because he was "just crazy for some girl." Sometimes Dadaist theater merely comes across as silly. That's part of the intention. But it's not the final hope.

Still, Devo was in command of the New York audience. These were strangers and, even as Bob Lewis watched, understanding how far Devo had come from the Creative Arts Festival days, and even as his old girlfriend Bobbie Watson took snapshots, and even as Sherry Casale wondered if her husband's radiology career was ending, and even as reliable Ed Barger ran the sound board, a whole new world was opening up. At Max's, during the song "Praying Hands", Mark went into the audience with his microphone after singing about the occupations of the left and right hands – "while the left hand's diddlin', well, the right hand goes to work." He began to confront bar patrons about their own hands as the band played the hyperactive instrumental interlude.

"Let's find out what people at Max's Kansas City do with their hands," he said, approaching a member of the audience. "You, sir – what is your left hand doin'?"

"Smoking a cigarette," came the reply.

He approached a woman.

Are We Not Men?

"You – what is your left hand doin', baby?"

She chirped something in response. Apparently it rubbed Mark the wrong way, prompting him into action.

"Hey – hey! O.K., don't be a spud. Don't be a spud," he said in rhythm with the band. And immediately, he began chanting: "Spud, spud, spud, spud," with one of the band members following suit.

Devo had become precise in handling adverse reactions. They – and now, significantly, Mark – were confident in what they were doing and aware of their role as the Dr. Moreaus of the stage. This was their show. And when they threw that in New York's face, New York seemed to eat it up. This was Devo's field research in the quest to understand humanity.

"We were not really pop musicians; we were scientists, we were musical reporters," Mark said years later. "We were influenced probably more so by multimedia pop artists and conceptualists of the time than influenced by the music that was on the radio. Visual artists – people like Andy Warhol, artists of the '60s that were dealing with concepts and ideas – that's what we wanted to be a part of, as opposed to sitting down with one guitar for the rest of our lives writing songs. We saw the whole world and technology and all things natural and unnatural as potential material for getting our message across."

So the message was getting across, whether fully understood or not. Jerry, writing 15 years later in the *Mongoloid Years* liner notes, recalled his reaction to the New York shows. Even he, perhaps the most ambitious of the Devo members, realized that this commercial acceptance was a double-edged sword. In the intervening years, that realization became even stronger.

"Though the lights are brighter it's the beginning of the end," he wrote. "Suddenly DEVO's proto-cyberpunk multimedia sensory attack is embraced as Entertainment. An audience of Big Apple spuds, peppered with record biz 'earmen' (tipped off by a snappy column in Alan Betrock's *New York Rocker* magazine), swallow huge doses of de-evolution in an instinctive effort to develop cultural anti-bodies, much like rats learning to live with DDT. Sexy nerds with a sonic plan, DEVO's shows at Max's introduce us to the benefits of artistic license in the pre-AIDS/PC era. On stage, girls rip the yellow Tyvek (TM) suits from our bodies. Backstage, they complete the ritual with post-performance orgasmic gratuities in the dressing room. The urgency is necessary. Having been paid a total of $500.00, we are forced to dense-pak into our 1970 Ford van, along with our equipment, and lumber back to Akron during the night. The next day, our Rubber City phone starts ringing early. 'I'm sorry. What's that?' 'Who!?' 'Oh from Sire?' 'Elektra/Asylum?' 'Columbia?' 'Really!?' Record company 'hitmen' have decided that DEVO is the new girl in town. The fight begins to see which of them gets her."

The New York stand had been a success. As if to put an exclamation point on this, the band members went out after one of their shows and hung fliers for the already completed gig. Sonny Vincent, from a New York band called the Testors, saw them do this and wondered why. There was something de-evolutionary about this, but it also sent the message that Devo wanted to be remembered.

Everybody was exhausted as they loaded up in the van and the Datsuns and headed back to Ohio. They all fell asleep, including Ed Barger. Unfortunately, he was at the wheel of his van at the time. He ran through a New York red light, his head lolling back on the seat. He snapped back into conscious-ness just in time, cursing himself for coming so close to killing everybody.

Then it was back to Ohio, back to reality. The next night, after Max's, Devo had a show at the Pirate's Cove, with some local band called the Nerves.

Chapter 19

In mid-June, Devo played an in-store appearance at the Drome in Cleveland. The record store was owned by a guy named John Thompson, known around the music scene as Johnny Dromette. He and his shop had become a gath-ering point for the new Northeast Ohio rockers; David Thomas and Peter Laughner worked there, as did the founders of *CLE* magazine, an important chronicle of that unlikely wrinkle in musical time. The scene had remained collegial and, pretty much by necessity, somewhat insulated. Laughner had very briefly joined Television (naming his follow-up band Friction after one of the group's songs), but Devo's quickly growing national attention was the exception.

Back in Akron, Nick Nicholis, the singer for the Bizarros – an earnest and organized fellow – had taught himself how to start a record label and was making plans to release an album called *From Akron*, with the Bizarros on one side and Rubber City Rebels on the other. Tin Huey, by then, had whipped a crowd of outsiders into shape as a loyal audience, and the bands were all watching one another and learning. Like Devo, Chi Pig was pairing silly costumes and dances with off-kilter pop. The Rebels had benefited from the Dead Boys' comradeship – Rod Bent (soon to become Rod Firestone in a bratty nod to Akron's rubber royalty) had spiked his hair – and the band was playing originals like "Brain Job" and "Child Eaters" under cheeky stage names, with Clic and Bent joined by Pete Sake and Stix Pelton. Tin Huey's Mark Price was helping produce some of the bands in Akron's Bush Flow Studios. Everyone seemed to be working together and having a good time.

Devo's Drome appearance on the afternoon of June 19 was aired live on the radio, and would become a well-known bootleg, *Workforce to the World*.

Are We Not Men?

The band debuted its song "Come Back Jonee" that day. They returned to Akron amid plans for a second round of New York gigs in early July. Then it would be off to the Los Angeles showcases. But amid all this excitement, some horrible news came down through the grapevine. Peter Laughner, the world-weary singer-guitarist who had such restless potential, died on June 22, 1977. He was 24. The cause was acute pancreatitis related to his alcoholism.

❋ ❋ ❋

Devo set out for their second trip to New York, stopping on the way for a July 6 show at the Hot Club in Philadelphia. Hilly Kristal had helped groom a small, like-minded East Coast club circuit between New York, Boston and Philly. Bob Lewis, always the automotive connoisseur, drove his 1964 tan Oldsmobile Holiday 8 two-door coupe with a 355 Rocket V-8 engine (but alas, no power steering), parking it in front of the club on South Street. In the accompanying van, he had packed 5,000 copies of the "Jocko Homo" single for delivery to Stiff Records in New York. The emerging London-based label had agreed to take on distribution, Devo having quickly outgrown its Booji Boy label. So maybe there was a silver lining when the thief who decided to break into a vehicle that night chose Bob's car, and not the van. (Although it's unlikely that a street punk would've recognized any value in those stacks of silly-looking records.) Bob and Jerry's luggage got ripped off, and Jerry wasn't about to let it slide. With perhaps a misdirected sense of revenge, he stole a rare bottle of Napoleon brandy from the Hot Club's manager.

Devo returned to New York the following day for a three-night stand at Max's Kansas City, sharing the bills with Suicide and the Cramps. The Cramps, of course, had their roots in Northeast Ohio (and Ghoulardi). Singer Lux Interior was from Stow, which neighbors Akron, and had formed the band there with his girlfriend, Poison Ivy Rorschach. And Suicide, although bleaker and more dissonant, shared Devo's desire to smash rock tradition over the head, using synthesizers as part of their weaponry. New York was all about compression; nothing was building slowly in the Village by then. Things were exploding. So Devo returned, a month after its debut, as conquering heroes.

Bob delivered the cases of 45s to Stiff's New York office and he and the band had a long conversation that culminated in a deal with Stiff to release a second single. The shows went even better than the first go-round. Word had gotten out, and suddenly the Max's audiences were studded with stars – aging rockers who wanted to dig the new breed. Keith Richards showed up, crowing, "I wrote that song!" when Devo played "Satisfaction". Robert Fripp, Brian Eno and Frank Zappa checked them out. A drunken John Lennon

126

came up to Mark's booth after the band had finished and started singing "Uncontrollable Urge" in his face.

John Lennon! Singing our song?

After one of the shows, Fripp invited Eno and the band back to his place and offered his help. He liked them. And he and Eno were in a position to make things happen. The Devo guys thanked him in their quaint Ohio way. They were trying to keep their cool, but with the L.A. shows ahead, it was hard to know which cards to play, and when.

The band returned to Ohio and caught a night's sleep before departing for Los Angeles. This trip was going to be a little different. The entourage would be pared down because of the cross-country flight. Bob Lewis would not be included. By then, Bob had already sensed that he was being pushed aside by Jerry. Primarily through his handling of the single, and more generally through his long association with the band, he was emerging as a manager. But there was tension in this.

"I had already had told Eddie Barger and General Jackett, sitting in a van across from CBGB's, that if Jerry tried to screw me over there would be a reckoning – and had had a talk with Mark out at 'the ranch' about the fact that there might be consequences to Jerry's behavior – this was a pretty vague conversation, but germane."

The tension was not just between Bob and Jerry, though. Mark didn't like what was emerging as an ugly dissension. He was caught in the middle. He had come into the fold long after Jerry and Bob's early pairing, and he didn't know exactly what their history entailed. Friends in the small Devo circle were, consciously or not, choosing sides, and some informal diplomacy was necessary. Bob Mothersbaugh and Bobbie Watson were no longer dating, but still close. Before departing for Los Angeles, he talked to her about Lewis' exclusion from the California trip.

"Bob Mothersbaugh was expecting me to be upset," Bobbie said. "But he said I shouldn't be, that it didn't mean Bob was excluded, that this was just an audition. There wasn't anything concrete for Bob to be doing during the short period of time that they anticipated being there. And they only had a certain amount of money to get there and get back on. They wanted a tight budget. He anticipated that we would think it was all Jerry's idea. He wanted it clear that that was not the case, that they all agreed.

"Mark was the one assigned to tell (Bob Lewis)," she continued. "Mark and I had a discussion about his task. He said there was a lot of antagonism between Jerry and Bob and that it was understandable. At this critical time Jerry wouldn't want to deal with that, and Mark was going along with that because he didn't want to blow the chance. If negotiations started and something concrete came up, (Mark promised) he would fly Bob there out of his own money. He valued his input and (Bob) was obviously part of it. (Mark) did respect him as a friend.

"(Bob) was hurt. He was confused. He didn't know how to handle it. He didn't know whether to confront Jerry. He decided against that in the interest of the band because he wanted to see it happen. He believed more, he trusted that this would happen. He believed what Mark said, that he could have joined them out there but there were a lot of things to do here that kept him occupied with the marketing of the 45s."

So the five members of Devo, with Ed Barger along to run sound, left for Los Angeles. And Bob Lewis did not.

❀ ❀ ❀

Devo played their first A&M Records showcase on July 25 at the Starwood in Hollywood. *Slash Magazine*, L.A.'s counterpart to *New York Rocker*, threw a big party for the band, inviting lots of film and music industry people. Kip Cohen, the A&M rep who had arranged the shows, was waiting eagerly to see how this "de-evolution band" would come across live. Mark sensed, based on the response in New York, that these shows were going to go well. "Outside of New York, L.A. is probably the most devolved city goin'," he told a reporter on the eve of the Starwood gigs, "and we just haven't shown them explicit views of the gut, so we're goin' to take the surface off of Los Angeles."

These guys were going to explain Los Angeles to the natives? This seemed like a pretty heady claim, but Devo, at that moment, believed they could do no wrong. They took the Starwood stage, opened the show with *The Truth About De-evolution*, pulled down the screen, and launched into their set, confident and more controlled than ever in their stage presence. The jerky movements had become sublime; the interaction with the audience, the ability to put on a real show and the belief that this was what people wanted to hear had reached an apex.

Backstage at the Starwood, a short-haired, skinny, kind of hyper guy in glasses walked into the dressing room. Jerry didn't recognize him at first. The man introduced himself:

"I'm Iggy Pop."

Jerry apologized – this really didn't look like the guy he'd seen four months earlier at the Agora.

Iggy started singing "Praying Hands."

Mark looked at him, surprised.

"How do you know the words?"

"Cuz I've been listening to that tape you gave David," Iggy said.

That tape – the one he'd gotten in Cleveland. Apparently Bowie had thrown it into a bin with a bunch of other tapes, and while he and Iggy were in Germany mixing the *Lust for Life* album, Iggy had gotten bored with the crappy German radio stations and asked Bowie if he had anything to listen to. Bowie pulled out this tape and handed it to him, and Iggy immediately dug it. He had been learning the songs and had, in fact, been talking about recording the material himself. The label with the contact information had gotten separated from the cassette; all they had was the name – Devo. "They didn't think the band even existed," Mark said. "They just thought we were some art project or something. Which is kinda half-true."

So Iggy, who was back from Germany and had just gotten his first driver's license, was driving down Santa Monica Boulevard in his GTO. He passed the Starwood and saw the name on the marquee: Devo. He'd found them.

Accompanying Iggy backstage were dancer/burgeoning singer Toni Basil, actor Dean Stockwell and singer Ronnie Blakely. Basil, who would later score an MTV hit with the dance-oriented "Hey Mickey", asked the band who did their choreography.

"Everybody laughed and they pointed at me," Jerry said. "It was like, I never thought it was choreography, but she related to it... and wanted to know, 'How do you get them to do that step?' That was so funny. She totally got off on it. Then she wanted to choreograph us, but we didn't have any money to pay her."

Jerry and Toni hit it off almost immediately. The band was on another high – until they sat down with Kip Cohen. According to Mary B. King in *New York Rocker*, he told them, "On a scale from 1 to 10, you get a 10 for 'star potential,' 10 for stage presence, and 1 for songs." This was an odd situation to be in. A&M had been providing Devo with apartments while they were in L.A. But they were cutting off the lifeline, even as Iggy Pop – Iggy *fucking* Pop – was going ga-ga over them, and this super-cute dancer was flirting with Jerry and they were sure they were on the verge of conquering L.A. the same way they believed they had conquered New York. What were they supposed to do?

With no support, the band was ready to return to Akron. But Jerry smelled blood in the West Coast waters.

"There's no way we're going back," he told them. "This is it. We got to make this happen. We've got to be professional. We're just starting to sound good. We're just starting to play good. Nothing else matters."

So they fished around for places to crash. Jerry hooked up with Toni, who made some calls to friends and found places for most of the other guys to stay. Mark and Bob Casale were invited by Iggy to stay at his place in Malibu. All of this was a risk. But they were beginning to realize it was the risk of a lifetime. Jerry had just celebrated his 29th birthday, and Mark was 27. Neither of them had particularly promising careers waiting for them back in Ohio, and suddenly, before they'd had a chance to absorb the opportunities that were bombarding them, their pop biological clocks were ticking.

Jerry started working the phones. Toni Basil helped hook him up with management people, and used her influence to get club owners to return his calls.

"She helped me because she understood business very well," Jerry said. "She understood this town and how it worked. I was, obviously, theoretically understanding it and trying to be the manager. I didn't have the connections. So she would help get me the people, the numbers and the callbacks. I just started getting us more gigs so that we were making money. The Starwood wanted us back even though Kip Cohen said, 'Fuck you guys.' Then, she got me to see Marshall Burrows, and we got into the Whiskey and Myron's Ballroom. We had a little circuit going."

For about three weeks, Mark and Bob Casale crashed in Iggy Pop's living room. This was kind of like living in a dream and an opium dream at the same time. They were jamming with him at his house, the godfather of punk shaking his thing with the spud boys. "(Iggy) wanted to record our first album before we did," Mark recalled. "I was like, 'No, we want to do it first,' and he was like, 'Shut up, this would be so good for you.' He was crazy during that time.... I have tapes of Devo rehearsing in his living room in Malibu, and him grabbing the microphone... to sing wild shit over the top of our songs."

After the first rehearsal in Iggy's living room, he asked the Devo guys if they wanted to go for a swim. It was a terrible day, stormy, with huge, treacherous waves. They walked to the beach and looked out at the ocean, which bore no resemblance to the flat inland lakes of Ohio. The spuds wanted nothing to do with it. Iggy stripped off his shirt and dove right in, swimming about 150 yards out into the wild Pacific and back.

"Like it was a baby's bath," Ed Barger said.

Barger recalled Iggy as a savior who stepped in when the band needed support. But he was a wild one, nonetheless. "I'll never forget, he had a '65 GTO in the driveway," Barger said, "and he made us call him 'Jim'. (After his Christian name, Jim Osterberg.) There were sheets of paper about 12 inches wide that hung from walls about 20 feet high. He had a tall step ladder and was doing paintings on these papers. He had these gay guys that would light his cigarettes and care for his every whim. He would pour a pile of cocaine on the table and do it all. And not that anybody wanted any, but none was offered to us.

"Iggy wanted to learn some Devo songs for his upcoming tour. He invited us to his Malibu house to teach him these Devo songs. He wanted to do 'Praying Hands' and asked me to write the lyrics out. So, of course, I wrote them out and handed them to him. Iggy then crumbled the paper into a ball, shook his fist at me and yelled, 'Where are the lyrics?'

"He also had this beautiful girlfriend. The next day when we got there he had wrecked the GTO, and this beautiful girl had this big bandage on her face. Another time, we were practicing and Iggy came by with this black woman. Devo went into 'I need a chick' and Iggy took over on vocals. He sang, 'Iggy's got eight inches!' … 'Iggy's got nine inches!' … 'Iggy's got ten inches!' This poor woman understood he was making a fool of himself, and tried to drag him away as he pleaded, 'It really is!'

"I had lunch with Iggy (and maybe Alan Myers) on a good day. Iggy was pretty straight, and I realized this was an intelligent guy. I had seen the Stooges several times, so we had a lot to talk about. Years later, I saw him backstage at a Gang of Four concert, and when I said, 'Hey, Jim. How are you doing?' Iggy walked away, looking like, 'Who is this guy, and how does he know my name?'"

Devo was on the cusp of something. They were five fairly straight guys from Ohio, suddenly slogging around with rock stars and Beautiful People. They were by no means naïve, but this was a new world for them. One did not sleep on Iggy Pop's couch in Akron. And so they woke up every morning, rubbing their eyes, wondering what was happening to them.

Chapter 20

The Kip Cohen affair had proved to be only a minor speed bump. Devo got a booking right away at Mabuhay Gardens in San Francisco, then another a week later at Myron's Ballroom in L.A., then another, and another, and another. The first time at Mabuhay, the band drew less than 100 people. The second time, 400 new fans filled the club. Devo's effect was immediate.

As Sleepers' guitarist Michael Belfer told James Stark in the book *PUNK '77,* "I think Devo were one of the best live bands of that time. Me and a friend came up from Palo Alto to see what was going on and ended up at the Mab. Devo was playing that night. We got in and started milling around and noticed there was a movie screen hanging in back of the stage, which I had never seen in a club before. We weren't sure what was going to happen. All of a sudden their film, the one about devolution came on, and it had the audience transfixed. I remember my friend asking me, 'What the fuck is this?' It had a very intense feel about it. After it ended, it instantaneously dawned on everybody in the club that what we had just seen was the band that was about to come onstage and play. There was this incredible surge that happens where everything goes forward. It felt like gravity had been taken out of the room. They came out playing; it was sort of like being on acid, in the good sense of the word."

After less than a month in Los Angeles, Devo was becoming a regular on the club circuit. The band got booked three nights in a row – August 22, 23 and 24 – at the Starwood, the same venue where they'd played the failed A&M showcase. Then, on August 25, back in Ohio, something happened, very quietly, and without the band's knowledge. Bob Lewis filed an application to trademark "Devo".

He had promised a "reckoning." The keystone was set.

❋ ❋ ❋

Dean Stockwell, Toni Basil's friend, was into the band. In the grand Hollywood tradition, he knew people who knew people. He had a casual friendship with Neil Young, and decided one day to play him a tape of Devo. He played "Mongoloid" and "Satisfaction" on a cheap cassette player, and Young liked it. So Stockwell took him to see the band at the Starwood. It's hard to know how well they understood their connection then, especially as Young was a denim-and-flannel, post-hippie rock-and-roller who sometimes wore fur-lined boots and Devo, well – Devo was none of those things. But there was a connection. Young, in a famously spontaneous fit of anger and sadness, had written the song "Ohio" after the 1970 Kent State shootings. He and Jerry had been equally affected by the event, and had channeled their emotion into music. Young had been succinct in his musical response, Jerry less direct but more complete. But their reactions were the same. That Devo was here at all, playing the Starwood seven years later, had a lot to do with the "four dead in O-hi-o."

With the band's star rising, the fence-straddling between Ohio and California began to fade. Devo played steadily through September, with a four-night stand at the Starwood followed by another at the legendary Whisky-a-Go-Go. The Whisky had been the launching pad for the Doors, and had continued as a showcase for provocative up-and-comers. Its history was written into the menu, with a Joan Jett Take-Off drink ("a Runaway best seller"), the Cheap Trick Bun E. Burger (after drummer Bun E. Carlos) and, paying homage to KROQ's most influential disc jockey, the Rodney Bingenheimer Special (Tab cola). Soon, a Devo item would be added to the menu – a bowl of nuts and chips. (Potato, no doubt.)

Devo was sharing the bill with Blondie and a new, primitive but strangely endearing punk band called the Germs. Bingenheimer was a fan of this group, whose whiny young singer, Darby Crash, a.k.a. Bobby Pyn, was taking rock-and-roll destruction rather seriously. The three bands were scheduled to play an afternoon matinee before their regular evening sets. The Germs went on first, with Crash strutting onto the stage in a leopard-skin jockstrap. During a sloppy cover of Chuck Berry's "Round and Round", he began breaking bottles over his head, then hurled himself off the stage and into the glass shards below. He was taken to the hospital, stitched up, and returned in time to catch Blondie's set.

Despite Kip Cohen's flat-out rejection of Devo, the buzz had continued. Record label scouts were coming out to the shows. After one of the Whisky performances, Gary Jackett found a scrap of paper on the floor. He picked it up and read it: "Devo – these guys are going to be huge."

❃ ❃ ❃

With the band staying longer and longer in L.A., Bob Lewis was feeling more and more like he'd been cut off for good. Mark had promised that if things started to heat up, he'd see to it personally that Bob was brought back in. But now things *were* heating up, and Bob was still sitting at home in Akron. He wrote Mark a letter, outlining his quickly growing concerns. Mark was still not certain how much the band owed Bob. According to several members of the Devo circle, Jerry had been deceptive, or at least vague about what role Bob had had in developing Devo. So at first Mark was sympathetic, in part because he knew a blow-up between Bob and Jerry would be disruptive to the band's progress. But when news reached Los Angeles about Bob's trademark filing, Mark was as angry as the rest. He felt like Bob had gone behind their backs. Bob was in danger of painting himself into a corner, and he was going to have to be certain he knew what he was doing.

Ed Barger, meanwhile, was feeling secure in his position. He had extensive experience doing crew work for Belkin Productions, the Cleveland region's dominant concert promoter. He was very good behind the soundboard, knew how to run lights and handle the roadie chores. He'd built a sound tower for Pink Floyd, so he could certainly handle the setup at the Whisky. And Mark must have felt an allegiance to him, considering how supportive Barger and Marty Reymann had been early on.

"Like so many others, I was thinking if these guys were successful – I would get out of spudland myself," Barger said. "I knew Jerry was evil, but I was also convinced of Mark's talent. I still believe that Mark was a good person and would have shared with Bob Lewis and everybody had it not been for Jerry."

❃ ❃ ❃

Devo still made a good Halloween band, and the Starwood booked them for its "Super Halloween Punk-In" with the Mumps "and other surprises." As the band played that night to yet another full house, there must have been a grinning sense of satisfaction. It was two years to the day since they had been pelted with beer cans before clearing Cleveland's WHK Auditorium. One year before, they weren't even playing, still teaching Alan the set and working up this alchemy from their base metals.

Devo took a break from the almost nonstop schedule to fly back to New York for a pair of shows at Max's Kansas City in mid-November. By then, they were the toast of New York. The Akron contingent made the trip to meet their old friends in Manhattan. Susan Massaro and Bob Lewis were there to greet them. Things seemed different. Jerry was sleeping with a minor celebrity. Their old friends were telling stories about being Iggy Pop's room-mate and hanging out with Blondie. To Bob Lewis, California had once been the backdrop for writing *The Staff* essays with Jerry. Now it seemed like an entirely different world.

Although things were tense, Bob was still willing to help out. His driving prowess was put into use when the band was late for an uptown meeting with David Bowie. "It was amazing, like being in the Batmobile," Susan recalled. Bowie, back from Germany, had heard from Iggy that this band they'd been trying to track down not only existed, but was the best thing he had heard in a long time. Devo appealed to just about every aesthetic Bowie held dear. Their songs were artful; their performance was provocative. They were intellectuals who could also rock with intensity. They were thoughtful adventurers, just like him. He told them he was interested in producing an album. And, just to cement an already clear mythology, he asked to introduce them at Max's.

The band waited backstage with Bowie. Max's was packed; the smoky air filled with anticipation. Robert Fripp and Brian Eno were there. Susan, who just eight months before had scratched her way into a few seconds of face time with Bowie, was now standing in the Max's dressing room, chatting with the Thin White Duke as if he were one of the Rubber City Rebels. Devo stood there in their yellow suits, accustomed by now to the attention, but still electrified by the excitement of it all. They waited as David Bowie walked onto the club's stage.

"This is the band of the future," he announced in his cultured tone. "And I'm going to produce them in Tokyo this winter."

"And we thought that was a great idea," Mark said years later, "because we were going to be sleeping in the van that night."

This wasn't exactly true. The band was staying at the Chelsea Hotel. But still, this was something. It was a little hard to share the good fortune with the rest of the Akron crowd, the former "Devo-tees". Although not all of them could have expected to be included in the success, they had maintained their loyal friendship. Susan and Bobbie had moved from the Greenwood house to an apartment on South Portage Path in Highland Square. That had become Devo's Akron mailing address, and the former girlfriends had helped keep things together on the home front. Bob was still willing to lend a hand, and his help was being accepted. Before one of the shows, during the afternoon sound check, Bob Mothersbaugh had played guitar for Susan. But Bob was also, by then, seeing a Los Angeles girl named Maria, and she was there with him.

"It's honestly still very painful to think about this last trip," Susan said 25 years later. "Everything was different."

✳ ✳ ✳

And so the band returned to Ohio. Devo played a triumphant Dec. 3 show at the WHK Auditorium, the scene of the WMMS crime. The show, arranged by Johnny Dromette, was opened by Destroy All Monsters from Ann Arbor and the Styrene Money Band from Cleveland. The auditorium was still in dreadful shape, but the atmosphere had changed. Almost everything had changed. Bob Mothersbaugh's girlfriend, 20-year-old Maria Linda Borisoff, was pregnant. They were going to be married in four days by a Cuyahoga Falls minister. Jerry was not happy about this. According to Gary Jackett, the prospect "flipped Jerry out." Bob Casale had left his wife shortly before the trip to California, and, "part of the whole Devo thing was that we're going to get all these chicks. We're going to be a big rock band, and have all this fun," Jackett said, recalling Jerry's attitude. "Suddenly, Bob put a wrench into the plan. He was going to have to be a family man."

And Devo, though only a few months removed from the local scene, were now, for all intents and purposes, rock stars. "Devo was stunning that night," said Tim Story, who was sitting behind the soundboard with Johnny Dromette. The show was polished. The band was tight. Every aspect of Devo's performance had benefited from the incessant gigging in California. They returned to Akron, finally, that night. Mark, reunited with Marina, slept in a spare room in Bobbie's apartment, the so called "dark room." He hadn't slept so well in months.

✳ ✳ ✳

Less than a week later, Devo was zigzagging across the country again, first for a show at Mabuhay Gardens in San Francisco, then back to Max's. Brian Eno came to the New York shows. He wanted to talk to the band.

After leaving Roxy Music in 1973, Eno, former foppish glam rocker, had become famous, not only for producing Bowie, John Cale and Robert Fripp, but also for the way he produced. He was all right brain, a Zen master who used the studio as an instrument. He didn't just record bands, he sculpted them. He quizzed them. He told them to make it sound like water, and then when it sounded like water, he told them to turn it upside-down. The English musician had, by the time of this meeting, been courting Talking Heads, the artiest of the CBGB's bands and, in many ways, the group that had the most in common with Devo – the weirdest of the accessible bands, or the most accessible of the weird bands. Either way you turned it, Eno was not going to pursue the Dead Boys. But he was going to pursue Devo.

He asked to meet with them for lunch the following day in a hotel room overlooking Central Park. The five band members were there, along with Ed Barger. Barger already had a long-distance relationship with Eno. The only phone number Eno had for Devo was at Man Ray Studios, and when he called there, it was usually Barger on the other end. So, there in the New York hotel room, they ordered room service and they talked.

"Brian Eno was a quiet guy, and the discussion over lunch was more about people feeling each other out," Barger said. "Devo was wondering what this guy wanted from them, and Eno was like a scientist observing the spuds under a microscope. Devo was always suspicious of everybody. Eno was as weird as Devo, and enjoyed seeing the spud squirm. Like them, he took pleasure in watching the experiment go wrong."

The band didn't have a record contract yet, but Eno offered to front the money and said he and David Bowie would produce an album. The rest would follow, he said. Of course it would.

Shortly after this meeting, Eno sat with a British reporter and talked about his next project. Devo, he said, has "the best live show I have ever seen. What I saw in them always happens when you encounter something new in art – you get a feeling of being slightly dislocated, and with that are emotional overtones that are slightly menacing as well as alluring.... I am very interested in knowing why that happens... and I spend as much time in that sort of reflection as I do in the work. You see, in this work, you arrive at attractive positions for which sometimes you have no defenses.... When you make a piece of work, you are postulating a little world of your own, with a set of rules, and you try to see how they work. Then, how do they apply to real life? That's where the 'Oblique Strategies' come in – employing accidents as a part of the work to make the connection. In both Devo, Talking Heads and myself, I see an interest in working out the terms of what that perception is."

The "Oblique Strategies" were tarot cards Eno employed in the studio. He would set them out before a musician he was working with and gesture toward them – pick a card, any card. The card would contain an instruction: "Honor thy error as a hidden intention," for example. The "oblique" part consumed the strategy part. This would be a far cry from General Boy's "nose-to-the-grindstone" ethic, a far cry from Mrs. Fox's organ lessons, a far cry from the nuns at St. Patrick's. But Devo was already a far, far cry from Ohio.

Chapter 21

The blizzard began during the midnight shift, after an evening of rain, when school kids and snowplow drivers were sleeping. The bottom fell out of the barometer, the wind took people's breath away, and before they could draw another, Akron and the rest of Ohio were paralyzed by the storm of the century. A small plane tumbled like a child's toy across a field at Akron Municipal Airport. Giant trees snapped like matchsticks. Store windows shattered, power lines fell, water pipes burst and snowdrifts buried cars. It seemed to happen all at once, and it would not go away. By dawn on Thursday, January 26, 1978, the entire region was frozen. Streets were indistinguishable in the white landscape. The wind, gusting to 75 miles per hour, drove snow against every surface, and had pushed the temperature from 34 degrees at 5 a.m. to 13 at 6 a.m. Nothing looked right; nothing sounded right; nothing felt right.

The members of Devo woke up that morning in their temporary lodgings at Susan and Bobbie's Portage Path apartment house, which had become Devo's informal headquarters. They looked out the window to find the biggest snowflakes they had ever seen, the size of 50-cent pieces. It just kept falling. Schools were closed; many businesses, too. The tire companies kept the factories open, though. Workers who could make it in would be able to stay as long as they pleased; plenty of coffee and free heat. Hard times had begun after the 1976 strike, and everyone knew this work was becoming more and more precious. Just two weeks before this snowstorm, Goodyear production workers had been stunned by the news that Akron's largest tire company was closing its main plant, ending car tire production in Akron and putting 1,380 people out of work.

"Akron is a dead town," one worker had said after the announcement. And this blizzard seemed to prove it. The storm was going to cause problems for Devo. The band was supposed to play its "farewell" show that night at the Pirate's Cove, but getting to Cleveland seemed impossible. And in the growing frenzy to sign Devo, Dave Robinson of Stiff Records was supposed to be flying in to Ohio the next day with Island Records' Chris Blackwell. Would the airports even be open? Meanwhile, Devo had a lot of work to do. In Susan and Bobbie's cozy brick apartment, the band had set up a chart in a highly organized attempt to sort out the record deals that were being tossed at them. Coming from record executives' mouths, everything sounded like milk and honey. On paper, none of it looked particularly appealing.

Are We Not Men?

Warner Bros and Island had made serious offers. There was a lot of money involved. And Devo, still without an experienced manager, was left to its own devices. In the Voyager laserdisc *DEVO: The Complete Truth About De-Evolution*, Jerry explained the agonizing process in an essay called "Drooling For Dollars."

"(T)hose six-figure deal numbers were mind-boggling to Rubber City bottomfeeders used to living hand-to-mouth. What to do? Keep cool! Hold on to your gene pool! Remember the lessons learned at good old Kent State University (besides '4 dead in O-hi-o') – i.e., research the situation. We read a book by Arista Records chief, Clive Davis, entitled, *Inside the Record Business*. The irony of one of the record business' most notorious 'hitmen' dispensing tips on success was lost on DEVO. So, as fledgling Punk-scientists, we did as he suggested. We made a chart to analyze and compare the offers.

"It didn't take us long to figure out that what you see is much more than what you get when it comes to record deals. Both of these on DEVO's table smelled fishy. As in the fifth DEVO commandment – 'in the end it made no difference.' Let me explain. All record deals are basically the same. They sign you. They promise you a lot of money down the line where the numbers escalate during each 'option period' following the 'initial period' which guarantees you one, or sometimes two albums. Of course, the option to continue is always theirs. And, of course, it's during the 'initial period' that the money you receive and the percentage of profit that you own of your album is at its lowest. Since all the money that you ever receive to record, make videos, tour, etc., is a recoupable advance against your percentage of your record sales, you are immediately in debt. And since standard accounting practices in the music business are only slightly less sleazy than those in the film business, you have about as much of a chance as a one-legged man in a butt-kicking contest of ever seeing any money."

The deal from Warner Bros looked more attractive on the surface, but it had a catch. It included a set of middlemen called the Bewlay Brothers, who would siphon off some of the money in a production deal. The Bewlay Brothers were actually a front for none other than David Bowie, whom Jerry has called "the most charming reptile I've ever met." Bowie's lawyer, Stan Diamond, had offered to represent Devo free of charge if Devo would accept the Bewlay Brothers portion of the deal. Devo recognized the conflict of interest, and the fact that the cash-flow proposal would leave Devo on the hook financially if the band didn't meet its advances. So, although Bowie had championed the band and helped them reach this point, they were in the awkward position of having to hold him at bay.

"Being scalped by an artist that you admire was more horrifying than having the job done by a big time executive," Jerry wrote.

This was an awful lot of math for a bunch of art majors and former bar band members. The snow outside seemed to reflect the overwhelming numbers the band was trying to sort out. Devo and its close circle of friends talked it through. Mark and Jerry went to the library. They studied law books. There was no way they were going to let themselves get screwed. Or at the very least, they wanted to understand how badly they were getting screwed. Devo's distrust of the music industry seemed written in their DNA; it began early and stayed with them throughout their career.

Bob Lewis, despite his growing suspicion that Jerry was trying to push him aside, remained willing to help. He had worked as a roadie the day after Christmas, when the band played a Cleveland Agora show with the Dead Boys. And he was handling the marketing of singles to Stiff Records. Stiff was set to release "Jocko Homo"/"Mongoloid" in the United Kingdom in a few weeks, and was preparing to put out a second single, "Satisfaction" b/w "Sloppy", right on its heels. The "Satisfaction" single would be released on the Booji Boy label, but distributed by Stiff. The English label, growing in reputation as a new wave powerhouse, also had a special interest in yet a third 45 – with "Be Stiff" on the A-side and "Social Fools" on the B-side. "Be Stiff" – wouldn't that be a perfect corporate anthem?

The band decided that afternoon to try to make it up to Cleveland for the Pirate's Cove show. As they loaded up their gear in a snowy driveway, they packed a copy of their latest film, for the song "Mongoloid", which was to make its premiere that night. This "new de-evolution film," as *Scene* called it, was directed by Bruce Conner, a respected experimental filmmaker. The band had met him through Toni Basil in Santa Monica. She played him "Mongoloid", and he flipped for it, offering his services without ever having seen the band. The film was a series of vintage black-and-white movie stills set to the music. It carried echoes of Mark's artwork, using old images cut-and-paste style in a new context, with evocative effect. The four-minute film would be marketed through unusual means. It was sold by San Francisco distributor Canyon Cinema, Inc. as an educational documentary, "exploring the manner in which a determined young man overcame a basic mental defect and became a useful member of society." The marketing materials described the film's "insightful editing techniques (that) reveal the dreams, ideals and problems that face a large segment of the American male population... (with) background music written and performed by the DEVO orchestra."

Devo made its slow, careful way up to Cleveland. The snow continued to fall through the night. Plows were unable to keep ahead of it. Everyone got there and back, but the next day, they would have to drive to Cleveland again. The big cheeses were coming to town.

※ ※ ※

Friday wasn't any better. Gov. James Rhodes, announcing that President Jimmy Carter had signed a declaration of emergency, said, "Ohio is in trouble." Countless people were without heat or power. Three people had died; snowplows were stranded; and a trucker on a roadside near Akron was buried under a 20-foot snowdrift, surviving on melted snow with a tube stuck through the window for air.

When Chris Blackwell, the Caribbean-born president of Island Records flew in from the Bahamas, he was still wearing beach clothes as he touched down in icy Ohio. Devo picked him and Dave Robinson up at the airport, Blackwell was shivering in the back seat, wide-eyed, wondering what manner of place had spawned this Devo band. As soon as they got to Akron, the natives drove him to a department store to buy some proper clothing. Hey, this is winter in Spudland, the Devo boys tried to explain.

They finally made it back to the Portage Path apartment, rubbed the cold out of their hands, and sat down to talk. Jerry and Mark liked Chris Blackwell. Although, on this day, they seemed literally to come from different worlds, Chris, to Jerry's recollection, was "charming, personable and pleasantly low-key." Island's offer had its benefits. There was one sticking point, however. Because Island was based in England, Devo would come out on the short end of the "reduced foreign royalty rates," part of the boilerplate language in most record contracts. By signing with the English label, Devo would make less money on records sold in the U.S. This was a real problem, because they knew they could expect up to 70 percent of sales in the United States.

Jerry thought this through. What if they split up the deal? They could ask Warner Bros to take on the band for America, Canada, Australia and Japan, and give Island the rest of the territory. He knew Devo had some leverage now that Brian Eno had arranged to produce the album. Devo had clout. It was time to play the hand.

Chris hung out with the band and their friends, learning about Akron and hearing about the little explosion in the local scene. Debbie Smith and Sue Schmidt of Chi Pig dropped by, and got to talking with the Island president. He asked how they got their name. They explained that it came from the sign in front of a barbecue joint. "Chi," for chicken, and "Pig" for ribs. Chris thought that was pretty cool, and wondered if they had ever tried to get their hands on the sign. A light bulb went off. And with that, the little group – two quirky new wave girls and a famous record company president – set off into the snowy Akron night to try to steal the Chi Pig sign. They failed, but the fact that he was willing to go along suggested that maybe Chris Blackwell was the kind of guy who could understand Devo's appreciation for the absurd.

Devo was impressed with Blackwell. Maybe he wasn't the "baby-faced killer" that a Warner Bros executive had described. Maybe he was just a regular guy who happened to be in a position to make them all rich and famous. Mark and Jerry and the others weren't jaded yet. Despite the teachings of devolution, the sobering lesson of the Kent State shootings and all the rest, Blackwell seemed to offer hope that maybe there was some sanity to the music business.

Then a very strange thing happened.

Chapter 22

A week or so after Chris Blackwell's Akron visit, the phone rang in the Portage Path apartment. It was Richard Branson, the president of Virgin Records. He said he wanted to fly Devo to Jamaica, that he had a deal to discuss. Mark looked out the window at the still-dismal snowscape. Jamaica? That sounded pretty good. They probably have palm trees or something there. So he got off the phone and asked who wanted to go to Kingston. Jerry was in the midst of an ongoing fight with his girlfriend, Linda Waddington. Bob Mothersbaugh was newly married and Alan was getting close – they both wanted to spend these waning days in Akron. So Mark and Bob Casale took Branson up on his offer.

In a reversal of Blackwell's wardrobe schizophrenia, the two Ohio boys boarded their flight wearing snowsuits and big winter hats. They touched down in balmy Jamaica, peeling off the layers to expose their February-white midwestern skin to the tropical sun. This was not a bad deal. They were being treated like rock stars, even though they still had no deal. The plane tickets alone had cost something like $300 apiece, money neither Mark nor Bob could have come up with on their own. The two friends had talked on the flight. Virgin's entry into the bidding could only help matters, and they wanted to make a good impression on Branson. They knew he was emerging as a mogul of no small stature. So they wanted to be cool, to let him know that they already had good offers, and yes, Mr. Branson, we'll certainly consider Virgin as we sort through all these lucrative deals, but we're not some hicks from Ohio who will jump at the first carrot dangled before us. We know what we're doing.

Mark and Bob checked into their hotel, chucked their hats and coats and freshened up. Kingston, Jamaica, was an intimidating place. Mark had never been there before, hadn't ever seen anything like this. He looked out of his hotel room window and saw a Great Dane in rigor mortis on the roadside as people went about their business, sidestepping the dead dog with hardly a notice.

It was with this image that he and Bob went down the hall to the room where they were to meet Branson. They walked in and were greeted by this millionaire and his minions – all these young South American guys who were pushing to make Virgin a major player. As impressive as meeting Branson was, though, Mark and Bob's eyes widened when they saw the huge pile of marijuana on the table. Despite Kent's liberal post-hippie milieu, drugs were still a rather precious commodity. Even more rare was good pot, which, Mark suspected, this probably was. They were in Jamaica, after all. Back in Ohio, someone would score a little stash, and everybody would stare at it for a week, discussing its potential quality. "I hear this African stuff's supposed to be really hallucinogenic," someone would comment, even though it had probably been plucked from a roadside in Mexico. Finally Saturday night would come, and a roomful of people would roll a pencil-thin joint and pass it around, trying to catch a buzz.

"I think I'm high," they'd say. "Maybe I'm high. Yeah, I might have felt something. My throat's definitely feeling raw."

But here, as Mark and Bob tried to maintain an air of sophistication, someone was rolling a joint the size of a cigar, lighting it, and handing it to them. Mark took a hit. Definitely not Ohio pot. Bob took a hit. The joint went around and everyone loosened up a little, even though Mark was still trying to stay focused so he could make some intelligent response when Branson started breaking down his deal.

"What do you guys think of the Sex Pistols?" Branson asked.

"Well, we like them," Mark said. In fact, he explained, Devo and the Pistols had partied together just a few weeks before, when both bands were gigging in San Francisco. While Devo's shows were building toward a climax, the Pistols were in the midst of their implosion. It was, in fact, the week the two bands met that the Sex Pistols played their last show, on January 14 at the Winterland Ballroom. Johnny Rotten finished the concert with his trademark whine, uttering the immortal last words, "Ah-ha-ha! Ever get the feeling you've been cheated? Good night." Three days later, they were finished. Mark told Branson he was really sorry about what had happened, that he thought the Pistols were cool, and really thought highly of them.

Branson smiled.

"Well, I'll tell why you're here," he said. "Johnny Rotten is in the next room, and he wants to join Devo. He wants Devo to be his new band after the Sex Pistols."

Mark squirmed. He looked down at his shoes. Branson continued.

"And if you want to make that announcement, we can go out to the beach – we've got all the British press here – *Melody Maker, Sounds, New Music Express* – and we can go down to the beach and make that announcement right now."

Mark looked at the huge joint in his hand. Was he hearing this right? Maybe it was the pot. Maybe this Jamaican stuff had done a number on his head. He looked up at the smiling Branson, realizing for the first time how very large the man's teeth were. They seemed to glisten. This was a carnivore. And Mark began to blush, embarrassed for everybody in the room, and for Johnny Rotten in the next room. And then he began to snicker. And he looked at Bob, who also began to snicker. And quickly the snickers turned into belly laughs. It was like one of those moments in church, where the harder you try not to laugh the more impossible it becomes to stop. They were laughing like a pair of nincompoops. Full, round, holding-the-stomach, tears-running-down-the-cheeks laughter.

Mark tried to stammer out some sort of answer, but the pot and the absurdity just made him laugh more.

"Really, Richard," he said, trying desperately to regain his cool, "I'm not laughing at you."

Finally, Mark and Bob managed to explain that it would never work, that Devo had great respect for Johnny Rotten, but it wasn't what Devo had worked for all those years. They parted, and Mark and Bob went back to their room, staring and not saying a word. They'd blown it. Not only that, but they were now certain that they were surrounded by sharks. It was going to be Devo against the world. And the world was becoming a very strange place indeed.

＊ ＊ ＊

And so it was off to Germany. Ed Barger dropped the band off at the airport, and they waited anxiously for the plane that would carry them into Brian Eno's waiting arms, and into their future. Jerry had gotten sidetracked making one last telephone call to Linda. They talked – and talked, and talked. Right through the boarding call and the boarding and the takeoff. As Mark and the others lifted off for Germany, Jerry found himself booking another flight. He'd be at least half a day behind his bandmates.

Devo wasn't paying for any of this. Despite the increasing industry lust for the band, they remained nearly penniless, having subsisted on club shows for a year. But they looked good on paper. They were getting flown around the world, and everything seemed like just a matter of time. Eno was paying for the studio sessions. Warner Bros had been kind enough to front the money for the flights. It didn't seem to matter at the time. Money was invisible. All that mattered was that they were headed to Conrad Plank's legendary studio. Housed on an old Victorian farm in Wolperath, not far from Cologne, the studio had become legendary as a landmark of the krautrock movement. Kraftwerk had recorded its first album there, the record that Jerry had loved listening to back in the apartment above Guido's. Plank had worked with GuruGuru, Can and Neu – bands that had pioneered electronic music and set a tone for Devo to carry forward.

Already, even before arriving in Germany, the band was looking past this first album. On a piece of paper torn from a spiral notebook, they had plotted out the songs for the first two albums. At the top of the page was scrawled, "Intelligent suggestions based on (an) exhaustive pole." While the contents of the albums would change somewhat, it was clear that Devo had a plan and was ready and able to produce at least two records based on their impressive warehouse of material.

Album #1: "Satisfaction", "Too Much Paranoias", "Praying Hands", "Uncontrollable Urge", Mongoloid", "Jocko Homo", "Social Fools", "Be Stiff", "Gut Feeling/Slap Your Mammy", "Sloppy" and "Come Back Jonee".

Album #2: "Anthem", "Clockout", "Timing X-Soo Bawlz", "Pink Pussy", "Blockhead", "Wiggly World", "Gates of Steel", "Secret Agent Man", "Space Junk" and "Smart Patrol-Mr. DNA".

The songs weren't yet listed for the third record, but a potential title was there: *The Golden Energy Album*. Devo's sound was still dominated by guitars, but the plan was to move beyond them. Electronics were advancing quickly, and Devo's futuristic bent – the *Jetsons* half of "*Jetsons* meet the *Flintstones*" – was lassoed to their engine. "We saw the whole world and technology and all things natural and unnatural as potential material for getting our message across," Mark once said.

The plane touched down and Devo reunited with Eno. David Bowie had originally wanted to be involved with the production, but he had just begin working on a film in Berlin. He had offered to handle production in his down time, but that didn't sound like a very efficient way to move forward, especially with so much riding on the finished product. Devo and Eno had decided to put the cart before the horse by recording without a contract, so they would need to get down to business. But that first day, without Jerry, all the band could do was set up equipment and jam.

"Holger Czukay (of Can) was hanging out most of the time," Mark recalled. "So, we have a tape of four-fifths of Devo jamming with Holger and Brian Eno. David Bowie was hanging out, so he picked up a guitar for a little bit. So it was just the seven of us, playing music at Connie Plank's studio."

Czukay, who had recently left Can, recalled walking into the studio one evening after dinner, holding a cup of coffee. On a whim, he picked up a bass guitar and started playing "Yoo Doo Right" a Can song. The members of Devo turned on their amplifiers and joined him. "Out came something I had missed with Can for a long time," Czukay recalled, "a punky punchover strike along a railway which needed to get urgently aligned – to characterize the musical situation in a few words. The guys obviously didn't know about 'Yoo Doo Right' and so their playing was more characterized by the forwarding dirtiness of the eighties than the ending process of the revolutionary sixties.

"But what was most important to me and why I will never forget this happening was the fact that Devo didn't care about making mistakes at all. When they got out of rhythm synch by accidental obstacles, they got back again in shortest time. After 30 minutes or so, the session stopped and I had a feeling like Jesus Christ rising up to heaven. Unbelievable!"

※ ※ ※

Eno was especially excited to get started. He'd loved Devo's shows in New York, just as he had loved Talking Heads' shows. Now he was in a position to produce both bands. In each, he saw an artistic sensibility he could relate to, bands that were open to new sounds, that were interested in expanding rock music's vocabulary. This fitted with his ability to "play" the studio as an instrument, to experiment with the sound by running it through synthesizers, even as the music was being played live. As a producer, he was on firm technical ground, but his greatest interest was in allowing creative accidents to happen.

By the time Jerry arrived at Connie Plank's studio, everyone was beginning to feel comfortable. Bob Mothersbaugh had found an oddball German amplifier, and was experimenting with its sounds. When he touched his finger to the metal tip of his unplugged guitar cord, a cool sound came out, sort of a cross between a bleep and a whistle. It was different than a synthesizer sound, and as the band jammed on "Uncontrollable Urge" he added that sound near the end. That was the kind of thing Eno loved. But what he didn't realize was that this band, so full of ideas and creativity, had also become very calculated. There were very few loose threads to unravel and discover what lay underneath. That scrap of paper with the albums mapped out was the very type of planning Eno tried to avoid.

Devo had brought along a box full of previous studio tapes. They had become very good in the studio, and they had a clear idea of where they wanted to go in these sessions. Eno, for his part, had brought the "Oblique Strategies" cards, and, more broadly, an oblique strategy. He wanted to do what he typically did – pull things inside-out, turn them upside-down, hold them up to a mirror, strip them down and build them back up. As the sessions began, he started to recognize that there was a fundamental difference of opinion between him and Devo. They knew what they wanted to do, and he knew what he wanted to do. Almost immediately, tension crept into the isolated studio.

"'Anal' is the word," Eno said years later. "They were a terrifying group of people to work with because they were so unable to experiment. When they turned up to do this record in Germany, they brought a big chest of recordings they'd already done of these same songs. We'd be sitting there working, and suddenly Mark Mothersbaugh would be in the chest to retrieve some three-year-old tape, put it on and say, 'Right, we want the snare drum to sound like that.'

"I hate that kind of work. I just do not see the point of trying to replicate such peculiar circumstances: the snare drum sounds good like that because all the other things around it are like they are, so do you really want to replicate the whole thing? 'No, we want to have that snare drum, but the guitar sound we want like this' – and it was back in the chest again for another tape! This seemed impossible, foolish and stupid. Stupid in that it was a waste of time: here we are in another situation, another time, another place, why not do something for this situation?

"Their picture of recording, for me, was very old-fashioned, like a Platonic Ideal of recording, that somewhere there existed the ideal state of this song, and they thought they could identify several of the ingredients, they were in the chest there somewhere, and my job as a producer was to try to re-make these ingredients and fit them back together. A nightmare. I'd be sitting there at the desk, and there are EQ's, echo sends, all those kinds of things, and my hand would sort of sneak up to put a bit of a treatment on something, and I could feel Jerry Casale bristling behind me. It was awful! He would stand behind me all the time, then lean over and say, 'Why are you doing that?' As if you can know why you do something before you do it, always!"

Meanwhile, the studio phone provided constant distraction. The fact that Devo was in Connie Plank's studio, recording its album with Brian Eno, had turned the heat up even higher. Warner Bros was calling. Virgin was calling. A&M had gotten back into the hunt. They all wanted this album, and their offers were escalating. Someone walked into the studio one day with the new issue of *Melody Maker*. Devo was shocked to find its picture on the cover. Stiff was getting ready to push the singles hard. Things were growing beyond their control, but at least they were growing in the right direction.

Bob Casale and Mark had left Jamaica believing they'd ruined their chances with Virgin, but Branson had only grown more persistent, almost obsessive in his pursuit. And Warner Bros was right in lockstep. During the Eno sessions, a Warner representative showed up at the studio and asked if the band needed some walking-around money. Sure, they said. Money, after all, was invisible. So they each got a little wad of cash, maybe a hundred bucks apiece.

Their studying had paid off. Devo was still acting as their own manager, but by now, Stan Diamond, David Bowie's lawyer, was working with them in the negotiations process. The band had a good strategy. They wanted to try to work out two record deals, each with separate territorial rights. That way, if the band didn't do well in one part of the world, the losses wouldn't eat into the profits from the other territories.

There was one major sticking point, however. Bob Lewis, back in Akron, had the trademark to Devo. Stan Diamond, realizing that no record deal could be finalized without the band owning rights to itself, drew up a set of papers – an "Assignment" – allowing rights to transfer back to the band. He contacted Bob about this and sent him the papers. Bob wasn't sure what to do. He had filed for the trademark to protect himself, but if he stuck to his guns, there might be nothing to protect himself from. Devo could get dropped before even being signed. And he didn't want to screw his friends. He had invested seven years in Devo – only Jerry had been around as long – and he wanted to see it come to fruition. He understood how important it all was. So, in what he later described as "a moment of weakness", he put his signature on the document. Devo was free.

Chapter 23

If being in a band meant just playing music, life would be pretty simple. But those days were long gone for Devo. By March 1978, the de-evolution band had plenty of field research to prove its notion that moving forward can also mean moving backward. Devo was being bombarded by offers, the arcanum of negotiation, legal details and, of course, the immediate task of completing their debut album. Amid all this, the phone rang yet again at Connie Plank's studio. This time it was Stiff Records. The "Mongoloid" single was making waves, and the label was about to release "Satisfaction", the second of the three singles it had planned for the spring and summer. Although Devo had rock-solid street credibility in New York and Los Angeles by then, the band remained an enigma in London, Stiff's prime territory. So Stiff wanted to book some shows before Devo left Europe. The month of February had been spent recording and the album was turning out well. Devo agreed to take the March 9-12 bookings. But there was a problem. They had no stage gear – neither costumes nor equipment. So they made a phone call to Akron.

Are We Not Men?

The loyal old spuds on South Portage Path sprang into action. Bob Lewis submitted applications to the Akron Federation of Musicians to allow the band to play in England. He and Susan and Bobbie and the others boxed up some yellow suits and black gym clothes and shipped those and the stage gear off to Europe.

With temporary visas and the album in the can, Devo arrived in London on March 6. Although Abba's "Take a Chance on Me" was No. 1 on *Melody Maker*'s U.K. charts that week, the country was primed for the raw energy and studied weirdness of this band from a place everybody seemed intent on pronouncing "Ak-rawn." The first show was scheduled for a club called Eric's in Liverpool, with concerts to follow at Leeds University, the Free Trade Hall in Manchester and the Roundhouse in London. Mark, having had his musical epiphany years before, watching the Beatles on *Ed Sullivan*, felt as though he'd reached some hallowed – if not particularly romantic – place. Liverpool was a dingy, gray industrial port town. As he took all this in, a music journalist asked him what "Ak-rawn" was like.

"Actually, it's a lot like Liverpool," Mark responded. He was, of course, referring to the landscape. But the reporter went away with the impression that Akron might be a Liverpool-esque musical hotbed. A seed had been planted that would soon begin to show strange flower back in Ohio.

Devo played their first show, not certain what to expect. The U.K. punk scene, inflamed by the likes of the dearly departed Sex Pistols and the emergent Clash and Buzzcocks, was becoming increasingly violent. Devo's yellow janitorial suits may have seemed cheeky back in America, but here they seemed downright sensible, what with all the gob flying about. American bands wondered about the British punk custom of spitting on a band to show its appreciation; Devo was about to do the same. Eric's, having seen its share of hooliganism, had installed a cage around the stage as a security measure. When Devo took the stage that night, playing live for the first time in well over a month and the first time off American soil, they found themselves surrounded by the wildest scene they'd ever experienced. Punk rockers were hanging off the sides of the cage, screaming and spitting. It was intimidating and exhilarating, all at once. The band never even saw what Eric's looked like, as they were surrounded by this wall of bodies for the entire set. It could have been an *Island of Lost Souls* outtake.

The following few nights erased any doubt – Devo was on fire. Word spread quickly through the compressed English scene that this band David Bowie had gone bonkers over was the real deal. They were intensely controlled on stage, but the music was primal and frantic. Devo had a sonic assault and sense of humor equal to the Sex Pistols. Devo, like many of the British punk bands, also had a message. It wasn't as directly political as the Pistols' middle finger-waving anti-government rants, and it's likely that the subtlety and intellectualism of the "Idea" was lost amid the hysterics.

But at this moment, none of that mattered. In less than a week of concerts, Devo had managed to drive its reputation right through the bars of that steel cage and directly to the ears of Richard Branson and all the others. Somebody had to get this record. It was time to finalize the deal. Devo returned to Akron at the beginning of May. Branson was ready to go, and he engaged the band in a series of secret meetings. Devo had favored one particular aspect of his offer. He was willing to include a film production deal as part of the package, which would help Devo fulfill one of its original intents, to pursue the project as a full manifestation of artistic expression.

"Devo was about art," Mark said years later. "We were multimedia from the beginning. That's what interested me about Andy Warhol. He wasn't limited to just being a printmaker. He was also a photographer, produced the Velvet Underground, made feature films – he was even a fashion designer. He was more interested in concepts and ideas. That's how we saw ourselves."

In fact, that's why the band had been so excited about being aligned with Bowie. He seemed to be the next incarnation of Warhol, and Devo wanted to take it from there. So when Branson was ready with his offer, Devo was ready, too. The Virgin Records contract had everything the band wanted. After the U.K. shows, Branson upped his financial offer. He included the film production package. He was willing to split up the world's territories into two separate contracts. Mark and Jerry and the others had done their homework. They knew this was an incredibly good deal. So they signed with Virgin.

Almost immediately, Warner Bros went ballistic. Wait a minute, they said. Jerry made a verbal agreement with us. We have already put money into Devo. Remember the plane tickets? Remember the spending money? That was all in good faith. Apparently, the band had gone so far as to O.K. a press release announcing Devo's intent to sign with Warners. In late May, Warner Bros sued Virgin and Devo.

This was a sobering moment. Everything had built up so incredibly well. The band had a nearly perfect contract with Virgin. Everybody was going to get rich. Devo was going to be able to make art for the rest of their lives on someone else's dime. They all turned to Richard Branson. Don't worry, he told them. I can handle this. He flew Jerry and Mark back to England for the proceedings and put them up on his houseboat while he went to court with his lawyer, Ken Barry. What he found at the other table was a regiment of grim, dark-suited English barristers hired by Warner Bros. The American company was going to play hardball.

Are We Not Men?

As Branson recalled in Terry Southern's book *Virgin,* "Their lawyer cited a case from 1934 where Bette Davis had been successfully prevented from working because it was claimed that she made a living in other ways besides acting. Due entirely to this previous ruling, apparently the judge decided in favor of Warner Bros." Adding insult to injury, Branson continued, the judge who had set the precedent in 1934 was his grandfather. Virgin was against the ropes. More wrangling followed. Virgin and Warner Bros huddled outside the courtroom, looking for some sort of resolution.

As all of this was going on, Mark and Jerry nervously waited on Branson's houseboat. According to Mark, Branson "ended up going in and saying, 'Look, I offered them more money than I want to pay them. I'll make you a deal – here's what we'll do. I don't really want them for the U.S. I don't have a company in the U.S. – You take 'em for the U.S. and the rest of the world and I'll take them for Europe. That's what I got, that I can handle... and we'll make 'em a new contract. We'll tear up the old contract that I wrote, and we'll give them something new.' (Of course) they gave us a deal that wasn't as good as the deal we had originally signed with him. Warner Bros was O.K. with that – they got us for the U.S. and that's all they really cared about. And we got two shitty record deals."

Jerry had a somewhat more optimistic impression of the outcome. As he wrote in *Drooling for Dollars,* "One of the ironies though, after hip capitalist Branson and corporate Bros. Warner finalized carving up DEVO's collectively owned carcass, we got what we wanted – a world-wide record deal with two first-class corporations."

The ultimate outcome was that Devo's debut album would finally be put into production. They had settled on a title, *Q. Are We Not Men? A. We Are Devo,* borrowing the key phrase from the band's anthem, "Jocko Homo". The epithet that had once been little more than an inside joke was becoming a catch phrase.

It was already clear that Devo no longer belonged to Akron. Now the band was becoming certain they didn't belong *in* Akron. In mid-May, Devo met with a local attorney named William Whitaker to discuss incorporation in Ohio and California, confirming their intention to relocate soon to Los Angeles. Whitaker had been a Kent State student at the same time as the band members, although he was not a Devo insider. But he, like some of the others, had been interviewed by James Michener for his book on the May 4 shootings, quoted under the pseudonym Paul Probius. So he helped the band tie up some of its final loose ends in Ohio. Devo, having seen a bit of the world, recognized the importance of this decision. Record companies, Mark once said, "didn't really understand us and they didn't like the music.

We were afraid that if we stayed in our hometown we really would be a one-off thing – we'd do one album and be buried quickly." The spuds' survival instinct pointed west.

Devo's calculated defection from the local scene both reflected and influenced a series of significant changes in Akron. By spring 1978, the Crypt had folded after the rubber worker who owned it was offered $14,000 for his liquor license. But by then, the scene had found an unlikely foothold in a larger national venue. Akron was becoming known as a hotbed of new wave, helped in great part by the "discovery" of Devo. The previous December, the Rubber City Rebels had decided to escape the hellish winter and drove out to Los Angeles. Thanks in part to their friendship with Mark Mothersbaugh, the Rebels got booked into the Starwood. Their manager then came up with a brilliantly mischievous plan to draw some attention. On Christmas Eve, he donned a pair of coveralls and climbed up onto a billboard catwalk above the Sunset Strip. On the whitewashed background, he painted, "Rubber City Rebels, Akron, Ohio." The billboard stayed that way for days, long enough to draw the desired attention. A Sire rep, perhaps recognizing Akron as sudden mark of credibility, attended the Starwood show. Seymour Stein soon came to see them, and before long he drew up a contract. But the Rebels pushed their luck a little too far, making demands on Sire that didn't sit well with Stein. He dropped them, but the attention was enough to score an eventual deal with Capitol.

Meanwhile, the Dead Boys had become a fixture in New York's Bowery, and the bands that had stayed local were plying their trade in a an odd boom town. The decidedly parochial Pere Ubu were signed by Blank, a new wave imprint of Mercury, and the Bizarros were about to do the same. Chris Butler had been kicked out of the Numbers Band for spending too much time on his burgeoning Waitresses side-project, and had joined Tin Huey, which was also being courted by the major labels. Just about every original band in Akron was being eyeballed. The groups were riding on Devo's yellow synthetic coattails. When Tin Huey entered negotiations with Warner Bros, Mark shared the details of Devo's deal, and the band, scaling down the numbers to suit their own realistic expectations, used the contract as a template.

And so Robert Christgau came to Akron. The influential *Village Voice* writer had been hearing snippets of what was happening in a place never considered a hotbed of original music. Butler had written him a letter; Nick Nicholis had sent him the *From Akron* two-band album. Christgau made a few phone calls, arranged to crash at Nick Nicholis' house, and ventured into the industrial Midwest in March. When his long feature appeared in the April 17 *Voice*, it captured the Akron-Cleveland-Kent scene at perhaps its highest point. Christgau explored why Northeast Ohio, of all places, had become such a fertile breeding ground of avant-garde rock and roll.

He gave some credit to WMMS, which in its free-form days had played the likes of the Velvet Underground, Captain Beefheart and Soft Machine. (although scenesters undoubtedly would have argued this point; WMMS virtually ignored the local bands inspired by those groups.) In conversations with Nicholis, he also observed that Ohio, unlike New York, offers unlimited garage and basement space, allowing bands to practice and evolve and experiment more thoroughly. He gave props to Johnny Dromette's record store – "a more impressive new wave outlet than any in New York" – and to Jim Ellis' *CLE* magazine.

More than anything, though, he captured a moment in time. Stiff Records, aided by a local musician and man about town named Liam Sternberg, was working on an Akron compilation, which would also include a teenage singer named Rachel Sweet, whom Sternberg was grooming. Everyone was *about* to happen, and the harsh realities of disappointing record sales, infighting and the splintering of the club infrastructure were not yet a factor. No, Christgau instead found the charming sincerity of Nicholis and the sweetness of the Chi Pig girls, all in their finest state.

Christgau's Akron visit coincided with Devo's first London gigs, so he instead found himself the guest of Bob Lewis, "their quasi-manager and long-time conceptual collaborator," and Susan Massaro and Bobbie Watson, who introduced themselves as Susan Devo and Bobbie Devo. The writer described the girls' Portage Path apartment as a Devo "commune," and wrote about the band almost in the past tense, as if their stardom was a foregone conclusion.

"When a Warners exec told (Devo) that he liked to sign one 'art band' for every act he knew was going to sell three million," Christgau wrote, "he was politely asked what art band would balance off Devo."

Chapter 24

One night in May, Neil Young finished playing a concert at a San Francisco venue called the Boarding House. But his night was far from over. He was in the midst of making a rather baffling film called *Human Highway* with his friend Dean Stockwell, who had first turned him onto Devo. He had decided to include Devo in the movie, and had fronted them some money for costumes. Devo had gone to Kmart and bought $136 worth of cheap cowboy outfits, which they were wearing that night, May 27, at Mabuhay Gardens, when Young walked in.

The club was packed. Devo, everyone knew, was probably about to graduate to larger venues when the album came out. Young had arranged for his film crew to be there, and the cameras were rolling when he made his way onto the stage at the punk club, offering a bewildering juxtaposition of rock cultures. Like the old saying about cats and their owners, it was hard to discern who was entertaining whom. Devo introduced Young as "Grandpa Granola". The audience, upon recognizing the hippie icon, began chanting a play on his name:

"Real Dung! Real Dung! Real Dung!"

(This, for a man later reputed to have played guitar while standing in a bucket of manure to get the right "feel".) Young was tossed into the audience like a human beach ball. Devo returned for an encore, with Booji Boy wrenching the guts out of "After the Gold Rush".

Devo was enjoying this collaboration, recognizing its strangeness and seizing the opportunity to be aligned with a big rock star. The band members referred to Young as "ancient history up close." And late the following night, the strangeness and the opportunity went haywire. After another show at the Boarding House, Young met the band at a studio called Different Fur. He had dubbed this ensemble "Neil Young and his All-Insect Orchestra". Mark was wearing his Booji Boy mask and a diaper with the cryptic phrase "Rust Never Sleeps" scrawled onto the cloth. They had borrowed a baby crib from a woman who lived next door, and Booji was sitting inside it. With the cameras rolling, Young plugged in his guitar and started to play a new song then called "Out of the Blue", which would become famous later as "Hey Hey, My My (Into the Black)". The song wasn't finished yet, and he and the band locked into the riff.

Despite Holger Czukay's previous reverence, Devo wasn't much for jamming. It wasn't their nature. Although they were all fine musicians, and although they put their hearts into their music, Devo was too much of the head to lay into the groove and give the groove back. By this time, they had so consciously removed themselves from rock tradition that cutting loose with Neil Young could only be done with a postmodern sense of irony. But the simple chord pattern lent itself to raunch and feedback, and the song carried on and on for twelve psychedelic minutes.

When Booji Boy came to the line, "This is a song about Johnny Rotten", the connection was just too weird, considering the proposition that had been floated in Jamaica. He changed it to "Johnny Spud". And as the tune devolved, Mark/Booji tossed in the line "rust never sleeps". Young, as he wailed on his guitar, loomed threateningly over Booji Boy's crib, Booji cringing from the sensory overload. The scene closed with crib upended and Booji Boy and Neil Young in a tangle of limbs.

This would become the nightmare sequence in *Human Highway*, in which

Are We Not Men?

Young plays a mentally challenged mechanic at a soon-to-be-closed roadside gas station. His character, Lionel Switch, is obsessed with a singing idol named Frankie Fontaine (also played by Young) and yearns to be a pop star himself. The disjointed script – much of which was made up as the cameras rolled – follows his reveries, with oddball musical numbers and an assortment of quirky characters, including Stockwell as the gas station owner. In addition to their cameo as the All-Insect Orchestra, Devo play a regiment of nuclear plant workers. As they haul drums of toxic waste out of a warehouse and onto a truck, the band, dressed in bright red coveralls, breaks into a cover of the Kingston Trio's 1959 feel-good hit, "It Takes a Worried Man". The song continues as the truck is loaded and rolls down the highway. Booji Boy, dressed like the other workers, rides in the back with the bins of waste, accidentally knocking one onto the road. And so the world ends in a beautiful atomic accident, followed by a twisted Busby Berkeley-esque musical number. It was a shining moment for Booji Boy.

"He's the infantile spirit of de-volution, basically," Mark once said of his alter ego. "He kind of represents pure de-evolution. He's a beautiful mutant.... He does let that nuclear waste drop while Devo's on the way to the dumping site. It falls on the highway, but he's not malicious in any sense.... He didn't mean it."

Young would work on the film off and on for a year or more afterward. It was finally released in 1982, to relative indifference and general head-scratching. The movie, originally intended as a tour documentary, had gotten completely out of control. Dennis Hopper, who played a short-order cook, drove the cast crazy with his rants, once accidentally stabbing actress Sally Kirkland with his chef's knife, leading to a lawsuit that she eventually lost. (When another actress testified in the trial, she was asked what the movie was about. She had to admit she had absolutely no idea.)

Actor Russ Tamblyn, who played Lionel Switch's bumbling sidekick, drove Jerry up the wall with his physical schtick. At one point in the filming, Devo pulled their nuclear waste truck up to the gas pump, where Tamblyn was the attendant. Jerry described the moment to Jimmy McDonough for his book, *SHAKEY: Neil Young's Biography*:

"The way Tamblyn played it was like a clown in the circus – tumbling, twisting, turning, fighting with the gas pump, falling down with it. In every successive take, he would ham it up more and more. I couldn't take it anymore. I went, 'You're a fuckin' evil clown!' Suddenly Russ gets real serious – 'I don't have to take this from that fuck.' That's the take Neil should've used, because everything... stops."

McDonough summed the movie up this way: "Neil Young has spent a lifetime creating mind-bending trips, but *Human Highway* would prove to be a doozy even by his standards. The film would start out as a sixteen-millimeter rock and roll road movie and wind up an end-of-the-world nuclear comedy, eating up four years and $3 million of Young's own money in the process. The movie was 'maybe the only not-smart financial thing Neil ever did,' said one of the stars of the film, Dennis Hopper. 'It went on and on and on – it was like once a year we knew what we were doin' – we were gonna go make *Human Highway*. It was just a great fuckin' party.'"

As production of the film dragged on, Young and his band Crazy Horse would complete what many consider a masterpiece, *Rust Never Sleeps*. Young, throughout his career, has listened to and allowed himself to be influenced by young rock innovators. In the late 1970's, Devo were among his favorites.

When he went back to the film of the night at Different Fur, Young picked out the line "rust never sleeps" that Mark had been singing in the squeaky Booji Boy voice. "It caught my ear," he said later. "I thought, 'Wow, right off they wrote better lyrics than I did.' I can relate to 'Rust never sleeps.' It relates to my career. The longer I keep going, the longer I have to fight this corrosion."

The source of the line isn't exactly clear. Several press reports said that the members of Devo had worked in advertising and had written the line as a slogan, possibly for Rustoleum. But Devo never worked in advertising. Peter Gregg and Ed Barger said the slogan came from a sign on the auto rust proofing shop that Marty Reymann's brother David owned in Akron, across the street from the go-go bar where Jennifer Licitri danced. This might make more sense. Before Marty built Man Ray, Flossy Bobbit had practiced in David Reymann's garage, where the wooden advertising sign apparently had been moved and hung on the wall. But according to David Reymann, his company never used the slogan "Rust Never Sleeps". And the truth may never be known, as the sign has since been recycled as the planking on David Reymann's porch.

Jerry offered a plastic-reality explanation. "Both stories are true," he said.

Regardless, it came from Devo, and it became the title of Young's next tour and the resultant live album. It also served as the slogan that would apply to his career for decades, as he continued trying new sounds and finding new bands from which to draw inspiration, jamming with Pearl Jam and exploring the depths of feedback with Sonic Youth. Young took more than just those three words away from the session with Devo. The incomplete "Hey Hey, My My (Into the Black)" had taken on a new edge, and when Young took it into the studio to work it out, he brought the film along.

"We went to play 'Hey, Hey', and we weren't hittin' it that good," Crazy

Horse guitarist Frank "Poncho" Sampedro recalled in *SHAKEY*. "Neil showed us the film of him playin' it with Devo. I didn't think we could ever play it that good, but that inspired us to play harder. From then on, we played the shit outta that song."

The collaboration with Young was tangled up with a new business relationship. Devo, to that point, had been operating without a professional manager. Young's manager, Elliot Roberts, was in tight with Warner Bros, and Young turned him onto them. (Roberts also played Frankie Fontaine's pompous English manager in *Human Highway*.) Devo remained suspicious of all aspects of the corporate rock structure, but recognized the need at this point for some experienced guidance. But not without skepticism.

When asked about the relationship, Jerry sarcastically told *Melody Maker*, "We put out a questionnaire and Elliot was the first to answer the questions correctly. We had them fill in the second half of Devo maxims like 'Wear gaudy colors, or (avoid display),' Devo lyrics, Devo thoughts. Apparently Neil had really informed Elliot about us. He was boned up on us and answered all the questions. So we went to see him in Hollywood. It seemed like the time. His office was all wood-grained, laid-back and mellow. Just what Devo needed!"

Bob Lewis, meanwhile, was sitting home in Akron, still half-expecting a role in the management. When he heard about Roberts taking on the band, he realized that what he had suspected all along was becoming true. He was cut out of the picture. And so he began to prepare for battle.

Chapter 25

There's a phrase from the *Little Rascals* that Devo has always been fond of applying to themselves: "Hey, kids – let's put on a show!" From Jerry's tampon coat to the white sheet tacked up to the wall for film projection to the thrift-store Booji Boy mask, their do-it-yourself bent had always run toward the homespun. So maybe it's not surprising that when the time came to make another film – even with a record company budget – the old ways prevailed.

They decided to make the "Satisfaction" film in Akron, where they knew how to operate. Chuck Statler was brought in from Minneapolis to direct, and the band arranged to use the stage of the Akron Civic Theatre, a downtown landmark, for the performance footage. The old movie house, built in the 1920s, was one of the few remaining "atmospheric theaters" in the country. When the house lights went out, stars and moving clouds were projected onto the vast ceiling. By the late 1970s, the ornate, Moorish Civic, like much of Akron, had fallen into neglect. It wasn't as bad as Cleveland's

WHK Auditorium, but was limping along on a small budget, with a handful of dedicated preservationists seeing to its care. There was a lot of crossover between the local crowd that supported the Civic and the local crowd that supported Devo. They seemed to be able to understand the importance of what the mainstream ignored.

Devo took some of their budget money and went shopping for wardrobes. They chose the local Gold Circle, part of a regional chain of discount stores, sort of a B-version of Kmart. They had an idea of what they wanted as they started sorting through the racks, using their highly trained sense of kitsch to spot just the right combination of double-knits, bad slacks, white plastic loafers and leisure shirts. They dragged these treasures back to the dressing rooms and began trying out the combinations, looking in the mirrors as they affected their dance moves. With the whole entourage making a big commotion, the manager finally came back and told them to get out of the store.

"Hey, we're spending lotsa money here, making a purchase," they argued. So he sent a couple of salesmen over to keep an eye on them as they continued sorting through the merchandise.

"We outfitted the band in a total double-knit, religious evangelist, middle-class salesmen's uniform... some damn cheap clothes!" the band recalled later that year. "All for $186.00 for 5 people."

Once again, the "Devo-tees" were recruited for supporting roles. Selma B. Smith, the mother of Debbie Smith from Chi Pig, would play an angry mother in a house dress, with a rolling pin and hair curlers. Her anger would be directed toward Mark, trying to score some late-night couch action with Linda Waddington, Jerry's girlfriend. In the back seat of a car driven by General Boy, Mark would try to cop a feel from Jenny Licitri, another of Jerry's old flames. Licitri, who worked as a go-go dancer, was nicknamed "Boob" – but not for the obvious reason. She had been fond of Yogi Bear's pal Boo Boo as a kid, and the name had stuck.

The performance part of the film showed Devo in the yellow suits, playing with the controlled, mechanical precision that had become their trademark. Mark wanted a guitar that looked like Devo sounded. He borrowed Bob Lewis' prized blonde Telecaster, the one he had bought from the Fender salesman at Dayho Electric. Mark sloppily duct-taped a boxy frequency analyzer to the front, with cables hanging down and extra guitar strings dangling from the headstock, so it looked like something from a mad scientist's home studio.

The most striking footage was of a tall, lanky punk from California known as Spazz Attack. As the song plays, Spazz, dressed in garish red pants and a bondage collar, throws himself into a flip, landing flat on his back. He looks

157

like he's being electrocuted, mirroring a scene with Booji Boy in a playpen, wearing a shiny silver spacesuit. As Mark yelps out "baby baby baby baby baby baby baby baby baby baby baby baby…," Booji sticks a fork into a toaster and shakes spasmodically.

As riveting as the *Truth About De-evolution* film had been, this new clip was Devo's definitive aesthetic moment. It was funny and entertaining, but it also made an authoritative visual statement. Here was a band that looked like it sounded and sounded like it looked, and it didn't look or sound like anyone else. This was a somewhat brave position, considering that the bands then dominating the musical landscape were groups like Boston, Foreigner, Journey and Styx, acts calculated to "sell three million" and also calculated, it seemed, to be indistinguishable from one another. There was a purposeful facelessness to those bands. They had been groomed as product, and even though Boston sang "More Than a Feeling," there seemed to be little actual feeling in their music. Emotion and drama were crafted for the stadium stage. Songs that seemed to say something really said nothing. Journey's hit lyric, "Any way you want it, that's the way you need it" came across as the defining statement of a genre intended to appeal generally to everyone, while specifically (and by design) appealing directly to no one.

Devo was also purposely faceless, but to far different effect. Their emotional distance was intentional, not a byproduct of the corporate rock aesthetic. So with General Boy as their leader and the likes of Spazz Attack in their elite forces, Devo was ready to make an assault.

All of this must have been rather confounding to the record executives preparing to sell the band's debut album. Art bands were supposed to eschew all aspects of business, except for the receipt of advances and royalty checks. But Devo was the art band that also boldly declared a commercial intent. On June 6, 1978, Mark applied for articles of incorporation with California's secretary of state to create Devo Inc. It was an if-you-can't-beat-'em-join-'em gesture. Devo recognized the insanity of the record business, but rather than run from it, they decided to mimic it internally, with the hope of the greatest financial reward.

❀ ❀ ❀

As Devo was filming the "Satisfaction" concert sequence, the band ventured out of the Civic Theatre and into downtown Akron for a photo session. Bobbie Watson, who had photographed them many times already, was there, along with another local photographer, Janet Macoska. Chris Stein from Blondie was in town visiting, and he also took some shots. The band posed in a nearby bus shelter, a wide concrete structure with a modernistic oval opening. They also ventured down to a local joint called Chili Dog Mac, a few doors north of the Civic, standing in front of the sign in their yellow suits.

It was as though the band wanted to mine this rich landscape one last time before pulling up stakes and relocating permanently to Los Angeles. "Akron's a good place to be from," Jerry once said sardonically, calling it "boot camp to the world." Now they were leaving.

One of the last things they plucked from their surroundings was the cover image for the upcoming album. Mark had included a picture in *My Struggle* of golfer Chi Chi Rodriguez, copped from a package of practice golf balls. The smiling Rodriguez, in his trademark porkpie hat, hearkened back to Jerry's "American Dream" installation/performance for the M-A-T-E-R art class. Graphically, it screamed, "Devo." It seemed, even in its careful representation of a sports icon, to suggest that mutation lay beneath the cheery veneer. When the picture was taken out of its original context, it had a strangely enigmatic presence.

The picture was initially chosen without regard to its source. It had been used on a line of golf products distributed by the Kent Sales & Manufacturing Company. The designer, Richard Blocher, worked for the local Fred Bock Advertising Agency. Blocher, coincidentally, was a close friend and golf partner of Susan Massaro's father. He had drawn the original illustration with colored pencils. Mark had spotted it several years before and tossed it in with his massive collection of found images.

The band had already used the picture as the cover for the "Be Stiff" single on Stiff, but when the artwork was presented to Warner Bros, there were immediate concerns. First was the problem of copyright. And, according to Jerry, the company's manager of business affairs was a golf fan and felt Devo was making fun of poor Chi Chi Rodriguez. So the band offered to contact the golfer and ask for his permission. In a weird set of local coincidences, Rodriguez's agent was Eddie Elias, a sports marketing legend who lived in Akron. But with deadlines pressing, the company decided instead to have its art department alter the image sufficiently to avoid legal problems.

"And after some resistance from us," Jerry said, "Mark and I decided okay. So Mark gave the art man a picture that he had pulled out of a newspaper of some artist's conception of a computer generated mélange of faces from the last four presidents – Nixon, Kennedy, Ford and Johnson... and showed what they'd look like if they were one man. Now this was truly in keeping with the Devo spirit as much as the Chi Chi image. So we said, 'Okay, take the lips from this president, that eye, that hairline and include it in Chi Chi's head.'"

From there, everything veered into quintessentially Devo absurdity. A

Warner executive, looking at the airbrushed image, decided it still resembled Rodriguez too closely. According to Jerry, he "personally altered our album cover by crossing the eyes off of Chi Chi, taking the scoop marks out of the golf ball, so you couldn't tell it was a golf ball, and changing the hat band, because he maintained that every golfer knew that was Chi Chi's hat. He sent his version back with a message saying, 'Here,' with a messenger waiting – 'sign off on this and you guys got the green light – you can have your album cover.'"

Meanwhile, Rodriguez had granted permission to use the original image. But by then it was too late. The plates had been made and the presses were ready to roll. So Warner Bros decided to pay Rodriguez $2,500 just to keep everyone honest, and Rodriguez asked simply for a box of records.

"His response from his lawyer was, at the end, when he got his box of records: 'Hey, this doesn't look like me,'" Jerry continued. "He at least, being good natured, didn't press charges for defaming his image. We were able to come out with something that – by the corporate interference and misunderstanding of the business side of Warner Bros Records – actually unwittingly produced something far more DEVO than the original… image of Chi Chi's much more handsome face over the golf ball."

Rodriguez, years later, recalled the transaction in a newspaper article. "I had never heard of them when my manager told me they called," he said. "They seemed like nice kids with some crazy ideas about music, but I never did meet them. I tried to listen to their music, but I felt sorry for them. I couldn't understand what they were saying."

In late June, with the album almost ready for release, Devo flew to Knebworth, England, to play in front of the largest crowd they'd ever seen – an estimated 120,000 people. The "Midsummer Night's Dream" Festival also included Genesis, Jefferson Starship, Tom Petty, the Atlanta Rhythm Section and Roy Harper. Devo was still a club band, without a proper road crew and without any practical preparation for such an event.

"Hey, kids – let's put on a show!"

The band members dressed themselves in gray coveralls and hung out with the roadies just offstage, watching the other bands. When Devo's turn came, these five men in workmen's clothes walked out and set up the equipment in front of a vast sea of people, then ran off to the mobile dressing rooms, changed into their yellow suits, and ran back onto the stage, to the same vast sea of people, with no idea they'd just been watching the same quintet hauling gear.

For all the canniness of preparation, however, the show was a monumental failure. The Knebworth audience had its ears ready for old rock standbys.

Devo at first confused, then incited the crowd, which completely trashed the band. Devo retreated from the thunderous booing. They ran back to the dressing rooms, changed back into the coveralls, ran back onto the stage, and broke down the equipment. General Boy would have been proud.

Chapter 26

Q. Are We Not Men? A. We are Devo! was released in England in late August, 1978, and came out in the United States two months later. With its October release, Devo embarked on their first proper tour, a grueling stretch of American and European dates that would carry into early 1979. By then, the stage show had reached its apex. The floor was covered with a sheet of black plastic, like a giant trash bag. Mark, as Booji Boy, would crawl underneath and emerge by tearing a hole in the plastic and wriggling forth, as if from the womb. The lighting was intentionally weird, with bright green fills from one side, orange from the other, and 1,000-watt television lights shooting from below, all playing off the yellow suits. Bennett "Bud" Horowitz, the band's lighting designer, found some adjustments in order for this new kind of rock band. "I was used to lighting people to make them look good," he said. "Devo, Jerry specifically, wanted to look as ugly as possible."

Somehow, it worked. Devo had gone forth with the dual intention of sticking to their iconoclastic guns, and of convincing the world that this was the way rock and roll should be. They didn't want to be outsiders in the traditional sense. They wanted to be the outsiders who set the template for the mainstream. They wanted the nerds to overthrow the jocks. Kiss, with considerably more bombast, had embodied the same attitude. Gene Simmons has said over and over that his band's act was not only the right way to present rock and roll, but that anyone who ambled onto a stage in jeans and a T-shirt (or worse, flannel) was doing it wrong. Devo had worked on this course for too long, and now they wanted to take the world with them.

Certainly, Neil Young was a convert. He had begun his *Rust Never Sleeps* tour not long after his collaborations with Devo, and had even taken to calling himself Neil 2. As he and Crazy Horse cranked out their folk-raunch for aging hippies and standard-issue rock fans, he would take a break in the set and walk across the stage with a big "DEVO" sign, asking the audience, "Have you got it yet?" As Susan Whitall wrote in *Creem* magazine, "His hippie fans shake their ponytails and stoke their pipes, pondering. Several men in lab smocks roam the stage, musing and taking notes." Young repeated this interlude when he played the Richfield Coliseum, nestled between Akron and Cleveland, on Sept. 22, 1978. Bob Lewis was at the show, one of the few who actually did "get it." After the concert, he was to meet with Elliot

Roberts, who managed both Young and Devo. Bob went to Roberts' hotel room along with along his lawyer, William Whitaker, who had helped Devo with their incorporation papers a few months earlier.

Roberts wanted to resolve the tension between Lewis and the band, or at least to reach some kind of settlement that would get rid of this growing distraction.

"I don't think there was any raging hatred against Bob Lewis," Alan Myers said. "Unfortunately, he just wasn't able to reach an agreement on what sort of compensation he might be due. Bands go through that a lot with former members. As I understood it, in the case of Bob Lewis, it was more about his role in the conceptual development of the Devo philosophy. Of course, I wasn't there until later, so I don't have firsthand knowledge of Bob's contribution or expectations."

Bob was expecting some kind of meaningful part in Devo Inc., a creative or managerial position. But Elliot Roberts, of course, already had the manager job. As they discussed Bob's future, Roberts offered a job racking records in Cleveland, a low-level promotional position. Bob flatly refused.

Roberts, according to Bob, responded, "You'll never work in this town again!" Which was fine with Bob, because he wasn't particularly interested in working in Cleveland in the first place. According to Bob, however, Roberts had misrepresented the Warner Bros offer, possibly opening up a long stretch of headaches in the process.

"In later discussions with Peter Gregg and then Jerry, this rather interesting tidbit comes to light," Bob said. "When Roberts came to try to settle – he was *supposed* to make an offer of an in-house job at Warner Bros in California, acting as a special liaison for the band's interests. This would have been a relatively highly paid position which, if I were able to work with the Warners' people, would have greatly benefited the band and myself. Instead, Roberts offered a job racking records with Warners in Cleveland. Why? Who knows? Jerry isn't a big Roberts fan, that's for sure. Who knows what would have happened if Roberts had done what he was supposed to do. As far as I'm concerned, Elliot's failure to properly transmit the offer was the reason it didn't get worked out more amicably."

Devo, meanwhile, was focused on more immediate concerns. A few days into the tour, the band was scheduled to play two songs on *Saturday Night Live*, which represented by far the biggest exposure they'd ever received. This would be the second show of the season, coming on the heels of the Rolling Stones' appearance the week before. It was a strange juxtaposition, considering that Devo's first song would be their cover of "Satisfaction". Or maybe it wasn't so strange. It was because of a series of coincidences and chance meet-

ings, ironies and mutations that Devo was there at all. In a directly chrono-
logical sense, this *was* de-evolution.

The band arrived at the NBC studios, mingling backstage with the Not
Ready For Prime Time Players, the group that had made the Lorne Michaels-
produced program an unlikely hit. John Belushi, Dan Ackroyd, Laraine
Newman, Gilda Radner, Jane Curtin, Garrett Morris and Bill Murray had
become stars. Their skits were repeated in classrooms and offices each week;
SNL was driving popular culture as much as any other entertainment of the
late 1970s. Even though there was a certain anti-establishment edge to the
program, Devo was a dark horse. With the exception of the "Midsummer
Night's Dream" festival, they had never played to more than 1,000 people.
And they had never been on mainstream radio. But on this night, millions
would be watching.

One of them was General Boy. Robert Mothersbaugh Sr. had gone out
that week and bought a VCR, a new bit of technology that would allow him
to capture one of his proudest moments as a father.

"That was really important for me as a father to see, because I knew then
that Devo had an audience," he said. "I knew that my sons could make a
buck and that they'd be all right."

Ed Barger, who had remained as the band's sound man, recalled Jerry
making a snide comment about the beloved Rolling Stones backstage "and
everyone on the show was bummed." This was probably a result of nervous
energy. The whole band was excited about this appearance. Jerry and Dan
Ackroyd had shared a laugh over the fact that, a year before, when Jerry had
sent a tape of the de-evolution film to him, Ackroyd had thrown it in the
trash. So this appearance was a victory in many ways. Jerry, to celebrate, had
made his first cocaine purchase, saving it for after the show. When he saw
Belushi backstage, he thought he'd be a nice guy and offer him some.

"Don't mind if I do," Belushi said, pulling a glass straw from the pocket
of his Blues Brothers jacket. He stuck the straw into the vial and snorted the
entire contents. Jerry's face went blank as Belushi handed back the empty vial,
laughing.

The host that night was Fred Willard, star of the TV show *Fernwood 2-
Nite*. He and Ackroyd performed the first skit, a parody of a low-budget law
firm called Two Guys Who Are Lawyers. That was followed by a segment
in which Belushi played an aging Hollywood stuntman. As it wound down,
Devo took their places on the stage, waiting nervously in their yellow suits
through the commercial break. Lorne Michaels came over to the edge of the
stage. They were on in 30 seconds, he said. Millions of people were watching.
"Don't fucking blow it," he advised. "Ten, nine, eight, seven..."

Are We Not Men?

The commercial break ended. Fred Willard, standing on the set, looked into the camera. "Ladies and gentlemen," he said, "Devo!"

"Then the lights hit us," Jerry said, "we can see the audience and they can see us, and we have to go. It was the most adrenaline I've ever felt in my life."

And despite the adrenaline, and despite the butterflies and the pressure and everything else, Devo delivered. The performance that night was as perfect as anything they had ever done. Every movement was controlled, giving the illusion of frantic action, when actually they were hardly moving. Jerry, especially, appeared to be a robot, executing precise half-turns, twitching as though he was drawn in stop-action animation. Although their specific personalities were obscured by the yellow suits and 3-D glasses, the collective personality was mesmerizing. These were not rockers who closed their eyes and bobbed their heads and poured out the love. These were funky bone machines. They were electric, and electrocuting. The song stopped on a dime and everyone froze, Jerry waiting a long beat before jerking the neck of his bass upward, then snapping his left hand up in a wave, as if to announce, "Take me to your leader." Then he dropped into a bow and popped back up, in subtle, twisted homage to the Beatles' *Ed Sullivan* gentility.

And then the show went on. Devo returned later in the night, this time in a clip from *The Beginning Was the End*. Booji Boy delivered the documents to General Boy, and then it got weird. This band that had seemed to crack open pop music half an hour before went hallucinogenic with "Jocko Homo". They weren't just goofing. They were saying something. And it wasn't clear whether this was a joke or a bold social statement, and that was exactly the point.

This had been the rarest of opportunities. It didn't matter to the masses that some of the world's premier hipsters dug Devo. That would have done them fine in the year-end top ten lists, but it never could have planted the seed that was planted that night. Without this national appearance, Devo might have passed as a super-cool inside joke. But now the world had seen exactly what a new wave band looked like and acted like. These weren't the raw English punk rockers dressed in a shredded version of some previous rock fashion. This was something entirely new, vaguely disturbing but wholly entertaining.

V. Vale, publisher of the fanzine *Search & Destroy*, talked about this in James Stark's book *PUNK '77*. "At first, when punk rock started, when we walked down the street wearing our black leather jackets, people would yell out 'Fag!' at us. They thought we were gay or something, me and my friends. They knew something was going on that they didn't like, but they didn't know what to call it. Then in 1978 there was like a 'consciousness' shift because people would yell out, 'DEVO!' I guess Devo were the first band to get some national recognition; they were heard by these kids from the suburbs who would drive into San Francisco Friday and Saturday nights just cruising around yelling at people."

That "Devo" had become a new kind of insult was a sublime compliment. An announcement had been made. The shrink-wrapped yellow albums appeared, with Chi Chi Rodriguez bravely smiling. Devo took the *SNL* moment on the road. Every seed of a densely structured past was in flower. Devo would, in some ways, get better, but they would never be more perfect. This was the beginning and the beginning was the end.

Tail:

1979-present

Eyes All Around

KRK Ryden

Chapter 27

And so the tour began. Real roadies. No more quick-change into coveralls to break down the stage. No more clunky vans. The financial support from the record company was nice, but at the same time, it was becoming more evident that the suits really didn't know what to do with Devo. Press releases painted them as a joke. They didn't fit in the new punk marketing niche, nor did they fit neatly into the ill-defined "new wave" bracket, an amoebic category attempting to embrace everyone from the Knack to Echo and the Bunnymen to Nina Hagen. Thus, after a series of East Coast shows following the *Saturday Night Live* appearance, Devo landed in Canada.

"I remember going to Toronto for the first time," Mark said. "We got off the plane, and there were five older people, one heavyset guy, a short little heavy-set guy, and a woman, and a tall guy with a mustache and somebody with long hippie hair, and they're from the record company. They've got on homemade Devo outfits that they made up for the occasion. One of them's got rubber galoshes on, another one's got, like, Beatle boots, a couple have swim goggles on, and they're jumping around, up and down like pogo sticks, going, 'Whoo, whoo, whoo, whoo, we're Devo'... and we're going, 'What the fuck is this?'

"It turns out they're Warner Bros people. They're, like, so proud that they go, 'We've been preparing the city for you guys all week. I tell you, we've been going downtown to McDonald's, and we've been jumping up and down, going 'Whoo, whoo, we're Devo!... Oh, my gosh, you wouldn't believe the response. I mean, people are saying, 'Fuck you, you assholes' – I mean, it's so great, you know – it's like we really got this town worked up for your concert tonight!'"

"We're going, 'Ah, Jesus, thank you so much.' We realized that we were really going to be in it alone. Even when they tried to help, they always made a mess."

The show went on nonetheless. Devo dropped back into Cleveland for an October 30, pre-Halloween show with Willie Alexander and the Boom Boom Band, whose guitarist, Billy Loosigian would later play in the Dropkick Murphys. Devo's old friends, Chi Pig, rounded out the bill, probably due in part to the fact that Mark was romantically involved with Debbie Smith. But that wasn't the way the night was supposed to go. Originally, the Police, who were touring the U.S. in a station wagon, were supposed to open, but Devo had them dropped.

By early November, Devo was on their way to Europe, for shows in

Germany, Scotland and England. Around this time, the band was having trouble with the quirks in the synthesizers and wireless systems. Jim Mothersbaugh was brought in from Ohio to work as an electronics tech. He'd been doing electronics engineering out of his dad's basement. Just 25 years old, with nothing to lose, he was thrilled to be joining his brothers in their grand adventure. There were sold-out dates; the band was on a high. With Christmas approaching, they were feeling the back end of all that hype. It was grueling, but exhilarating. Jim recalled the exuberance of experiencing all of this for the first time.

"(Mark) would actually have a cassette player, and right before the plane would land – he had this (recording) of Godzilla, and planes crashing into buildings with people yelling, 'Oh, Godzilla! Godzilla!' And he would hit it, and play it really loud! Everybody on the airplane is looking around, and they'd be yelling across the aisles because they're strapped in. 'Turn that thing off! Turn that thing off!' And my brother would be like, 'Up? Up?' You'd just be sittin' there in hysterics laughing. And Jerry and Mark would have contests on the flight to take their airline food... these pieces of meat... and cut them into different shapes – body parts and things like that. (They'd) have contests and pass them around to everybody. Always strange and interesting stuff going on."

Jerry, meanwhile, continued to be an abrasive and controlling presence. His sense of confidence and direction had been a key factor – probably *the* key factor – to the band having arrived at this point. But it also led to confrontations. Interviews would sometimes turn uncomfortable when he started messing with reporters' heads. This helped lead to an antagonistic relationship with the British press, which took to questioning and criticizing the Devo "philosophy." And Jerry was always riding Ed Barger about the sound. Because of the wireless microphones, Mark and Jerry could roam the hall during sound check, listening from the audience's perspective. They would meticulously pick apart the mix, working and working until it was perfect.

Barger had taken Jim Mothersbaugh under his wing. He was experienced not only in the technical aspect of touring, but, perhaps more importantly, in the survival aspect. He guided Jim and watched out for him. "When we traveled on the road," Jim said, "Ed was like a brother to me." Jim could relate to Jerry's treatment of Barger. He'd had already had his own battles, having been driven out of the band by Jerry's bullying. He didn't regret having given up the drum throne, and recognized that Alan Myers was a far superior musician. And besides, he said years later, "I look at the life and times of Devo, and it's not as though you hit utopia there."

Barger often used a dry sense of humor to roll with the punches. As he and Jim sat behind the board during a sound check one afternoon in England, Jerry was yelling about the mix.

"Eddie!" he said. "Make us sound like the Beatles!"

Barger turned to Jim and rolled his eyes. "Yeah, sure," he muttered, continuing as he had before.

❀ ❀ ❀

On December 26, Devo filed a lawsuit in California against Bob Lewis. The move was strategic. The band and their lawyers figured if this was going to go to court, better to make the first move so the proceedings would take place in California. That way, Bob would have to front the money to bring witnesses, most of whom lived in Ohio, out to the West Coast. The relationship with Bob had deteriorated significantly. His meeting with Elliot Roberts had been a punctuation mark in a years-long dialogue. Now with a set of corporate lawyers in the picture, there was no more messing around. Bob's insistence on a piece of the pie had been a drag and posed a threat to the band's relationship with Warner Bros, and the band and the record company were ready to be rid of him once and for all.

Meanwhile, the reviews for *Q. Are We Not Men?* began to appear, and the band was finding itself as confused as the critics and some fans seemed to be. In *Creem* magazine Readers' Poll, Devo's debut was listed as Best New Wave Album of 1978, ahead of releases by the Ramones, Elvis Costello, Patti Smith and Blondie. But readers also put Devo at No. 3 on the "Worst Group" list – even as they gave them the No. 3 spot on the "Best New Group" list. Lester Bangs (perhaps not surprisingly, given his straight-punk sensibilities) called Devo "tinker-toy music", while *Rolling Stone* praised the album's sense of authority. "Devo," reviewer Tom Carson wrote, "presents their dissociated, chillingly cerebral music as a definitive restatement of rock & roll's aims and boundaries in the Seventies."

Amidst all this, the band returned to the States, and to Akron. A January 4, 1979 show at the Akron Civic Theatre was billed as Devo's Homecoming Concert. The event was written up in the hometown paper, the *Akron Beacon Journal*, but it was clear that the mainstream still didn't quite get it. Devo was – and maybe always would be – trapped between wanting to be accepted by a mass audience and wanting to change the way that audience thought about music, about performance, about the condition of their lives. But it was hard for audiences to get past the band's sound and presentation. They were the group that had done that weird Rolling Stones cover, the ones in the yellow suits with the baby mask. Not a lot more was getting through. The title of *My Struggle* was proving to be an ironic truth.

Are We Not Men?

The band's families eagerly awaited this show at the downtown landmark. General Boy, still aglow with the *Saturday Night Live* appearance, was going to see living proof of his boys' success. Akron teenagers bought tickets to the concert and rode their bicycles downtown. "We had kick-ass seats," recalled Mark and Bob 1's cousin Alan Mothersbaugh, who was 12 at the time. "And a whole row – my uncle, all my dad's family was at this thing."

Devo, meanwhile, was somewhat ambivalent about this homecoming. Coming home to what? The place that, with precious few exceptions, had shunned and antagonized them? It was ironic that the show was promoted jointly by WMMS, the radio giant at whose Halloween party three years before the band hand been pelted with beer cans, and by Belkin Productions, the regional goliath of concert promoters that probably would just as soon have been shilling a Springsteen show. Devo's last Akron gigs had been at the Crypt, which was an outsider joint by necessity. Even though "Akron" had become part of the band's calling card, part of its quirkiness, it was also a place they recognized they'd had to escape. But now they were back.

In the familiar surroundings, they loaded in their gear, Ed Barger running the soundcheck, just as he'd done at the Crypt. They hung out with family members and old friends backstage. They were interviewed by a Kent State graduate student named Scott Lee Powers for a thesis he was writing. As they basked in this triumph and all its ironies, a stranger approached. A U.S. marshal. He thrust an envelope at the band. Before they knew what was happening, they'd been served with a lawsuit. Bob Lewis was asking for $1.5 million in compensatory damages and $1.5 million in punitive damages. He was suing them for theft of intellectual property.

"I talked to Mark about (Warner Bros assigning Elliot Roberts as Devo's new management), and he said that Jerry was the boss," Bob recalled. "It wasn't a high-pressure thing, it was just a quiet resignation on the rest of the band's part. Mark said, 'He's got to do what he has to do, and so do you.' Right away, I asked them to change the name of the band, to relinquish all of the intellectual property related to Devo. The General, the bios, manifestos, graphic design, philosophies, characters, even the Poot. Jerry wasn't interested. So… I filed the lawsuit Lewis v. Casale, Mothersbaugh, Mothersbaugh, Casale, Myers, Devo Inc."

The band kept the lawsuit quiet that evening. It may have been unsettling, but they weren't going to let it destroy this moment. "It did not seem to affect their performance," Ed Barger said. "At their worst, Devo was always great live." This was true. Devo was as polished and urgent that night as they had been on the TV a few months before, putting a charge into a downtown that had fallen silent.

Bob Mothersbaugh, who played with a wireless guitar transmitter, ran down the aisle of the theater during a guitar solo. "We were like, 'Bobby! Bobby!'" Alan Mothersbaugh said. "He put his pick in his mouth and shook our hands real hard, all in the middle of this song. We were so excited. He had that guitar that had been customized, cut down so it was like a thin plank of wood. My dad – he's like, 'That's a real expensive guitar – and he didn't care, he just shaved the shit out of it.' You know, that depression-era thing."

Twenty or so years before, central Akron had been full of nightlife, enjoying the ripple effect of young tire builders with money in their pockets and a Saturday night to blow. But by 1979, the ugly term "Rust Belt" was emerging, and, although no one wanted to admit it, Akron was right in the middle of it. Tire-building – the backbone of the local economy and the local psyche – was fast becoming a local anachronism. The jobs had moved south, to "right-to-work" states. The short-term gains of the 1976 strike had lasting effects. There was no way Akron's blue-collar workers could continue to dominate every aspect of life here, as they once had. And downtown was a dark and empty place. A bar called the Bank – formerly an actual bank, now a ratty but cavernous nightclub with marble bathrooms and a huge, ornate vault that served as a storeroom – had begun to book the Numbers Band, and would soon become the local new wave haven. On any given weekend night, all up and down Main Street, the only noise and the only light came from there.

But on the evening of January 4, the noise and the light emanated from the Civic. Devo delivered. The band that almost no one had seen before came home and conquered. And then they left. Devo never played Akron again.

❅ ❅ ❅

The tour continued through January and February. In March, the band's film for "Come Back Jonee", with Devo in the same black "fascist cowboy" outfits they'd worn with Neil Young, debuted at the Ann Arbor Film Festival. And then Devo, after a breathless year, returned to the studio.

Duty Now for the Future had already been scripted. The songs, the second choices after the *Are We Not Men?* A-list, were road-tested and tight. The band was finished with Brian Eno, but not with the David Bowie connection. Ken Scott, who had helped produce *The Rise And Fall Of Ziggy Stardust And The Spiders From Mars,* was at the helm, and the band quickly cranked out the 13 songs that would comprise their second album. The record sounded very much like the debut, which wasn't surprising, and certainly not to Devo, who knew exactly where they were going. The first two records would come from the years of material the band had bankrolled. The third record would be the real step forward.

The cover art for the European version of *Duty Now for the Future*, like

171

the cover for *Are We Not Men?*, was lifted from the pages of *My Struggle*. A silhouette of a man, head cocked, is backset by the ellipsis of an atom and what appears to be the line drawing of a lab beaker. Once again, the band's graphics were succinctly rooted in a storehouse of images that captured a retro-futurism.

The American release, meanwhile, featured a cover that served as a commentary on the band's new status as a commercial entity, plastered with enough bar codes to drive a record store clerk crazy. Devo was product now. They knew it, and they wanted to make sure their consumers knew it too. The back of the album was perforated so a fold-out stand would allow proud owners to display it on a tabletop like a family portrait. "We made 50 cents an album," Mark commented, "and I gave up 10 cents of that so this cover could be perforated."

This second album was calculated, but the music didn't suffer. Devo's B-list was as good as their A. "Smart Patrol/Mr. DNA" mirrored the "Gut Feeling/Slap Your Mammy" medley, and kept up with it step-for-step, with driving guitar crunch bringing up the rear. "Secret Agent Man" was as apt a turn on a classic as "Satisfaction" had been. The album may have lacked the grand statement of *Are We Not Men*, but in terms of songs, this was just what fans wanted and needed.

With the record in the can, the band immediately lit out for Japan, landing on May 20 and playing the first show in Osaka. The Japanese dates continued right up to the release of *Duty Now for the Future* in June, a mere nine months after the first album had appeared. And the touring continued, night after night after night. Back to California, on through the Midwest, out to the East Coast, down South, through Texas, back across Europe and into the winter.

Chapter 28

There is an Ohio brand of televangelism, strangely rooted in sincerity despite its polyester attire. There are no mascara-streaked scandals, rather a legacy that seems to fit comfortably with the rubber-company bowling leagues and early-bird specials at the chicken paprikash restaurants that pepper Akron's cultural landscape. On the Akron UHF stations in the 1970s, one could pick up both Rex Humbard and Ernest Angley. Humbard, with entirely biblical implications, began to build a tower toward the heavens in 1971, planning to put a rotating restaurant up there in the sky, an all-you-can-eat buffet in service to the Lord. But he ran out of money before he was done, and the half-finished spire still stands, with all its biblical implications intact. Angley, meanwhile, was more of an Appalachian faith healer in go-to-meeting clothes.

Early on Sunday mornings, kids waiting to leave for church had the choice between watching a locally produced professional wrestling show, *Davey and Goliath*, or Angley's program, in which an endless procession of mostly elderly believers waited in line to be healed. They'd make their way up to the front of the stage on walkers and in wheelchairs, where Angley, thick-haired, with a softness to his mountain twang, would ask why they had come to him.

"I've got arthritis. I haven't walked in years," a woman might say.

Angley would place his palm firmly on the forehead, raise his eyes heavenward.

"Say Jeee-sus!"

"Jesus."

"Devils – out!"

The patron would fall backward, into the arms of dark-suited henchmen who seemed AWOL from Elvis' entourage. Freed from her affliction, she would regain her composure and announce that she did, indeed, feel better.

The Devo boys had seen this. Mark and Bob and Jim Mothersbaugh, awaiting their weekly Sunday school lessons, had watched and learned. "I think Ernest Angley is sometimes kind of funny," their father said, "but tell that to somebody who's gone there and gotten cured – or somebody that's gotten helped by him and blessed by him. They'll think you're a bad person for saying that. He lets himself open for a little ribbing, and of course, Jerry and Mark did it."

They did it by reinventing themselves as Dove, the Band of Love. Despite the constant touring and the seeming reliance on old material, Devo's creativity and sense of performance art remained surprisingly fluid. Dove was the alter-ego of a band that already was an alter-ego. Outfitted in mustard-yellow leisure suits like Century 21 salespeople shilling lunar real estate, Dove was intended to be a feel-good, up-with-people commentary on the coming Reagan-era optimism, the logical descendant of Jerry's old *American Dream* performance piece at Kent State – and of Ernest Angley.

The band had played in this guise only a couple of times before their New Year's Eve 1979 show at California's Long Beach Arena. Dove would open the show that night, followed by X, the smooth, driving L.A. punk band with beatnik/rockabilly roots, and then Devo, who were closing out their *Duty Now for the Future* dates with a short West Coast "Fountain of Filth" tour. The band was drawing audiences of about 2,000 fans by then, and it's likely that few recognized the headliners who walked out onto the stage early in the evening, politely picked up their instruments, and began to strum a clean, snappy version of "It Takes a Worried Man", the same song Devo had played in their nuclear waste-handler's uniforms in *Human Highway*. They all wore accountant's visors on their heads and stepped merrily in unison as Mark came out, took the microphone, and snapped his fingers to the beat while crooning that he "won't be worried long".

This easy-listening performance was the advancement of the original Devo intent. It was certainly more subtle and vastly more tuneful than the "headache solo" from the Creative Arts Festival, but it was a challenge nonetheless. Were they serious? Was this really some new band with a fresh-morning-sunshine message? The audience was left to figure it out for themselves, because Devo was never willing to blink. They had remained, in Mark's words, "punk scientists." This was an experiment in human behavior as much as a musical exercise. Devo already had been criticized for being condescending to its audiences, for treating those who didn't "get it" with disdain. That wasn't really fair. Kiss approached its fans with the same attitude – you either were in the Kiss Army or you weren't. This was calculated to make a vast fan base feel special. Neither Devo nor Kiss minded being popular, but both wanted their fans to feel smarter or cooler for having discovered them. In Devo's case, the criteria were somewhat more strict. To really understand the band, one had to buy into a complicated philosophy that included understanding the artistic intent of something like Dove, which epitomized the old "plastic reality." But the journey was entertaining enough that the challenge didn't seem unfair. The sexy nerds were shuffling a deck that could use a little shuffling.

X, meanwhile, was not among the converted. Guitarist Billy Zoom recalled his band having to play off to the side of the stage at the New Year's Eve gig, with no monitors and restrictions on the number of sound board channels they were allowed to use.

"As far as the members of Devo are concerned," he said, "they never spoke to us, and I just remember them being a bunch of stuck-up prima donnas. I saw them play several times when they first hit L.A. They were a tight band, and always had great sound, but I was never really into their trip, and they weren't friendly."

Before the show, Mark had given his old friend and former roommate Ed Barger an inscribed copy of *My Struggle*. Inside the cover, Mark had written, "Although others remain incredulous, you know, for you were there." Barger had been with Mark since long before the two had ever heard of Devo, and he was one of the few from the Akron contingent who had proven himself valuable enough to remain as part of the inner circle. He had always been willing to speak his mind, but his talent behind the board, which previously had drawn praise from Brian Eno, kept him in good standing. So there he was, having traveled the world with the band, working the board in Long Beach.

Devo played their set, which included what is believed to be the first live performance of a new song called "Whip It". After the concert, Jerry came out to the house mixing board and congratulated Barger for a great show, something he had never done before. And then, shortly thereafter, Barger was fired.

The act was done by management, but Barger blamed Jerry. The congratulatory comment after the show, Barger said, "was like the Mafia Don setting me up for the kill." Barger never learned exactly how his firing transpired, whether there had been a vote or whose pressure had led to it. In retrospect, he realized that Mark's presentation of *My Struggle* – which contained artwork Mark had done but credited to Barger – was a sort of pre-apology. It didn't soothe him. But he also recognized the dynamics within the band. Jerry was in most ways the leader, and he and Jerry had never gotten along.

"I would speak my mind with Jerry, and Mark had to deal with the ramifications of my actions," Barger said. "You can see the position it put Mark in. I was doing what he should have been doing. He had the power, but no real guts. The only way to get rid of me was for Mark to finally give in to Jerry. Mark sold his soul to Jerry when he finally sold me out."

❊ ❊ ❊

Right around this time, Bob Lewis sent a letter to his old friend and professor, Ed Dorn:

"Briefly – present status... Bobbi Watson, myself, and a girl named Susan Massaro have got a video-tape business going – doing industrial tapes, promotional tapes, training tapes for (for example) golfers, doing some taping of Ronnie Harris, a local middleweight now ranked #2 in the world, etc. etc. I've also been doing freelance cinematography with the Jerry Smith Studio out of Milwaukee, doing commercials for TV stations in Pittsburgh, Cleveland, Utah, Chicago etc. etc. I'm currently working as a law clerk part-time, and we hope to move into legal applications of video tape (depositions, wills, presentation of evidence etc etc). Got some songs on an album called *Bowling Balls from Hell* coming out on Clone Records (under the stage-name Hurricane Bob – from the tropical storm of the same) and have even been doing some writing.

"In re. Devo," he continued, "the boys have currently exhausted all avenues of delay, harassment and procedural fencing – and trial is scheduled in Federal District Court for late March. In the meantime, hopefully they'll make big bucks and decide to settle for same."

Bob had successfully argued that the significant part of his involvement with Devo had taken place in Ohio, and that the trial should be held there, giving a huge boost to his ability to fight his case.

The *Bowling Balls* album he referred to was part of the ongoing attempt from within the tightly knit local scene to make itself heard. Released on Nick Nicholis' local label, it was a cross-section of the unconventional, arty music being concocted in Akron basements and garages. In addition to the contribution from Hurricane Bob (which included Bob Lewis, the members of Chi Pig and Numbers Band saxophonist Terry Hynde), the record included cuts from Chris Butler's side project the Waitresses, and collaborations between Tin Huey horn player Ralph Carney and Pere Ubu vocalist David Thomas. By then, many of the Akron bands had been signed and had released their debut albums, but nobody had gotten a lot of attention, and certainly not at the level of Devo. The Rubber City Rebels were doing well as a Los Angeles club band, and Doug Fieger from the Knack had agreed to produce their Capitol Records debut. The Stiff Records Akron compilation had been released – with a tire-scented scratch-and-sniff cover that featured the "Shine on America" mural. Rachel Sweet's new wave/country hybrid had caught the ears of some industry types, as had the Waitresses. But the coattail effect was not as strong as many had hoped.

Chapter 29

Nineteen-eighty had arrived. "The Eighties." The decade that seemed like it was going to be as modern as any that had come before, that would capture some future already imagined by Orwell and Reagan and Devo. The slogan for the last leg of the band's tour had been: "The '80's – We're for It!" Events of the recent musical past had made this decade seem like a blank slate. For idealists, a lot had been wiped clean by the punk rock revolution; for realists, the fact that the music industry had found a way to make a buck off that revolution meant there might be some temporary creative breathing room. *Rolling Stone* had declared that Devo's "shriveling, ice-cold absurdity might not define the Seventies as much as jump the gun on the Eighties." The band seemed as poised as any to define a new sound. Devo had finished with the archival approach of their first two albums, and were ready to move ahead with what promised to be the most significantly creative period of their career.

They were working on songs that had more conventional pop polish than the previous recordings. Mark had taken a riff from a Chi Pig song called "Pimple on My Plans", and he and Jerry had reworked it into something called "Gates of Steel".

"Since Mark and I were an item, we would get together and fool around jamming in the basement or this other rehearsal studio at Highland Square," Debbie Smith said. "Later, Mark called one day claiming to have written the tune, but asking for permission... honor among thieves. The music was the same, but Jerry wrote new lyrics and we worked out the money and percentage."

Devo's addition to the song was significant in continuing the message of de-evolution. To an upbeat, simple riff, the lyrics slip in the fatalistic darkness of Oscar Kiss Maerth. "We pay to play the human way," Mark sings, before continuing with, "The beginning was the end (of everything, now)." And then it's on to a discussion of apes and the devolutionary notion that the primate will "repeat until he fails."

Although the music was becoming shinier, the lyrics kept their bite. "Freedom of Choice" begins by imploring the listener to grasp this basic American ideal, but ends by pointing out that no one seems to want it. Devo was trying to find a balance between the old eggheaded explorations of the human condition and a burgeoning pop sensibility. Jerry had learned early that being subversive required a platform – the SDS wasn't going to get anything done by holding secret meetings in a house on a hill. By extension, Devo's passive-aggressive approach to song craft was reaching its pinnacle. Mark, too, understood the dynamics of mischief and defiance. In the days following the breakup of the Sex Pistols, and before the Johnny Rotten/Devo trial balloon had been floated, Mark had a conversation with the sneering, confrontational punk icon. He'd suggested that Rotten lose the safety pins and shredded shirts and adopt a corporate approach, that screwing with convention was edgier than spitting at it. Perhaps in response, Rotten dropped his stage name and John Lydon formed Public Image, Ltd., defining the post-punk aesthetic in the process.

Although *Girl U Want* was given serious consideration for an album title, the third Devo release would be called *Freedom of Choice*. "We wanted to make a thoroughly American album," Jerry said, "and let them know that we understood what was going on because they thought we didn't. *Freedom of Choice* is a statement that there isn't any and that people don't want any." The album's title and theme were directly influenced by Eric Fromm's book *Escape From Freedom*, which had presented the same theory, that people would rather be told what to do than think for themselves. The band would self-produce the album, in association with Robert Margouleff. Margouleff was a giant in the world of synthesized music. With his partner Malcolm Cecil, he had invented and built TONTO, described in the liner notes of *TONTO's Expanding Head Band: TONTO Rides Again* as, "the world's first (and still the largest) multi-timral polyphonic analog synthesizer." As a producer, Margouleff had overseen groundbreaking records by Stevie Wonder and others.

This would be the first opportunity to move in the technical direction that Devo had envisioned for years. Technology was an exciting frontier; its potential was huge. "The guitar became such a symbol of the flaccid state of rock and roll," Mark said about a year after the *Freedom of Choice* sessions. "We're not picking on the guitar as an instrument. It's just something people tend to misuse. It's not a big devil in itself."

Jim Mothersbaugh and his growing expertise in electronics were a valuable addition to the studio. He watched the band's direction change as the recording progressed.

"The first couple of albums, all the music had been written prior to ever going into the studio," he said. "The tunes pretty well had been worked out. I mean, we refined and changed things, but all of a sudden the production techniques were changing and you found yourself doing more composition (in the studio). Plus, technology was just exploding. You were being afforded more tracks to record on. I mean, it was nothing to take two twenty-four tracks and link them up back then. You had a different production technique coming in. Jerry never liked being confined just to a bass guitar. I think if they could have actually perfected synthesized bass guitar back then, he would have enjoyed it. He liked the raw, gritty bass sounds that came out of a Moog keyboard and things like that.

"Mark was doing more up-front singing, and so Bob Casale became logically sliding into the position of doing a lot of the extra keyboard parts. It really was just a matter of logistics. Mark had sort of slid into more of the up-front performing person, whereas he was behind a keyboard in the old days through the entire show, virtually. So positions changed, technology changed, and the way you make albums and things like that really changed a lot."

One of the songs that best fit the band's new groove was a hooky pop tune called "Whip It". The lyrics took a Dale Carnegie, pull-yourself-up-by-the-bootstraps approach, very much an outgrowth of the aphorisms that General Boy had preached in the Mothersbaugh home back in Ohio. Against a cold, galloping beat and a frail synthesizer line, Mark and Jerry traded lines in a nasal twang as they sang about "going forward" and "moving ahead", about grasping problems and turning them into something positive. They never let on whether they were being ironic; Mark had always embraced the same work ethic as his father, and it's entirely possible that he was being sincere, but the perceived sado-masochistic double entendre of the song would eventually overwhelm any examination of what the lyric was actually about. Musically, this was the kind of song that would define *Freedom of Choice*, a bookend to the equally catchy "Girl U Want", a frustrated lust song in the tradition of "Gut Feeling".

There was an authority to this new collection of music, although the vibe was much different. Gary Jackett, who was still working with the band at the time the album was being written, listened with disdain. "I can remember the first rehearsal Eddie (Barger) and I heard 'Girl U Want' and 'Whip It'. We were just horrified," he said. "We had to ask, 'What are you guys doing?' We fell out protesting the direction Devo was taking with 'Girl U Want' and 'Whip It'. Devo had moved to LA. The first album was out, and because 'Satisfaction' was kind of a novelty hit, Jerry kept listening to the radio. The Knack was getting a lot of airplay on the West Coast. They obviously had a big impact on him."

Ed Barger continued: "I heard 'Girl U Want'. I told Jerry and Mark it was an obvious sellout – it was The Knack's 'My Sharona' just twisted. Jerry said, 'You have no right to an opinion.' I said, 'Fuck you, Jerry. If you want to sell out, go right ahead!' That was the end of Devo as a musical group. They sold out to money and corporate greed. Devo proved de-evolution is very real. They devolved from the best music to the worst, and managed to self-destruct. Jerry would always say, 'When we make some money we will get back to the 'old' Devo,' but that never happened."

But of course these were Devo's decisions to make. And whatever objections there may have been from the outside regarding the musical direction, and whatever the commercial intent, there is a lasting artistic purity to the album. It is focused and clean and very much a musical statement that defined its moment and would influence the sound of the 1980s.

Perhaps no statement would be more lasting than the visual approach. Devo had adopted one of Kraftwerk's most successful and intriguing tactics, changing the band's look and theme with each new record. And so it was that the red "flowerpot" hats became an icon of the era. As with so much of Devo's aesthetic, the energy domes had roots in the high and the low. They were inspired chiefly by one of Bobbie Watson's *Little Lulu* comic books. Bob Mothersbaugh recalled a red helmet being worn by Lulu's friend Tubby during his violin lessons, protecting him from the horrible screeching sound. Mark recalled "a martian who came down and he had a 'cancellator helmet' that was very similar looking." Either way, and very much like Professor Zool's devolution machine, the band was far from content to let the meaning end on the comic pages. This was Art Devo.

As the helmet was being designed, Jerry recalled his days at St. Patrick's, looking upward to distract himself from the foul-smelling stuff the janitor had used to absorb vomit in the hallways. The Art Deco, ziggurat shape of the hanging light fixtures had a graphic fineness and solidity that had always stayed with him. And so the hats would have ridges. But these weren't just hats. They were "energy domes."

Back at Kent State, Jerry and Bob Lewis had studied Wilhelm Reich, an

Are We Not Men?

Austrian psychiatrist who had come up with the idea of an "orgone box." Reich postulated that the world was filled with energy – "orgone" (with "orgasm" as the root word) – that could be collected in a special cabinet. By sitting inside, one could absorb that energy.

"In fact," Bob Lewis recalled, "Charles Swanson (the Black Mountain art historian) may have even had a rudimentary orgone box among his treasures."

Jerry explained that the red hats were an extension of the orgone idea, that they were intended to collect and focus energy into the brain. He certainly must have realized that few people were going to buy this explanation, but he also wasn't the type to strut onto a stage wearing an outrageous costume without having some high intellectual ideal. The tampon coat was not just a coat covered with feminine products; it was an "experiment involving the phenomena of dreams." The Gorj mask was the springboard for an entire persona, complete with prayer cards. It had always been thus.

Now, the record company had just gotten used to the yellow suits. There was some not-unexpected resistance when the new look was unveiled, but Devo was sure of their direction, and sure that a striking new look had to accompany the new album. The band enlisted a Los Angeles design group called Artrouble, led by photographer Jules Bates. Originally, Bates' partner David Allen had created a purely graphic design for the cover, without photography. But the band decided to pose for photographs, wearing silver suits and the red energy domes. The suits were designed by Jerry and custom tailored in material alternately referred to as "aluminum naugahyde" and "barstool fabric."

For the photographs, the band members positioned themselves between American flags to capture the American theme Jerry had suggested. Bates' favorite shot was of the band with their heads bowed, so the tops of the domes faced forward. But eventually they settled on a photograph of the band members facing forward, unsmiling, their hands pointing rigidly downward, like German Expressionist robots.

Years later, singer-songwriter Beck recalled the impression the image made. "I wasn't sure if they were an army, a gang, or a specialized task force of geological engineers," he said. "Whatever they were, when this came out, I wanted to enlist. There was something so satisfying about their regimented chaos. I'd love to see some of these new-school rock bands step up to this level of concept."

Devo had been successful enough to be allowed to wallow in its high concept. They weren't losing money for the record company, and there seemed to be a base of fans that embraced all the "weirdness." This relationship suited the band well enough. Whatever commercial ambition they had was countered by artistic ambition, and they felt they had settled into a niche that served both. *Freedom of Choice* was released in May 1980, and Devo immediately flew off to Japan to begin another tour. Although "Freedom of Choice" (b/w "Snowball") was the album's first single, when the band appeared as the musical guests on ABC's *Fridays* late that month, they performed "Whip It". The flowerpot hats and that sharp, mechanical, oddly danceable beat were finding their way into the American consciousness.

Chapter 30

"Whip It" was released as a single in October 1980. It was an immediate hit. On October 4, the song reached No. 14 on the *Billboard* Pop Singles chart. This changed everything. Devo was now conspicuous, which, considering their attire and their intent, was neither unexpected nor unwelcome. But they were conspicuous in a micro, consumable sense – "Whip It" was like a Devo McNugget. Window washers were whistling the tune. People were tossing around "Devo" and "Whip It" as catch phrases, e.g. "You're so Devo." Rock jocks were reveling in the sexual innuendo of the lyrics, e.g. "I'm whippin' it good, har-har-har."

Warner Bros had pushed Devo hard. The debut album had sold half a million copies, but *Duty Now for the Future* had been somewhat of a disappointment, selling less than 250,000 copies. So *Freedom of Choice* was proving to be the hit record both the band and the label had expected when they had first joined ranks. Hit singles were not easy to come by, and were usually the result of a complicated business structure. There were programming consultants who acted as middlemen between record label promotional departments and radio station program directors. Two of the most powerful consultants of that time were Kal Rudman, who published a trade magazine called *Friday Morning Quarterback*, and Lee Abrams.

"If it hadn't been for Kal Rudman down in Florida, 'Whip It' would never have been a hit," Jerry said. "Lee Abrams hated us – hated our band, hated our music. Said it would never program on his five hundred AOR stations.... All it takes is, like, one Lee Abrams, and you can be dead."

Plenty of industry insiders have asserted that this complex set of influences is corrupt, that cash is part of the game. In a series of articles for Salon.com in 2001, writer Eric Boehlert detailed the relationships: "Radio promotion firms – or 'indies' – serve as well-paid middlemen or lobbyists, paid by record companies to get their songs played on radio stations. (The middlemen are necessary as 'cut-outs': If labels paid directly for the airplay and stations didn't notify listeners, both would be in violation of payola laws.) The indies pay radio stations amounts in the six figures in return for an exclusive relationship – and invoice record companies thousands of dollars every time a station adds a new song to its playlist."

Donald Clarke and Stan Cornyn have both written books about the music industry, and both describe Rudman as a consultant whose considerable influence came with a price. Clarke, in *The Rise And Fall of Popular Music,* described Rudman as "a talented tip-sheet operator who took payola: Rudman had a real skill for picking hits, and took money for records he liked (why not?). The Network, the system of independent promo men of which Kal Rudman had been one of the midwives, had begun to take over. The major labels farmed out their promotion work so that the payola was kept at arm's length, and a handful of gangster types controlled what records were played on the most important stations in America."

"Whip It" was a good song. But there were lots of good songs released in 1980 – including other singles off *Freedom of Choice* – and only a handful became hits. What mattered was that Warner Bros was willing and able to negotiate these waters on behalf of this band for which they had high hopes. In his book *Exploding: The Highs, Hits, Hype, Heroes and Hustlers of the Warner Music Group,* Cornyn explained that radio program directors had taken to playing it safe. They would only push records that seemed to have the full backing of all the players involved. "One way to distinguish safe records," he wrote, "was to pick mostly from those that were getting labels' full attention, nationwide: displays hung in stores, national tours by the artists, a new album, too. The word used was 'priority.' Labels often put out, say, six new singles a week. So as not to offend its artists, a label had a secret 'priority' list, a piece of paper hidden, its existence deniable. (Warner Bros executive Russ) Thyret had one but could not admit it."

Shortly after the release and skyrocketing sales of "Whip It", Warners and some other industry heavyweights decided to get out of bed with the middlemen. According to Cornyn, in November 1980, Warners announced that it would no longer use independent promoters. CBS Records joined in this resistance. But without the influence of the "indies" record sales suffered, and eventually the "pay-to-play" practice resumed.

Did "Whip It" become a hit because of payola? There's no direct evidence that it did, but it seems more than possible. Would Devo have cared? Hardly. The band was long convinced that the industry was corrupt, but was also willing to play along. For "Whip It" to have connected with a vast audience through unsavory means would only have proved what Devo already believed to be true. If anything, the band would have been delighted; the "punk scientists" would have new data to back up their theories.

And the band was happy finally to have a hit. Although some fans – and Ed Barger and General Jackett – accused them of selling out, Devo saw things differently. Long before they'd had a hit, the band had declared that "being commercial is being responsible," that there was no point in making art without an audience. Shortly after the release of "Whip It", Mark said in an interview that "the cult aesthetic of liking only what's obscure is just as sick as being mindlessly led around by the nose. Take the Residents as an example. They are exactly what we don't want to be, and what we once were – an artsy band liked by a few people who consider themselves elite, or with it, or hip, while the vast majority of the people on the planet never hear about them at all. We aren't at all interested in whacking off like that."

Alan Myers concurred: "I think it's hypocrisy to pretend to communicate with people and then purposely be obscure so they can't understand you. I mean, there's no doubt some people will be magnetized by a band that purposely sets up some kind of obscurity. But that usually just hides a lack of content."

It's true that Devo had, since its 1976 incarnation, been commercially ambitious. But these declarations were complicated by the fact that the band had always been artistically ambitious, as well. Their attitude was that they were a product just like any popular band, but that their product was better. In fact, that's what *Freedom of Choice* was all about – getting consumers to recognize that Devo was giving them a quality alternative in the mass marketplace. Devo was convinced that they could change the system from within, that they could become rock stars without falling into the rock star stereotypes. The only television that had been smashed to this point was the one Flossy Bobbit (or God) had destroyed back in Akron, with distinctive artistic intent. Jerry and Mark had snickered at Joe Walsh's lifestyle even as they had tried to enlist his help. And, until this point, their drug use had been recreational. They had been proud to distinguish themselves from what they saw as a bunch of spoiled, disconnected, drug-addled musicians. "There's nothing special about a rock star," Jerry said in a magazine interview. "We're totally unglamorous, asexual geeks." To which Mark added, "Our hotel rooms are cleaner when we leave them than when we show up!"

But they had started making more money. And with it came a seemingly inevitable increase in chemical intake. Drugs began appearing as a byproduct of success. "There were tours where, you know, it just got to the point where, everywhere you showed up people were offering you cocaine – every kind of drug," Mark said. "Any kind of drug you can imagine came through the mail to our fan club. Everything, you know, like peyote buttons and acid. (Fans would say), 'I grew this weed in my backyard in Hawaii. What do you think of it? I named my dog Booji Boy…'"

Jim Mothersbaugh was still working as a tech, although he had begun consulting with Roland, one of the premier developers of musical electronics. He saw the effect of the drug use, especially with his brother Bob and with Jerry. Bob Mothersbaugh had been a heavy drinker even in the pre-Devo days, but alcohol was enough a part of the lifestyle of being a rock musician that nobody seemed to recognize that he might have a serious problem. The increasing drug consumption was mostly closeted, and Jim wasn't part of it, but he could see a change.

"There was a spell where a few of the guys were really messing with cocaine and alcohol really bad," he said. "And it was pure torture working around them, and being around them because, it's really one of those things where if you're not part of that scene and part of what's going on with that stuff, you don't fit in. When we all lived in Akron, nobody was messing with the stuff, and I don't think for the first couple tours that it really surfaced very much. And then, just about, in the last times I was going out on the road, you could tell there was some of it being used, because the personalities were really stupid. It really makes you stupid."

Gary Jackett saw the change, too, and its effect on the music being made. In Akron, the band's intentions had been pure. But success had opened the door to corruption. "They were anti-big record company. They were anti-rock music. And they were anti-drugs," he said. "The whole Devo philosophy was not the typical philosophy. That's part of the reason why Jerry cut everybody off that he knew in the old days. He didn't want anybody around that knew the truth. The coke use actually started around 1979 or '80 because Devo finally had some money. They couldn't even buy their own equipment until they signed with Warner Bros. Before that, no one could afford real drugs. Cocaine was $100 a gram, and if you wanted it, that was what you paid. You couldn't get a $20 bag. Mark was never into it, but Bob1 had problems. He had the double whammy of both alcohol and cocaine, and would get out of control. Jerry was able to walk the line.

"I think it totally affected the Devo product. It pinpoints the thought process, it doesn't expand it. Their albums took longer because you just start nitpicking at everything. You don't want to talk about it, but for so many years Jerry would go, 'Oh, them Eagles, doing all that cocaine. It's disgusting. We'll never be like them if we make it.' Both bands got into the marching powder, and ended up doing the same dumb things. In the recording studio, where Devo used to go in, do a song and knock it out… they'd now go in, piddle and fuss, and Jerry would listen. He'd do a little bit of, 'If only that note was…' And it was funny because Jerry and Don Henley are so similar in that way. Henley was the same in the studio. They'd start and then the blow – it would open them up to infinite possibilities. If you listen to the music, it gets littler and littler as the albums progress. All of that intellectualism kind of leaves, and you end up with electro-pop dance music. That's Mark's music, and there's nothing wrong with Mark's music. But, it wasn't what Devo was, with that hard, angular, angst-out stuff. They tried to become a pop band."

And they did become a pop band. Devo was everywhere that summer and fall. On magazine covers, in radio interviews, on *American Bandstand.* The song "Uncontrollable Urge" was shot live for use in *Urgh!: A Music War,* a film that documented a slew of post-punk bands, from the Police to Pere Ubu. A San Francisco show was taped for *King Biscuit Flower Hour. Freedom of Choice* was certified gold in November.

Jerry tried to capitalize on this success by using it as a springboard for one of the band's long dreamed-about goals: a feature film. In December, he registered a 13-page treatment with the U.S. Copyright Office for a motion picture called *The Devo Movie,* an updated version of George Orwell's *Animal Farm,* with music by Devo and their alter egos Dove and Evil Clowns. The Japanese band the Plastics and Spazz Attack's band the Hu-Boons were also included in the treatment. The members of Devo would all play roles in the film. As the synopsis explains, "By combining elements of horror, science fiction, and social satire with low budget techniques in a conscious aesthetic, everyday life on earth is portrayed as life on 'another planet.'"

Devo also had storyboards for an hour-long television show; they were making conceptual videos with every album, something few bands did at the time; and they were hoping to start a film company, to realize their ambition of becoming a multimedia entity, a modern, high-tech incarnation of Andy Warhol's Factory.

But sometimes the visuals worked against them. The video for "Whip It" featured Mark with a bullwhip, cracking it at a blindfolded woman wearing red lingerie. He's cheered on by beer-drinking jocks and bimbos in cowboy clothing, and the band had intended for this to be a mockery of mainstream, narrow-minded misogyny. But it was hard to get around the fact that Mark was, after all, cracking a bullwhip at a woman in red lingerie.

"In America most of the networks didn't want anything to do with (the 'Whip It' video)," Jerry said at the time. "We managed to get it on Don Kirshner's late-night ABC show and some cable networks, but most of them completely misunderstood Devo. America is a Christian country, so they are heavily into sado-masochism. They didn't realize we were purposely parodying the kind of cowboy, macho-sexist mentality which is prevalent here. We were treating America the way Fellini treated Italy. The fact that we were taken literally by people was poetic justice. It kind of proved our point. They can't get enough videos of Rod Stewart singing between a girl's legs in a tight bikini. As long as it's male-oriented, soft-core innuendo, it's O.K."

Chapter 31

Even as Devo was enjoying some of their greatest moments, the Bob Lewis lawsuit had continued to loom like a ghost in the background. As Bob had gathered ammunition, he'd managed to track down a tape of the interview conducted by teenager Michael Hurray back at the 1977 Akron premiere of *In the Beginning: The Truth About De-evolution.* Bob realized that this obscure bit of evidence could well be his secret weapon, and he and William Whitaker were planning to save it for the courtroom. Meanwhile, the depositions continued, filled with testimony from Bobbie Watson, Susan Massaro and others, detailing their perceptions of Bob's importance to the development of the band's concept.

Bob's deposition took place in an 18th-floor conference room at a Century City law office. Robert Mangels, the attorney for Devo, asked Bob what made him think he was the one who had come up with the Devo concept. Realizing his answer might change the course of the whole thing right then, he dropped the bombshell prematurely. He told Mangels there was a tape on which Mark had professed Bob's importance. Mangels appeared taken aback, Bob said, and demanded that the tape be produced.

A couple of days later, during another deposition that was observed by Jerry and Mark, Whitaker set a tape deck on the table. He pressed play. The old cassette rolled. Hurray asked his question.

"Who started the original idea of Devo?"

"Him," Mark clearly replied. "Bob Lewis."

Bob looked across the room, at his old friends and their attorney. As he recalled it, Mark looked baffled, Jerry was enraged and Mangels looked deflated.

On Feb. 13, 1981, the record company settled with Bob. Part of the agreement was that the amount never be revealed, but Bob did acknowledge that it was "into the six figures." A few days after the settlement, he wrote a letter to Ed and Jennifer Dorn: "As for the good news of which I spoke, I got a call on Friday the 13th from DEVO HDQ, saying essentially 'Uncle,' and while I think that the major tragedy of the affair still lives on in the bifurcation of vision, and in the breakdown of the 'trust', the settlement which we effected will at least release me from the grinding stone of abject poverty, and might supply both the room and the capital needed for the projects now simmering on the back burners."

Patrick Cullie, the old friend who had tried to help Devo in the early days, heard about the settlement. He had risen in the music industry ranks, working in various management roles with Joe Walsh, the Rolling Stones, the Eagles and Carole King. From his perspective, the lawsuit and the settlement were justified. "I wholly supported Bob's lawsuit," he said, "and was as pleased and amazed as anyone when they won. Intellectual property in the music business is a concept that idiots like Don Henley only recently have deigned to bless the world with. Hey, one steals licks, riffs, grooves from everyone else. We all stole from Chuck Berry, who lifted practically everything he had from T-Bone Walker. That's the evolution of music and it's righteous. But to abscond with a concept, say, a story about deaf, dumb and blind boy, a lonely hearts club band or devolution, is yet another thing, and those concepts deserve their fiduciary due. Bob got his and he deserved it. End of story."

The fallout for Devo was hard to take, however. The band's relationship with Warner Bros had been founded on a lawsuit, and now this one came just as the label was pushing the group toward stardom. Bob had hurt Devo. He realized it, and said years later that he took "no personal pleasure from the whole episode."

❃ ❃ ❃

Freedom of Choice continued to sell well. In May, Warner Bros released the six-track EP *Devo Live,* recorded the previous August in San Francisco, to extend interest in the album. In the meantime, the band was working on the follow-up. The pressure was different than it had been before. Devo had always been astute at recognizing irony, and it was beginning to dawn on them that "Whip It" could be an albatross.

"'Whip It' actually helped bring about the demise of Devo," Mark said years later. "Before we released 'Whip It', we were an art band, and our record company said, 'Look we've got these weird art types, like Frank Zappa…' We were making these little films, writing albums… staying in the black. After 'Whip It' they looked at us and saw dollar signs, and after that album (*Freedom of Choice*) they started intruding on the aesthetics."

The message now was that the band could have all the artistic freedom they wanted – as long as there was another hit. This was a difficult spot, especially for a group that felt it had so much to accomplish, things that had nothing to do with the *Billboard* charts. This fourth album would be self-produced, and as the sessions unfolded, the members continued trying to advance the technological basis of *Freedom of Choice,* with guitars moving further into the background. They came up with a title. The new record would be called *New*

Are We Not Men?

Traditionalists, a phrase from a tiepin Jerry had spotted at a sushi restaurant in Japan. The pin showed a businessman's arm from the shoulder down, with the hand holding a pencil and the words "New Traditionalists" written on the sleeve. This was an appealing concept for a band so interested in retro-futurism; Devo was not interested simply in novelty, but in finding new things that would have some sort of cultural resonance.

"There were a lot of bands around that were starting to sing popular music in their own language," Mark said, "rather than, say, Italian bands doing massacred versions of English lyrics. We started talking about what we need are new traditions, and so we called the album *New Traditionalists*."

They didn't realize until later that the phrase had a different, and very specific connotation in Japan. On a trip there, Mark ran into a Japanese friend.

"He goes, 'Mark! I do not believe what you call your album!' And I said, 'What do you mean? I got the name from a Japanese tiepin!' And he goes, 'You don't know! It's so embarrassing! New Traditionalists are worse than Yuppies! They are the worst! I cannot believe you call your album New Traditionalists!'"

So maybe the band had even found a way to create a new tradition from the very term. But the theme was set, and the new look was designed to help carry it. The energy domes would be replaced on this album with molded plastic hairpieces intended to evoke John F. Kennedy, whom, Mark said, "we respect as the last American president who was really pro-information and pro-exploration." This was not the first nod to Kennedy; the song "Come Back Jonee", from the first album, evoked "sad memories of JFK," Mark once explained. The outfits that went along with the hair consisted of gray trousers and blue T-shirts with "New Traditionalists" written on the sleeves over a picture of an astronaut's head. "We look like a maintenance crew in that outfit," Mark said. "We look like we're coming to do the plumbing at your house. That's the one thing in common in all our outfits. We always look like some sort of ground crew for an airline."

Musically, the new album continued to weave in some of the old themes. The lead track would be "Through Being Cool", a song that directly addressed one of the band's most persistent, and most socially important ideas – that it was O.K. to be a nerd, an outsider. In this case, there was a call to arms: "Eliminate the ninnies and twits. Going to bang some heads, going to beat some butts, it's time to show those evil spuds what's what. If you live in a small town, you might meet a dozen or two – young alien types who step out and dare to declare… We're through being cool." Although the song moves on to stronger suggestions ("waste those who make it tough to get around"), it served as an anthem for the kids who'd been picked on for wearing glasses, or who'd been bullied by a "Baby Huey," or who'd been teased for liking "Whip It". Devo, the band that had purposely chosen ugly stage lighting and had not shied away from their own braininess (or, in Mark's case, nearsightedness), had a new power in their popularity. They could, like Woody Allen, open doors of social acceptance for nerds.

The *New Traditionalists* sessions also produced one of the band's best and most poignant songs. With Jerry on lead vocals, "Beautiful World", over a heavy synth track with chiming guitar strokes, handles Devo's trademark cynicism with a light, almost melancholic touch. "It's a beautiful world we live in, a sweet romantic place," the song begins. Details of that apparent beauty pile up as the tune progresses.

Only at the end, and only briefly, is the truth revealed: "It's not for me." That statement seems almost apologetic, and so understated that it comes across as a softening of the previous stance that had turned off some critics, the notion that Devo was looking down at anyone who didn't see the world the way they did.

The album was in the can; the packaging was complete. As the band worked on videos, word was getting around that cable television was planning to launch a new channel devoted to music videos. And on Aug. 1, 1981, it happened – MTV came on the air at midnight, with the seemingly prophetic Buggles song "Video Killed the Radio Star". Devo initially saw this as a golden opportunity, the perfect forum for a band whose visuals were at least as important as their music. Not long before, Devo had been stringing up a bedsheet to show their films to club audiences, in a *Little Rascals*-esque prediction of what was to come. Now there was a proper outlet. MTV had perhaps 100 videos available to show at first, but Devo was happily ready to provide them with more.

It wasn't necessarily a match made in heaven, however. The National Organization of Women protested MTV's airing of "Whip It", claiming it promoted violence against women. Lily Tomlin found the video offensive and withdrew her invitation to have Devo make a guest appearance on her television show. Despite all this, the band went ahead with production of three videos to accompany the release of *New Traditionalists*. There would be clips for "Through Being Cool", "Love Without Anger" and "Beautiful World". Over the course of the first three albums, Jerry had been learning more about the technical aspects of direction through a trial-and-error process. And both he and Mark said years later, in *The Complete Truth About De-evolution* laserdisc, that "Beautiful World" represented the band's most complete and successful use of the medium. Jerry called it "my favorite video that we've ever done."

Are We Not Men?

The video's basis is a collage of archival footage, stretching back to the 1920s. Booji Boy watches a futuristic monitor as flowers spring into bloom and clouds race across the sky, vintage fashion models turn and the cockpit closes on a space car. The tone begins to change, as a soldier tosses a grenade, a bridge explodes and collapses and a woman tries to extinguish her flaming dress. And then it changes further, with quick cuts of a Ku Klux Klan rally and cops with nightsticks handcuffing an African-American man. There is an image of the Earth seen from outer space, followed by a starving child in its mother's arms. By the end, there is the chaos of street fighting and then a mushroom cloud. In a reflection of the subtly ironic lyric, the atomic blast gives way to the closing image of a baton-toting woman leading a marching band.

The video harks back to Bruce Conner's montage of black-and-white stills in the "Mongoloid" film, a simple but moving approach that was handled with a deft touch. Mark gave much of the credit to Jerry's vision and diligence. "'Beautiful World' may be our most complete, all-around, and at least privately successful video, and in no small part (due) to the fact that Jerry spent hundreds of hours going through archives, looking for these images and picking just the right ones," he said. "The way the scenes build up to the Earth and the starving child is such a great ambush, it makes the song so much stronger than the song ever was as a song by itself."

The band was able to completely control the video's content, in great part because MTV's commercial potential had not yet been realized. The channel wasn't even national yet, and there were many in the industry who thought it would be a novelty. But that would soon change, and the record companies would respond by insinuating greater control over videos. But for now, Devo was far ahead of the game.

"We were hoping that our strong commitment to visuals and to music were going to create a whole new way of thinking in music, that was going to allow us to be part of it, monetarily. We got to be pioneers," Mark said.

It would soon become clear to them that MTV, instead of broadening the artistic possibilities of popular music, was narrowing the form into homogenous commercials for new records.

"Devo has always believed in imagery with ideas and integrity," Jerry said in 1984. "We think the synching of visuals to music is probably the most important artistic phenomenon of this century, and we respect that medium. Most rock videos, though, don't seem to respect the medium. There's just too much of what I call 'puzzling evidence' – that all this ridiculous indulgence in gratuitous, meaningless imagery that has no integrity at all. It's mystifying, it doesn't mean anything and has no connection to the song. They hire these rock video directors as creative mercenaries to apply a fashionable visual aesthetic to the band. After a while it all gets so dumb and pretentious, watching MTV for an hour is like watching chimps-on-parade, or at best record-label baby pictures. It's a cheap, shallow approach that insults the intelligence of the audience. It's no different, really, than putting a pretty girl in a bikini on top of a station wagon so you can sell a lemon, you know?"

Chapter 32

Four albums in three years. It's no wonder Devo chose a weary worker's song for their next exquisitely mutated cover. In September 1981, simultaneous with the release of *New Traditionalists*, the band contributed Allen Toussaint's "Working in a Coal Mine" to the soundtrack for *Heavy Metal*, an animated rock film. The song wasn't on *New Traditionalists*, but would soon be included in the package as a bonus single. "Working in a Coal Mine" had been a hit for Lee Dorsey in the mid sixties, but once again, Devo aptly sidestepped soul and added machinery. The synthesized beat is accented by a spiky clang at the top of each measure, Bob 1's twangy guitar setting the whimsical foundation for the hiccupy lead vocals and the throaty declaration, "Lord, I am so tired. How long can this go on?" The choice of the song and its handling are as effective as "Satisfaction" and "Secret Agent Man". In this case, the band's blue-collar/intellectual dichotomy plays both with and against Toussaint's original idea. The spuds, the "dirty hard workers of the earth", really do seem tired. But there's also an ambiguity to the playful, catchy delivery. Sincerity was always too simple a notion for Devo, and the aesthetic tension in their treatment of the old chestnut was true Devo. With "Working in a Coal Mine" in their canon, it was evident that, for all their originality – and *because* of their originality – Devo was one of the best cover bands of the era.

The four-month *New Traditionalists* tour, which began in mid-October, covered the United States and Australia. By now, the electronic delivery of the music had become the trademark of a band previously known for its raw, shadowy punk energy. Devo was one of the few rock bands willing to admit that disco had added new artistic possibilities to music, and had embraced some of the technical contributions of the genre, especially the use of drum machines. The sound on *New Traditionalists* is heavily reliant on the use of the Linn drum machine; there's a brief scene in the "Beautiful World" video where Alan is playing what appears to be an Oberheim D-8 drum machine by hand. Devo was also getting deeper into experimenting with new technology on stage (they had, even in the early years, been one of the first bands to embrace wireless guitar transmitters), treating the computers and sequencers not as gadgets, but as tools to advance their vision.

Are We Not Men?

Partly because of the increased use of synthesized drums, Alan Myers was feeling alienated. "To me, things got kind of cut off from their root when we came out here (to California)," he said. It was all kind of a blur to me at that point because creatively it wasn't really hitting the core anymore. Artistically, what happened with the group pretty much after we got out here didn't resonate to me. It lost its life energy.

"When I first started playing with the group, the material that we wrote for the first couple of albums – we'd get together and there would be a lot of information, a lot to play with. But once we came out here, it was like there was somehow never anything, any joy, any happiness of, like, having any goop to play with. It was always like, 'Wow, what's going on here?' There is no texture here. It is almost like you can compare to the ground in Los Angeles and the ground in Ohio. There you've got earth, you've got grass, you've got something you can stick your hand in and play with. And out here it's dry and you need a hammer to make a dent in it. And I almost felt like creatively that was what it was like. It was like trying to take something and grow it in the barren ground. We forced ourselves to create *Freedom of Choice*. We sat in this little room and we just hammered out that record as a matter of survival. That was an act of will, that record. And then after that things just creatively became more and more parched."

This view ran counter to Devo's general "go forward, move ahead" philosophy. "We go where we go," Jerry said in a newspaper interview during the *New Traditionalists* tour. "Otherwise, we'd still be dressing in the yellow suits and playing that crude, edgy music. The risk is to do something totally different that makes as much of an impact as the first thing you did. And that's very hard to do."

Mark mirrored this sentiment in a separate interview around the same time. "There is always a chance that Devo's going to go down, that we will be sucked up by the business and made horrible, stupid and meaningless," he said. "That's what the whole game is. It's fighting for as long as we can before we go under."

Mark, meanwhile, had continued making visual art. On the tour bus and in hotel rooms, he whiled away the hours as he had as a young man in Akron, working in a small, portable format that suited his lifestyle. "I do visual art every single day," he said in 2001. "And for the last 25 years, it's manifested itself as postcards. I think it had a lot to do with touring and always being on the road. It's a nice format to work on postcard-sized images. I used to do mail art even earlier than that with people like Robert Indiana and Irene Dogmatic, who were kind of at the more famous end of mail art world. I've been doing painting and drawing and collages."

192

New Traditionalists failed to produce a hit at the level of "Whip It". "Working in a Coal Mine" peaked at No. 43 on the pop charts, but "Through Being Cool" and "Beautiful World" didn't crack the top 100. The album itself went to No. 23, just one spot lower than *Freedom of Choice*, indicating that the fan base had remained loyal. And even without a big hit, Devo remained a strong visual presence on MTV and in live television appearances. In the process, they helped influence a post-punk era that represented an advance in the presentation of music. The band never appeared out of uniform; both onstage and off, they managed to convey a thoroughly postmodern image. This was part of the notion of plastic reality, creating an image separate from the sentient humans making the music. There was little point in walking around in jeans and flannel to signify sincerity when that sincerity was being designed and promoted by publicists. Devo was a product and everybody knew it, including themselves, so why not keep the packaging interesting and consistent? U2 was just emerging at the time, and would soon become the epitome of earnestness. But even they would eventually adopt a Devo-esque stance. Their *Popmart* tour of 1997, an over-the-top commentary on consumerism, could easily have been designed by Casale, Mothersbaugh, et. al. (with "Too Much Paranoias" as the template).

As work began on the follow-up, the band toyed around with the idea of inviting guest lyricists into the mix. They put out a feeler to William Burroughs, whose novel *Naked Lunch* had greatly intrigued Jerry back at Kent State. Burroughs' twisted iconoclasm seemed an apt fit to Devo. On June 4, 1982, Burroughs sent a letter of response to Jerry, and included the poem "Pick Up Sticks", full of anachronistic gangster lingo. (A "stick" in gangster slang, is a legitimate job that one can turn to when the heat is on or crime isn't paying the bills.) Burroughs sent ten stanzas he had written while working on his book *The Place of Dead Roads*. The poem begins this way, and continues with the same simple rhyme pattern and theme:

"Your luck's gone bad, lad
Pick up your stick
And pick it up quick
Before you get a lick
From someone else's stick
When you're old and sick
Lean on your stick
You're hot as a rivet
Stink like a civet

Are We Not Men?

Grab that stick
A simple swineherd, officer'
OINK OINK OINK"

Burroughs' lyrics didn't make the cut. But Devo had also become intrigued by a poem written by an unlikely source – John Hinckley Jr. who was in psychiatric prison for the March 30, 1981 shooting of President Ronald Reagan. His act had been a warped attempt to impress actress Jodie Foster.

"It was kind of a dark period for us, anyhow," Mark said, "and we called up Bethesda Maryland Hospital where we read that he was staying. Wouldn't you know, just by being persistent and saying that we were with the band Devo – it either caught them off guard, or anyone could get to him – we actually got to John Hinckley and talked to him. He said that he was a Devo fan, which didn't make me feel good at first. He only bought the first album, so that was okay. We figured he had lost interest, so we wouldn't be next on his list.

"But he let us take a poem that he had written, and we used it for the lyrics and turned it in to a love song. It was not the best career move you could make. We had the FBI calling up and threatening us. They told us, 'Well, you know he gets 500 death threats a week, and his fans are going to be your fans, and you better not publicize this song.' Our record company called and said, 'Wait a minute, we're getting calls from the FBI. Is this really the John Hinckley they say it is?' My manager said, 'Mark, you can't do it. Neil Young never would have done it, Bob Dylan never would.' None of his other clients would have done it. Tom Petty wouldn't. It was like, why did we do it? But if people told us we couldn't, that just gave us all the more determination... you know, *Spinal Tap* syndrome."

So they did it, turning the poem into the song "I Desire". It begins by pledging allegiance "to the thought that your love is all that matters." It's an intense exploration of obsession and seemingly perfect love: "A smile I might bring you is more important than world peace." And at the end, however, comes a warning that "nothing is more dangerous than desire when it's wrong."

In retrospect, Alan Myers said, "I thought 'I Desire' was a good song. I think that was a cool thing. That was one of the better things that came out of the last few records. I don't understand why anybody would get uptight about the fact that it was based on a poem by John Hinckley. I think that art is art. I don't have a problem with that at all."

But the song and the problems it invited worked into a trend of weird things going wrong. Devo was used to being misunderstood, but now the misunderstandings were taking on heavier significance. The title of the fifth album seemed like a nod to this idea: *Oh, No! It's Devo*. This time, the band returned to using an outside producer, working with Roy Thomas Baker, whom they'd met on the Australian leg of their tour. Baker had added deeply layered sheen to albums by Queen and the Cars, and together they pulled a thicker sound from the machines, highlighted by the single "Peek-A-Boo!", an underrated, aggressive song that evoked Big Brother paranoia.

For this phase, the band adapted a simpler look, with sleeveless black outfits topped by wide round collars that came over the shoulders. (Many observers said they looked like toilet seats.) On the album cover, the band's bodies were replaced by potatoes, the first significant use of the spud image. The videos they produced reflected Jerry's continuing intention to use the burgeoning form not as a vehicle for a song, but as part of the song. "We had at this point totally abandoned story, and band hijacks and silly images alluding to story were a thing of the past," he said. "We were trying to get more pure about it all." So the clips from this album are modified performance videos, graphically clean, with rear-projected images that enlarge the music, rather than turning it into a soundtrack. In the "Peek-A-Boo!" video, the screen behind the band appears to open, revealing images behind. The first is a quick cut of the spanking scene from the original de-evolution film; the video also includes old pal Spazz Attack in garish devil/clown makeup. At the end, a pirate interacts with the band; when he kicks his foot forward, one by one they go tumbling off.

This marriage of video and musicians was exactly what Devo had envisioned even before it was possible. The band was trying more and more to work the same element into their live shows, an ambitious undertaking. "We had finally, even with our meager budgets and crude technology, been able to synch up and rear-project huge backgrounds in our live stage show, and play with them through click tracks in our sound system back to a modified 35-millimeter projector and 35-millimeter sound mag, (to) be able to play in sync," Jerry said. "Devo then represented a 3-D video game in concert."

The album was released in November 1982. The tour that followed would be billed as the first-ever "video-synchronized" rock concerts. The run of shows was kicked off by what seemed like an exciting possibility, another technological first. In a pay-per-view, closed-circuit television broadcast, Devo would perform the "First Time Ever Live 3-D Concert". The so-called 3-Devo show, originating from the New Beverly Hills Theater in Los Angeles on Halloween night, would be piped by the Campus Entertainment Network to nearly 20 colleges across the United States and simulcast on FM radio stations. The idea was for fans to don 3-D glasses and see something they'd never seen before. Unfortunately that's exactly what happened.

Are We Not Men?

In the days leading up to the show, the band was becoming nervous that the producer, Black Tie Entertainment, didn't have all the bugs worked out. Wall of Voodoo opened the concert and then Devo went on. It was a disaster. "What they had done," Jerry explained, "was assure us that they could 'live' run our sequences from… (a) projector through a sound system, and that they could keep it in sync with the backdrops. Of course, what happened, there was an offset, and someone deprogrammed the offset. So, from the beginning of the concert, the pictures and the sound were out of sync with each other. We were left on stage without being able to play to our own sequences – so we were, like, making it up as we went along."

From the opening notes of the show, Devo was hung out to dry. They knew it wasn't working, and they knew audiences would be scratching their heads, thinking this was the band's fault. The frustration was clear in Devo's demeanor. During a segment where Mark brought a woman from the audience onto the stage, he made a mockery of the technology that was supposed to be regarded as a breakthrough. He was every bit as funny as Ghoulardi, except that Ghoulardi's technical chaos was intentional.

Brian Schellenberger, a fan of the band, was watching at East Carolina University. "It was one of the lamest things I've ever seen," he said. "At our site, the signal was lost for a little while and replaced with a porn channel. Everybody cheered. That was the best five seconds of the show. Though it *did* introduce me to Wall Of Voodoo, but that was the only reason that the evening wasn't a complete and utter waste."

At the end of the show, Booji Boy appeared as always. But instead of his usual innocent declarations, he delivered a blistering tirade, far out of character. It takes a lot to make Booji Boy mad, but apparently the boy's got gumption.

Devo sued Black Tie Entertainment and won, but the incident seemed to be a harbinger of bad things to come. A month after the 3-Devo show, Jerry and five crew members were arrested following a concert in Houston. There was a dispute with the fire inspector, who had ordered the show to stop so the aisles could be cleared. Jerry reportedly told the audience, "The men with badges want to take us to jail; so, we need to clear the aisles so the little piggies don't take Devo away." Jerry was handcuffed right then, but when it became clear a riot would erupt, the band was allowed to finish the set.

"I spent nine hours in jail," Jerry said. "The cops just gloated; they loved it. They would demand that we talk to them, and if we didn't, we were reprimanded: 'Hey, DEVO, c'mere! I said COME HERE!' They tried to make me sing 'Whip It' for all the drunks in the drunk tank. Then the cops got on a loudspeaker system and sang it themselves, amid laughter."

It seemed like, to paraphrase Burroughs, the time had come for Devo to pick up their sticks.

Chapter 33

Jim Mothersbaugh, after several years of working back-and-forth as a Devo tech and a Roland consultant, had gone to work full time for the electronics company. The dabbler who had built an electronic drum kit from scratch had found himself at the cutting edge of music technology, an opportunity that would have been hard to imagine back at JB's. He was part of a team of Japanese and American engineers working on a groundbreaking new development called Musical Instrument Digital Interface, or MIDI.

At the January 1983 National Association of Music Merchants (NAMM) Convention, Jim and another engineer named David Smith successfully connected two digital synthesizers from different manufacturers, thus making MIDI a reality. This would be one of the most important advances in electronic music, and would change the way artists were able to play live and in the studio.

Meanwhile, back in Akron, Bob Lewis had embarked on a decidedly lower-tech venture. He had formed a business partnership with his attorney, William Whitaker, and Whitaker's new wife (and Bob's old girlfriend), Bobbie Watson. Bobbie had designed novelty sunglasses from the letters of "Ohio," so that the "hi" fit over the nose and the "O's" made the lenses. The OhiO Sunglasses were being marketed to amusement parks, state fairs and the like. Bob was moving on, finally, after all those years of fighting with Devo. He would soon become a consultant to the Syrian Defense Ministry through Janson Industries of Canton, Ohio, and would also freelance as *Rolling Stock* magazine's Middle East correspondent, reporting from Damascus, Syria.

The partnership symbolized a sort of Lonely Hearts Club of people who perceived themselves as having been shunned or betrayed by the band. Ed Barger, Marty Reymann, General Jackett – all of them felt left behind in some way, and most of them blamed Jerry more than anyone else. Jim Mothersbaugh, years later, likened the situation to people who had a tough boss and left the company disgruntled. There's no question that Jerry was the one who had overseen the organization, the CEO of Devo Inc., as it were. "He's leading the band, and has to make a lot of choices," Jim said. "Some of them are good and some of them are bad. That's a hard position. It's hard when you're running a business. Jerry's a loving, caring person. He sheltered most of the members of the band (from the difficult business decisions)."

It seems clear that he was hard to work with, at least at times. But it also seems clear that, without his diligence and ambition and vision, Devo would never have succeeded as they did.

By this time, Devo seemed like ancient history in Akron. None of the bands who had shared stages with them existed any longer. By 1980, the only one left locally was Chi Pig, and they disappeared soon after. The "Akron Sound" was quiet. Younger bands, playing at JB's in Kent, were vaguely aware that Devo had once stood on the same stage, but far fewer were marveling about the fact that Tin Huey and the Bizarros had played there as well. There was a lingering sense of frustration, as some of the late-'70s musicians tried to make a go of it in other bands. But it wasn't working. No one was paying attention to Akron anymore. And the city itself had slipped considerably, with tire production all but gone and much of downtown boarded up. In an effort to get tenants into downtown buildings, the city offered financial incentives, propping Monopoly-style posters in the window, suggesting one might buy space with play money.

Ralph Carney had found his niche with Tom Waits and was sporadically releasing solo albums. The Waitresses and Rachel Sweet had made a splash. Liam Sternberg was still working behind the scenes in the music business, and would eventually write the Bangles' hit, "Walk Like an Egyptian". But at home, all the promise was gone. For one moment, just as Akron was about to stumble, it seemed that this unlikely "Akron Sound" might be a thing to cling to, a new export. That Akron, as it was losing its identity as the Rubber City, might find some new sense of self in these scruffy, off-kilter rock and rollers. Not only did that not happen, but, except for a handful of people, nobody in town even knew such a possibility had existed.

❊ ❊ ❊

Devo's tour had ended and the band was facing an uncertain future. The contract with Warner Bros had expired, and the band's sales had declined incrementally after the *Freedom of Choice* apex. One bit of the past came full circle that summer, when *Human Highway* was finally released with a premiere party at Mann's Bruin Theater in Los Angeles. Bob Dylan apparently saw the film, and his ears must have perked up when he heard Booji Boy at the end, after the nuclear disaster, reciting, "The answer, my friend, is breaking in the wind. The answer is sticking out your rear." Dylan later made a cryptic request to Mark for a copy of *My Struggle*. Dylan's "people" called Mark and told him to expect a limousine to pull up at his house, and to have a copy of the book ready to hand off so it could be delivered to the airport and into Dylan's hands. Mark made the hand off, but he never heard another word on the subject.

In this period of relative inactivity, Devo wrote and recorded the theme

198

to a Dan Ackroyd bomb, *Doctor Detroit*. The bouncy dance number helped hold Devo's place in the MTV rotation and landed them on the flip side of a James Brown single, but it didn't represent any kind of artistic advancement. At about the same time as the song's release, there was some different musical activity going on in the Mothersbaugh family. Robert Mothersbaugh Sr., who had always had his own interest in music, registered a volume of song lyrics, co-written with a woman named Heather Miller, with the U.S. Copyright Office in Washington, D.C.

The *Human Highway* and *Doctor Detroit* associations were reminders that Devo had not yet fulfilled their hope of making a feature film. They were still talking about making "The Big Picture" and Jerry's continued interest in and facility for direction and production would have seemed to have placed the band in a position to see it through. Jerry had an idea to produce a story about the "Smart Patrol" taking the name from an early Devo song and applying it to a group of Devo-esque youngsters who would serve as a sort of updated Monkees. (With this vision, he predicted the "boy bands" who would become ubiquitous 15 years later, albeit with far less brainpower. The "Cute Patrol" they might be called.)

Devo did continue their presence on the small screen, however. They made appearances on *Late Night with David Letterman*, *Night Flight* and played Muffy's "new wave" bat mitzvah on the CBS Monday-night sitcom *Square Pegs*. In the episode, Devo is portrayed as punk rocker Johnny's "ninth-favorite band." The appearance reconnected Devo with Chris Butler's band the Waitresses, who had provided the *Square Pegs* theme song.

❋ ❋ ❋

After the longest period of dormancy since 1976, Devo had managed to work out a one-album deal with Warner Elektra Asylum (WEA) to release their sixth record. *Shout* came out in October 1984. There was new leadership at the record company, and there were hopes that Devo had some commercial life left. "They decided that after the failure of *Oh No! It's Devo*, it was sink or swim for the band," Jerry said, "so with *Shout*, it was the make or break album for Devo. At the time, none of us knew it would be the break album."

The record was self-produced. Again, synthesizers dominated in the studio, and the band, as a unit, was less involved in the process than before. Guitarist Frank Schubert, a friend of the band, said he had begun sitting in on the sessions. "I worked with the band from around 1984 through 1990. I played most of the guitar parts on the albums during that time and did a couple of tours," he recalled. "I am hesitant to talk about my friends in that wacky band. During the time that I played with them, it wasn't a good time for any of us."

Are We Not Men?

Jerry claimed not to have been aware of Schubert's role. "Frank was a guitar tech for Devo's early concert tours," he said. "Unless Mark kept it a secret, Frank never played on any Devo albums."

Devo's string of success with cover songs led to the idea of taking on the Jimi Hendrix classic "Are You Experienced?" This choice carried the same implications as the "Satisfaction" cover, the thoroughly postmodern band reshaping one of rock's cornerstones. Electric Ladyland would become Electronic Ladyland. The song, in Devo's hands, takes on a rich, trancelike tone, still psychedelic, but with an entirely new palette. The key phrase comes near the end, when Mark bends Hendrix's lyric toward devolution: "Not necessarily beautiful, but mutated."

For "Are You Experienced", the record company gave Devo their largest video budget to date, $90,000. Jerry would have the opportunity to experiment with what would become known as "morphing" – an innovative version of digital animation – and sophisticated graphics. He would be able to develop elaborate sets and costumes, while shooting on 35-millimeter film. Jerry worked on the video with Ivan Stang, a founder of The Church of the Subgenius, an irreverent "religion" that worshipped J. R. "Bob" Dobbs, a smiling, pipe-smoking 1950s advertising icon who represented the American Way. The Church of the Subgenius bore a number of similarities to the Devo philosophy, and Mark was among the converted. He mailed in his $20 to a post office box in Texas to become an ordained reverend, and would later wear the mask of Bob Dobbs at the church's debut "Devival" in Los Angeles.

The premise of the "Are You Experienced" film is that a metal peace sign, an apparent relic from some lost culture, is discovered by a group of street kids. They throw it away as junk, and it lands in Devo world. Mark, dressed in a white lab suit and riding his Honda scooter down a highway, passes through the gas it emits and is transformed into a hippie with a shag haircut and '60s sunglasses. He enters a laboratory where the other band members, dressed in the same lab outfits, examine him. The scene shifts to a live stage setting, where Hendrix impersonator Randy Hanson emerges from a coffin and plays a solo, with the hippie-fied spud boys, in spandex suits with bulbous shoulders and hips, acting as his backing band. The video is an elaborately surreal excursion. Shapes change, bodies float, realities warp; the song and the visuals are fluid and dreamy.

Shout had its moments, but there was a sense that the band was losing its steam. The songs were written on a computer and seem more like soundtracks to something – perhaps videos that were never made or ideas that no longer had the right conditions for incubation. Devo was trapped in a corner of their own making. By consciously removing themselves from rock traditions, they didn't have the conventional "comeback" devices to rely on. Bruce Springsteen and Bob Dylan, when these times came, could always sit in a dark room with an acoustic guitar and strum out introspective songs that the world would recognize as a return to their artistry. But Devo had no such roots to cling to. The final brilliance of Devo was that they had predicted this from the start, from before they were even a proper, working band. They had put themselves in a position of always having to move forward, but they knew that moving forward was moving backward. So "Are You Experienced?", while it was an interesting take on the original, was also an ideological return to the first truly sparkling moment of the band's career – the "Satisfaction" cover. The beginning was the end, and the end could only reflect the beginning. In that sense, the Jimi Hendrix song was a poetic choice.

✳ ✳ ✳

Devo's first and only Grammy nomination came in February 1985, for their long-form home video *We're All Devo*. This collection of greatest hits was augmented by a story line about Rod Rooter, a sleazy music executive who hates Devo, and his daughter Donut, who loves the band. Donut was played by *Saturday Night Live*'s Laraine Newman, whom Mark was dating during the filming. In a nod to their relationship, she counters her father's disdain for Devo by whining, "Well, I think they're sexy – especially Marky."

Timothy Leary also had a role, as Dr. Byrthfood, and Spazz Attack made another appearance. The pieces of the story had been shot during the *Human Highway* project, but never saw the light of day until they were salvaged in *We're All Devo*. The compilation joined another video collection, *The Men Who Make The Music*, which had been released in 1980.

In the hiatus that followed *Shout* and the Warner Bros years, Alan Myers left the band. It was 1986. Although there were allusions to an unspecified falling out, Jerry's later explanation was that Alan "lost the de-evolutionary spirit; he became un-Devo. His brain was unwashed; he was no longer Devo brainwashed. He wanted to stay home with his wife and his child and he didn't want the life anymore and the responsibility and the stress of the complete commitment of what it takes to make music in today's world. That's fine… if that's how he felt."

How he really felt, though, was creatively unfulfilled. He'd been feeling it almost since the day the band had moved to Los Angeles. Only when he was onstage did he feel like a vibrant artist. And now, with Devo in decline, he didn't want to do it anymore.

"A lot of what was good about us at the beginning was that we were human beings that were being machine-like," Alan said. "But you could tell that there was an energy pushing it. Then, when we were able to replace that with actual machines – the actual intellectual concept of doing that might have been stimulating or interesting to some members of the group, but in fact it lacked vitality. It was the new technology and that was something that certain members of the group felt was something that we stood for. And particularly artificial technology. It was a perfect example of an intellectual analysis of a situation getting in the way. We just tried to plug in these other methods of creating the material and actually performing the material. And that was not interesting to me. For me music is a tactile thing. And I am not really interested personally in programming and intellectualizing it."

✼ ✼ ✼

Jerry went to England and hooked up with Kevin Godley and Lol Creme, two of the most innovative video directors of the time. He worked on videos for Andy Summers, Rush, Jane Sieberry, the Cars and others. Mark released a solo album in Japan called *Music for Insomniacs*. The band did commercials for Honda and Coca-Cola to make enough money to continue working as musicians, accepting the jobs only under the condition they maintained creative control. Bob Casale, whose own studio expertise had grown over the years, produced a band called Martini Ranch and engineered an Andy Summers solo album, as well as the Police guitarist's soundtrack to the film *Down and Out in Beverly Hills*. Mark, working with Bob 2, wrote the music for a new TV show called *Pee-wee's Playhouse*, a vehicle for Paul Reubens' spastically innocent alter-ego, Pee-wee Herman. "I'd like to do more TV," Mark said at the time. "If it's the right show. And if we get the same kind of freedom we had on *Pee-wee*."

The only Devo music released in that four-year layoff was the *E-Z Listening Disc*, a collection of muzak versions of Devo songs that had previously been available from Club Devo, the band's fan club, on cassette and colored vinyl. This new CD version was released on Rykodisc in 1987.

✼ ✼ ✼

The band found a new drummer, David Kendrick, who had previously played with Sparks and Gleaming Spires. They signed with Enigma Records, accepting a contract that was an obvious step down from Warner Bros. With the small label, there would be very little money for videos or elaborate stage sets. But there would be another album, and the band realized, reluctantly, that the only way to do that was to re-enter the nasty world of the music business.

"We were already on the Titanic," Mark said later. "The day we signed, we walked in, looked around, and all the things that we'd been told by people that, 'Oh, they're gonna be the next A&M Records', we instantly knew that was wrong. We watched our career go down the drain, what was left of it, along with many other bands. For videos we had to make the most of our budgets, every penny. We even invested our own money in these things."

The band produced an album, *Total Devo*, that continued the trend of synthesized dance music. There were love songs, a cover of Elvis Presley's "Don't Be Cruel" and a single aptly called "Disco Dancer". It's not a bad album, but it failed to capture the imagination. Critics were unkind, the public wasn't buying it, and the label wasn't in a position to help much. Michael Azerrad, writing for *Rolling Stone*, closed his one-star review with the line, "If you listen closely, the bass drum on this record sounds suspiciously like a digital sampling of a dead horse being beaten."

Much of the album was made with a Fairlight synthesizer, which had emerged in the mid-1970s as the first digital synthesizer and had become a favorite of electronic bands. An electronic revolution was on the horizon, but Devo's aesthetic seemed stranded somewhere on the cultural *Island of Lost Souls*.

"It became all about the equipment," Jerry said later. When asked for an explanation, he continued, "It would depend on who you'd ask. It certainly wasn't my idea. That's all I'll say. I had this thing in 1983 that I really wanted us to do. I wanted us to use the Fairlight only for amazing, nasty, primitive, screaming, animal kinds of sounds. Build them and take a long time to do it, and even though they were on reel, the end result would be frightening. Build sparse sequencer lines and progressions and have everyone play to that. But of course there'd be so much room in there because everything wouldn't be filled up with sixteenth notes. Go back to, like, an 'outer-space caveman' idea. Well, that didn't happen, and I sure wish it had."

The band uniforms this time around consisted of simple red military-looking shirts and pants. No masks or headgear. The tour found them in clubs, including a November date at Peabody's DownUnder in Cleveland, formerly the Pirate's Cove, where Devo had played those early shows with Pere Ubu. The show was on election night, and General Boy stood outside the club in uniform, greeting concertgoers and thanking them for coming to see his boys.

Chapter 34

So that was it. The first song on *Smooth Noodle Maps* is called "Stuck in a Loop". As with *Oh No, It's Devo!* it was almost as if the band was willing to beat critics to the punch, commenting on the direction of their own career. It was 1990, and the band that had helped define the previous decade had run out of reasons to keep going. *Smooth Noodle Maps,* the second Enigma album, sounded – and fared – much like *Total Devo*. The single "Post Post-Modern

Man" was another punchy electronic dance-floor song, well composed, but unable to recapture any of what had once made Devo so compelling.

A year before, Mark had exhibited some of his postcard artworks at Psychedelic Solution Gallery in New York City. On one, he blamed Bob Dobbs, the smiling, pipe-smoking, Ward Cleaver-on-acid godhead of the Church of the Subgenius, for Devo's failures: "Bob Sez... Yes, I told Devo to write a song with John Hinckley - HA HA! But I didn't tell them to sign with that corrupt manager! It was their own foolish doings... Oh – I got an idea!! Hey, Devo! Why don't you switch record labels! Oh, sorry, forgot I already talked you into that one. Well – Can't you take a joke??? Come on – Spuds – Are We Not Men? You'll love parking cars in the afterlife. Oh – You're already parking cars? Well good practice." So that was it. Devo did not break up, and would make periodic appearances throughout the years that followed. But there were no new albums, and no sense that the grand construction of the thing had any more corollaries other than nostalgia. Meanwhile, Mark's work on the hip, quirky *Pee-wee's Playhouse* had been too perfect a fit for others not to notice. In 1991, the cable channel Nickelodeon launched a smart new animated children's show called *Rugrats*, with Mark as the music director. The show was a hit, and more and more offers came in for commercials and other TV work. Mark bought a building on the Sunset Strip, a round structure that formerly housed a doctor's office. He painted it lime green, and it became the headquarters of Mutato Muzika, a multimedia studio that encompassed exactly the range of work Mark had dreamed of before Devo turned him into a rock star. With Bobs 1 and 2 working at his side, Mark was scoring cartoons and films and was working at the cutting edge of interactive media.

The band was leaving their old life behind. With Mark's help, Bob Mothersbaugh had gone through a rehab program, and had emerged clean and sober, giving talks to groups about his successful recovery, trying to help others with the same problems. Mutato Muzika seemed almost like a haven of redemption, a way to continue the ideas behind Devo without having to deal with the hard truths of being in a rock band.

There comes a time in every pop music career when an artist has to look at himself and wonder what he's about. It's only in that answer that he can understand how to age gracefully. Devo was rooted in cartoons and commercials and loopy sounds and mutated visuals; the whole *Little Rascals* theme. Now Mark had found a new home in those things.

"Devo was greatly influenced by media," he said. "We were products of pop culture; we were fans of Andy Warhol and Roy Liechtenstein and all the Pop artists and the Dadaists. We were fans of TV commercials; we quote a Burger

King commercial on our first album, a song called "Too Much Paranoias". Kinda interesting, 'cause in my life now it's come full swing and now I work on commercials. When I first did it, I didn't know how many I was gonna do, and I spent a lot of energy doing things like putting subliminal messages in."

So Mark, always mischievous and subversive, the man who'd played a Godzilla tape on airplanes, was hiding messages like "Choose your mutations carefully" and "Question your parents", which could have been lifted from the "laws" the scroll across *The Truth About De-Evolution*. In a soda pop commercial, he scolded: "Kids, don't eat so much sugar." Mark and his little brother would sit in a boardroom with the advertising professionals, trying not to laugh as these commercials were previewed.

"I just put it, just below the threshold where you're gonna, like, wait a minute – 'I heard a voice.' And, you know, it's like, nobody notices it. Nobody says, 'Oh – wait a minute – stop that and run it back – didn't I hear a voice?'"

Bob Mothersbaugh had emerged as an equally talented soundtrack composer, writing music for the feature films *200 Cigarettes* and *Men*, for PlayStation games and more than 200 commercials. Mark wrote and produced music for TV's *Dawson's Creek*, *Tucker* and *Rocket Power*, among others, and scored *The Rugrats Movie*, *Rocky and Bullwinkle*, *Rushmore*, *Happy Gilmore* and *The Royal Tannenbaums*.

With *Rugrats*, Mark said in a 2002 interview, "I did the early ones and was just figuring out things, then Bob took it several steps further. He has a wider palette of instruments and a more sophisticated sound. Bob is much more adept at guitar and really good at rock stuff. If you listen to his *Rugrats* episodes, his scores are much better than mine. In Bob's music, I hear the influences of all the things he enjoyed on TV when he was a kid. I'll hear orchestral things that remind me of the *Little Rascals* or cartoons. He was into that. I liked old movies, so I used to tape movie soundtracks off the TV with a tape recorder. Then when you listened to it without a picture, it really emphasized the score."

Jerry did not move forward with Mutato Muzika. He did continue directing videos, working with Soundgarden, Silverchair and the Foo Fighters, among others. And he remained as eloquent about de-evolution as he had always been. When Reagan was in office in the 1980s, Jerry was the one to point out that de-evolution had come true. At each political and social turn, he found and expressed new evidence. And of course, the denouement of Devo was further proof.

"Even though we had always said from the beginning, very self-consciously, that the beginning was the end, and that the truth about devolution embodied that idea, the end always comes as a surprise," he said. "The specific end, you never understand, and you never can foresee, and that is the perverse joke of it all."

The band's legacy picked up almost immediately after Devo stepped aside. In the early nineties, Nirvana recorded "Turnaround", the B-side to the "Whip It" single. Soundgarden and Superchunk recorded "Girl U Want". Moby did a death metal cover of "Whip It". Growing numbers of rock bands paid homage. Guided by Voices singer Robert Pollard listed *Q: Are We Not Men? A: We Are Devo!* among his favorite albums of all time; punk orator Henry Rollins proclaimed that there are just two kinds of people: those who get Devo, and those who don't.

In the 1990s, Rhino Records released two volumes of *Hardcore Devo*, culled from the band's Akron tapes. There were *Greatest Hits* and *Greatest Misses* releases, a live CD of some of the band's earliest shows and a two-disc anthology. The band produced a computer game called *Adventures of the Smart Patrol*, which revived some of the ideas from the never-made Devo movie. In 1999, Mark released *Joyeaux Mutato*, an ambient Christmas album that was perhaps the most beautiful music he had ever made. And in 2001, Mark, the two Bobs and drummer Josh Mancell released a surf album under the name The Wipeouters. (Plastic reality was not dead; the band claimed to have invented the surf sound and recorded these songs when they were Ohio teenagers, and that surfing was a big deal on flat, frigid Lake Erie.)

Devo's periodic live cameos culminated in a series of Lollapalooza dates on the West Coast in 1996, now with Josh Freese on drums. They played the old show, starting in the yellow suits and relying heavily on the early material. Crowds went ape. The members of Devo were approaching 50, but there was a musical vindication, a feeling that the important sound of things falling apart still had relevance. Mark, at the time, called the reunion "healing, especially for the brother sets." A series of Midwest Lollapalooza dates followed in 1997, including a headlining show at Blossom Music Center in Cuyahoga Falls, a stone's throw from Mark and Bob's alma mater, Woodridge High School.

Mark and Jerry sat backstage before that concert at an outdoor picnic table, reminiscing about the old days, about Akron, about the smell of the tire factories and watching *Island of Lost Souls* on TV. By then, Akron had rebounded. The old Bank Nightclub had been torn down and a new minor-league baseball stadium had been built in its place, the centerpiece for a resurgent central city. New restaurants were opening; the Monopoly signs were long gone from the storefronts; and the polymer industry, appropriately synthetic,

206

had replaced the old tire industry as Akron's calling card. The Bizarros and members of Tin Huey, now middle-aged, were working on albums that had been left unfinished. Members of both bands, and the Rubber City Rebels, too, would soon play reunion shows. Pere Ubu was still releasing albums and touring. The Numbers Band, who had never left town, remained a fixture on the club scene 30 years after Jerry had come and gone as the bass player. Downtown Akron was no longer a ramshackle playground for the young. And even though many people thought the place had improved, there was also a message of devolution. The gentrification of Main Street had removed the gritty spirit that had made it so appealing to the young people who took it over when no one else wanted it. It had moved forward by leaving some of its soul behind.

Jerry, as always, recognized the irony in how things had changed. Devo had been heckled and harassed as a local band. And now they were headlining Blossom Music Center, which had once represented a seemingly untouchable aspect of stardom.

"More people are interested now than were then," Jerry said. "They're done beating us up, because we're basically unbeatable at this point. They did it already to us. Everything that could have been done to us has been done to us. And they kind of lift you up off the floor. Now there's a lot of people that have these fond memories of Devo; the very same people that hated us and wouldn't play us on the radio and were trying to keep us off MTV – now they all have these fond stories of Devo."

In the years that followed, there would be a show here and there, an acoustic set as Los Devos, a casual concert to open an Airstream trailer museum with the band dressed as rednecks. Devo was easing into history, still convinced that things could have gone better. There had been lawsuits and the absurdity of the music industry, the crazy screw-ups with John Hinckley Jr. and 3-Devo. Things were always falling apart, and Devo came to understand that in a more profound way than anyone – maybe even Devo – could have predicted.

"The music business is a hard business... and it's a nasty business," Mark said in 2001. "It's absurd, it's wasteful, it's childish, and it makes you feel bad as an artist. People are making big decisions about your life for you, and they shouldn't be. They throw money around... waste your money and lie to you about it."

For all of this, however, there would always be a depth and a purity to this band, even when things got shallow and dirty. Devo started as the soundtrack to something and ended as the soundtrack to something. They were two entirely different somethings, but this was a band brave enough to laugh, regardless of the story. The reason there seems to be a sort of tragedy to their devolution is because they knew it was coming, and because there had been so much behind it. For all the confusions of commerce, Devo was, and will always remain, one of the most well thought-out, most well executed ideas for a rock band ever to find a niche in the mainstream psyche. Despite all the planning, there were lots of accidents along the way, but maybe the biggest accident was that people, briefly, got it. And that they didn't really get it. Devo was one of the most misunderstood bands in rock history and in a way that made their idea richer. Jerry could laugh, as he had done back at Kent State, and that laugh meant there was something bigger going on. Mark could pull on his Booji Boy mask and make the apocalypse seem like a boo-boo. Five skinny guys could step onto a stage and make everything more urgent and more funny and more important than anyone could have expected.

There was a prize in the cereal box. All you had to do was buy the package.

Bibliography

Introduction

INTERVIEWS:
Jerry Casale, interview by Wil Forbis of Acid Logic, 2000;
Jerry Casale, interview by INKnineteen, May 2000;
Jerry Casale, telephone interview by Jade Dellinger, June 11, 2001;
Jerry Casale, interview by Brian L. Knight of *The Vermont Review* (date unknown);
Peter Gregg, posted on the MSN Spudtalk newsgroup, Oct. 29, 2001;
Bob Mothersbaugh, interview by Paul Provenza for checkout.com, 2001;
Mark Mothersbaugh, interview by Michael Hurray, March 12, 1977;
Robert L. Mothersbaugh, Sr., telephone interview by Jade Dellinger, July 26, 2000.
OTHER SOURCES:
Reverend B.H. Shadduck, *Jocko-Homo Heavenbound* (Roger, OH: Jocko-Homo Pub. Co., 1924); Encyclopedia Britannica (online).

Chapter 1

INTERVIEWS:
Robert Bertholf, telephone interview by Jade Dellinger, May 17, 2001;
Jerry Casale, interview by *New Vinyl Times*, v. 1 #11, 1980;
Jerry Casale, interview by Sharisse Zeff of *Upbeat*, August 1980;
Jerry Casale, interview by *Rolling Stone* magazine, 1981;
Jerry Casale, interview by David Giffels, July 18, 1997;
Jerry Casale, interview by INKnineteen, May 2000;
Jerry Casale, telephone interview by Jade Dellinger, June 11, 2001;
Jerry Casale, online audio interview for the Experience Music Project's special exhibition "(Un)common Objects," 2002;
Jerry Casale, interview by Australian 3-PBS 106.7 (date unknown);
Tim DeFrange, e-mail interview by Jade Dellinger, Sept. 10, 2000;
Peter Gregg, posted to Spudtalk newsgroup Oct. 18, 2001;
Peter Gregg, posted to Spudtalk newsgroup, Oct. 19, 2001;
Peter Gregg, posted to Spudtalk newsgroup, Dec. 11, 2001;
Peter Gregg, posted to Spudtalk newsgroup, Feb. 20, 2002;
Bob Lewis, interview by Jade Dellinger, Jan. 8, 2001;
Bob Lewis, e-mail interview by Jade Dellinger, Oct. 5, 2001;
Bob Lewis, e-mail interview by Jade Dellinger, Oct. 12, 2001;
Bob Lewis, e-mail interview, Oct. 16, 2001;
Bob Lewis, e-mail interview, Oct. 17, 2001;
Rod Reisman, telephone interview by Jade Dellinger, Dec. 15, 2000;
David Thomas, posted to www.projex.demon.co.uk/archives/heenan.html (date unknown);
Bobbie Watson, interview by Jade Dellinger, Oct. 15, 2001.

OTHER SOURCES:
Akron Beacon Journal, "Forever Ghoul," Oct. 25, 1998;
DEVO BIO(logical) Report Sheet (from *Shout* membership packet);
Tom Feran and R.D. Heldenfels, *Ghoulardi: Inside Cleveland TV's Wildest Ride* (Cleveland: Gray & Company, 1997);
Steve Love and David Giffels, *Wheels of Fortune: The Story of Rubber in Akron*, (Akron: University of Akron Press, 1998);
Ohio Department of Health records;
Rough Rider, 1966 (Roosevelt High School yearbook).

Chapter 2

INTERVIEWS:
Ed Barger, e-mail interview by Jade Dellinger, Nov. 29, 2001;
Bob Mothersbaugh, interview by *Guitar Player*, July 1981;
Mark Mothersbaugh, interview by Jettlag, Sept. 1980;
Mark Mothersbaugh, Live 105 Modern Rock interview, published in *Spud Magazine*, 1988;
Mark Mothersbaugh, interview by "E.K." for RocknRollreporter.com, 1996;
Mark Mothersbaugh, interview by TalkCity.com, Aug. 26, 1998;
Mark Mothersbaugh, interview by Victoria Reynolds Harrow for Northern Ohio LIVE, March 2000;
Mark Mothersbaugh, interview by Michael Pilmer, April 26, 2001;
Mark Mothersbaugh, interview by Brad Shank for *Music Alive!*, vol. 21, #1, Oct. 2001;
Mark Mothersbaugh, interview by E-Online HotSpot (date unknown);
Mark Mothersbaugh, interview by Diana Fischer for iCAST (date unknown);
Robert Mothersbaugh, Sr., telephone interview by Jade Dellinger, July 26, 2000.
OTHER SOURCES:
Jim Mothersbaugh, address to DEVOtional Fan Convention, Cleveland, 2001 (transcript);
Robert Mothersbaugh, Sr., address to Devo "Day of Atonement" Fan Convention, Cleveland, 2000 (transcript);
Robert Mothersbaugh, Sr., address to DEVOtional Fan Convention, Cleveland, 2001 (transcript);
"Mr. Potato Head," www.yesterdayland.com/popopedia/shows/toys/ty1048.php;
Gary Graff and Daniel Durchholz (eds.), *Music Hound: Rock – The Essential Album Guide*, (Detroit, MI: Visible Ink, 1996);
Booji Boy (a.k.a. Mark Mothersbaugh), *My Struggle*, (Cleveland: NEO Rubber Band, 1978);
Ohio Department of Health records; Oriflame (Woodridge High School yearbook), 1968;
Woodarian (Woodridge High School student newspaper), May 28, 1968.

Chapter 3

INTERVIEWS:
Robert Bertholf, telephone interview by Jade Dellinger, May 17, 2001;
Chris Butler, telephone interview by Jade Dellinger, April 10, 2001;
Jerry Casale, interview by *Search & Destroy #2*, 1977;
Jerry Casale, interview by *Newsweek*, Oct. 30, 1978;
Jerry Casale, interview by *Rolling Stone*, Dec. 10, 1981;
Jerry Casale, interview by Jeff Winner, March 11, 1993;
Jerry Casale, interview by "On Tour" (PBS broadcast – Sunshine TV/KCET-Los Angeles), August 1997; Jerry Casale, interview by David Giffels, April, 2000;
Jerry Casale, interview by Ron Kretsch of the *Cleveland Free Times*, June 14, 2000;
Jerry Casale, interview by Wil Forbis of *Acid Logic*, 2000;
Jerry Casale, telephone interview by Jade Dellinger, June 11, 2001;
Jerry Casale, interview by Brian L. Knight of *The Vermont Review* (date unknown);
Roger Casale, e-mail interview by Jade Dellinger (April 10, 2001);
Gary Jackett, telephone interview by Jade Dellinger, Jan. 18, 2001;
Bob Lewis, interview by Rob Warmowski, (c.1996, Posted

Are We Not Men?

online at http://www.geocities.com/SunsetStrip/8539/
bobL.html);
Bob Lewis, telephone interview by Jade Dellinger, Jan. 8,
2001;
Bob Lewis, e-mail interview by Jade Dellinger, Sept. 30, 2001;
Bob Lewis e-mail interview by Jade Dellinger, Oct. 12, 2001;
Bob Lewis, e-mail interview by Jade Dellinger, Oct. 16, 2001;
Susan Massaro Aylward, e-mail interview by Jade Dellinger,
March 5, 2002;
Bobbie Watson, e-mail interview by Jade Dellinger, Oct. 15,
2001;
Fred Weber, telephone interview by Jade Dellinger, Jan. 24,
2001.

OTHER SOURCES:
Akron Beacon Journal files, 1970; *Akron Beacon Journal*,
April 30, 2000, "Of Loss and Learning;" Edward Dorn, *Way
West: Stories, Essays & Verse Accounts: 1963-1993*
(Santa Rosa, CA: Black Sparrow Press, 1993);
William A. Gordon, *Four Dead in Ohio: Was There a
Conspiracy at Kent State?*, (Laguna Hills, CA: North Ridge
Books, 1995);
*The President's Commission on Campus Unrest Special
Report*, 1970; "Shut it Down!" (newsletter), May 1970.

Chapter 4
INTERVIEWS:
Ed Barger, e-mail interview by Jade Dellinger, Dec. 1, 2001;
Ed Barger, e-mail interview by Jade Dellinger, Dec. 6, 2001;
Ed Barger, e-mail interview by Jade Dellinger, Dec. 7, 2001;
Ed Barger, e-mail interview by Jade Dellinger, Dec. 13, 2001;
Ed Barger, e-mail interview by Jade Dellinger, Dec. 18, 2001;
Chris Butler telephone interview by Jade Dellinger, April 19,
2001;
Jerry Casale, telephone interview by Jade Dellinger, June 11,
2001;
Peter Gregg, posted to Spudtalk newsgroup, Dec. 10, 2001;
Peter Gregg, posted to Spudtalk newsgroup, Dec. 11, 2001;
Bruce Hensal, telephone interview by Jade Dellinger, June 18,
2001;
Gary Jackett, telephone interview by Jade Dellinger, Jan. 18,
2001;
Bob Lewis, telephone interview by Jade Dellinger, Jan. 8,
2001;
Bob Lewis, e-mail interview by Jade Dellinger, Sept. 26, 2001;
Bob Lewis, e-mail interview by Jade Dellinger, Sept. 27, 2001;
Bob Lewis, e-mail interview by Jade Dellinger, Sept. 28, 2001;
Bob Lewis, e-mail interview by Jade Dellinger, Oct. 5, 2001;
Bob Lewis, e-mail interview by Jade Dellinger, Oct. 12, 2001;
Bob Lewis, e-mail interview by Jade Dellinger, April 1, 2002;
Bob Lewis, e-mail interview by Jade Dellinger, April 3, 2002;
Bob Lewis, e-mail interview by Jade Dellinger, April 10, 2002;
Jennifer Licitri, telephone interview by Jade Dellinger, Oct. 18,
2001;
Dale McGough, telephone interview by David Giffels, Oct. 13,
2002;
Mark Mothersbaugh, interview by *Search & Destroy* #7
(1978);
Mark Mothersbaugh interview by Diana Fischer for icast.com
(date unknown);
Martin Reymann, telephone interview by Jade Dellinger, Nov.
7, 2001;
Rod Reisman, telephone interview by Jade Dellinger, Dec. 15,
2000;
Bobbie Watson, e-mail interview by Jade Dellinger, Sept. 25,
2001;
Bobbie Watson, e-mail interview by Jade Dellinger, Sept. 27,
2001;
Fred Weber, telephone interview by Jade Dellinger, Jan. 24,
2001.

OTHER SOURCES:
Adventure Comics #416, which re-printed the *Golden Age
March-April 1948 Wonder Woman* (issue #28);
Akron Beacon Journal, May 23, 1971, "City Charges
Obscenity in Films;" *Akron Beacon Journal,* Sept. 8, 1971,
"'School For Sex' Is Closed;"
Akron Beacon Journal, Sept. 15, 1971, "Charged With
Showing Obscene Film;"
Akron Beacon Journal, Feb. 25, 1976, "2 businesses hit by
robbers;"
Akron Beacon Journal, April 17, 1976, "Coventry man
indicted in Greenlese slaying;"
Akron Beacon Journal, May 10, 1976, "Evidence illegal,
case halts;"
Akron Beacon Journal, March 1, 1978, Akron police hold
suspects in N.M. robbery, slaying;"
Akron Beacon Journal, March 11, 1978, "Fistfight puts jail
inmate in city hospital;"
Mark Mothersbaugh, *The sad story of a very dead man ...
My Struggle, or life in the Rubber City* (manuscript);
Barbara Jo (Bobbie) Watson deposition taken on June 15,
1979 in the U.S. District Court Northern District of Ohio
Eastern Division case between Robert Lewis, Plaintiff –vs–
Gerald V. Casale, et al, Defendants;
Youngstown Vindicator, November 12, 1971, "Speeding Auto
Leaves Bodies Strewn on W. Federal."

Chapter 5
INTERVIEWS:
Ed Barger, e-mail interview by Jade Dellinger, Dec. 13, 2001;
Jerry Casale, interview by Jeff Winner, March 11, 1993;
Jerry Casale, telephone interview by Jade Dellinger, June 11,
2001;
Gary Jackett, telephone interview by Jade Dellinger via
telephone, Jan. 18, 2001;
Bob Lewis, interview by Rob Warmowski, (c.1996, Posted
online at http://www.geocities.com/SunsetStrip/8539/
bobL.html);
Bob Lewis, e-mail interview by Jade Dellinger, Sept. 26, 2001;
Bob Lewis, e-mail interview by Jade Dellinger, Oct. 17, 2001;
Susan Massaro Aylward, e-mail interview by Jade Dellinger,
Sept. 28, 2001;
Susan Massaro Aylward, e-mail interview by Jade Dellinger,
March 5, 2002;
Bobbie Watson, e-mail interview by Jade Dellinger, Sept. 25,
2001.

OTHER SOURCES:
Devo Rap Sheet (ca. 1976 press release); Eric Mottram, "Left
for California: the slow awakening," Sixpack 5 (London &
Lake Toxaway, NC, 1973);
The Staff 2 (Hollywood, CA, July 14, 1972) in the Collection of
the Eric Mottram Archives at King's College London, UK.

Chapter 6
INTERVIEWS:
Jerry Casale, telephone interview by Jade Dellinger, June 11,
2001;
Jerry Casale, interview by Brian L. Knight for *The Vermont
Review* (date unknown);
Patrick Cullie, e-mail interview by Jade Dellinger, April 8,
2002;
Gary Jackett, telephone interview by Jade Dellinger, Jan. 18,
2001;
Gary Jackett, telephone interview by Jade Dellinger, Feb. 2,
2001;
Tim Maglione, e-mail interview by Jade Dellinger, Aug. 15,
2000;
Mark Mothersbaugh, interview by Victoria Reynolds Harrow
for *Northern Ohio Live*, March 2000;
Mark Mothersbaugh, interview by Marshall Thomas for BBC

Rock Hour (date unknown);
Rod Reisman, telephone interview by Jade Dellinger, Dec. 15, 2000.
OTHER SOURCES:
Headley Gritter, *Rock-N-Roll Asylum* (New York, N.Y.: Delilah Books, 1984);
numbersband.com (band history of 15-60-75);
Shelly's magazine, (Kent, Ohio, Spring 1975).

Chapter 7
INTERVIEWS:
Robert Bertholf, telephone interview by Jade Dellinger, May 17, 2001;
Jerry Casale, telephone interview by Jade Dellinger, June 11, 2001;
Bob Lewis, telephone interview by Jade Dellinger, Jan. 8, 2001;
Bob Lewis, e-mail interview by Jade Dellinger, Sept. 30, 2001;
Bob Lewis, e-mail interview by Jade Dellinger, April 11, 2002;
Rod Reisman, telephone interview by Jade Dellinger, Dec. 15, 2000;
Marty Reymann, telephone interview by Jade Dellinger, Nov. 7, 2001;
Fred Weber, telephone interview by Jade Dellinger, Jan. 24, 2001.
OTHER SOURCES:
Robert Bertholf, deposition taken on June 14, 1979 in the U.S. District Court Northern District of Ohio Eastern Division case between Robert Lewis, Plaintiff –vs- Gerald V. Casale, et al, Defendants;
Booji Boy (a.k.a. Mark Mothersbaugh), *My Struggle*, (Cleveland: NEO Rubber Band, 1978);
The Daily Kent Stater, April 23, 1974; Devo, *The Complete Truth About De-evolution* (Voyager laserdisc 1993);
Edward Dorn, *Recollections of Gran Apacheria* (San Francisco, CA: Turtle Island, 1974);
Edward Dorn, *Way West: Stories, Essays & Verse Accounts: 1963-1993* (Santa Rosa, CA: Black Sparrow Press, 1993);
Chuck Klosterman, *Fargo Rock City: A Heavy Metal Odyssey in Rural North Dakota* (NY: Scribner, 2001);
Bob Lewis, letter to Ed & Jennifer Dorn, ca. 1974;
Mashin' Potatoes (compact disc), Beat Happy! Music, (date unknown);
Barbara Jo (Bobbie) Watson deposition taken on June 15, 1979 in the U.S. District Court Northern District of Ohio Eastern Division case between Robert Lewis, Plaintiff –vs- Gerald V. Casale, et al, Defendants.

Chapter 8
INTERVIEWS:
Jerry Casale, interview by Wil Forbis for Acid Logic, 2000;
Jerry Casale, interview by Donna Kossy for Puncture, 1995;
Jerry Casale, telephone interview by Jade Dellinger, Feb. 19, 2001;
Jerry Casale, telephone interview by Jade Dellinger, June 11, 2001;
Jerry Casale, 1978 telex sent to a (unknown) UK music magazine;
Devo (unidentified member), interview by Warner Brothers CyberTalk, Aug. 19, 1996;
Don Harvey, e-mail interview by David Giffels, June 26, 2002;
Bob Lewis, telephone interview by Jade Dellinger, Jan. 8, 2001;
Bob Lewis, e-mail interview by Jade Dellinger, Sept. 30, 2001.
OTHER SOURCES:
Akron city directory, 1974;
Oscar Kiss Maerth (trans. by Judith Hayward), *The Beginning Was the End: How Man Came into Being through Cannibalism – Intelligence Can Be Eaten* (NY:

Praeger Publishers, 1974);
Robert Bertholf, December 7, 1973 letter to Ed & Jennie Dorn;
The Daily Kent Stater, Apr. 23, 1974;
Reverend B.H. Shadduck, *Jocko-Homo Heavenbound* (Roger, OH: Jocko-Homo Pub. Co., 1924);
Bob Lewis, July 13, 1974 (postmark) letter to Ed & Jenny Dorn;
Jim Mothersbaugh, address to DEVOtional Fan Convention, Cleveland, 2001 (transcript);
Booji Boy (a.k.a. Mark Mothersbaugh), *My Struggle*, (Cleveland: NEO Rubber Band, 1978);
Donna Kossy, *Strange Creations: Aberrant Ideas of Human Origins from Ancient Astronauts to Aquatic Apes* (Los Angeles: Feral House, 2001);
Time Magazine, June 24, 1974.

Chapter 9
INTERVIEWS:
Ed Barger, e-mail interview by Jade Dellinger, Dec. 1, 2001;
Ed Barger, e-mail interview by Jade Dellinger, Dec. 4, 2001;
Jerry Casale, interview by David Giffels, July 18, 1997;
Jerry Casale, telephone interview by Jade Dellinger, June 11, 2001;
Patrick Cullie, e-mail interview by Jade Dellinger, April 8, 2002;
Patrick Cullie, e-mail interview by Jade Dellinger, April 10, 2002;
Peter Gregg, posted on the MSN Spudtalk newsgroup, Oct. 20, 2001;
Bruce Hensal, telephone interview by Jade Dellinger, June 18, 2001;
Gary Jackett, telephone interview by Jade Dellinger, Jan. 18, 2001;
Bob Lewis, telephone interview by Jade Dellinger, Jan. 8, 2001;
Bob Lewis, e-mail interview by Jade Dellinger, Sept. 27, 2001;
Bob Lewis, e-mail interview by Jade Dellinger, Sept. 28, 2001;
Bob Lewis, e-mail interview by Jade Dellinger, Oct. 5, 2001;
Bob Lewis, e-mail interview by Jade Dellinger, Oct. 11, 2001;
Bob Lewis, e-mail interview by Jade Dellinger, Oct. 21, 2001;
Mark Mothersbaugh, interview by David Giffels, July 18, 1997;
Mark Mothersbaugh, interview on E-Online HotSpot, (date unknown);
Jim Mothersbaugh, interview by David Giffels, Sept. 4, 2002;
Robert Mothersbaugh, Sr., telephone interview by Jade Dellinger, July 26, 2000;
Martin Reymann, telephone interview by Jade Dellinger via telephone, Nov. 11, 2001.
OTHER SOURCES:
Robert Bertholf, deposition taken on June 14, 1979 in the U.S. District Court Northern District of Ohio Eastern Division case between Robert Lewis, Plaintiff –vs- Gerald V. Casale, et al, Defendants;
Chestnut Burr (Kent State yearbook), 1975;
DEVO RAP SHEET (ca. 1976);
DEVO: The Complete Truth About De-Evolution (laserdisc), Voyager, 1993;
Island of Lost Souls (videocassette), MCA Home Video, 1993 (original release: Paramount Productions, 1932);
Bob Lewis, letters, ca.1974 to Ed & Jenny Dorn;
Jim Mothersbaugh, address to DEVOtional Fan Convention, Cleveland, 2001 (transcript);
Robert Mothersbaugh, address to DEVOtional Fan Convention, Cleveland, 2001 (transcript);
Booji Boy (a.k.a. Mark Mothersbaugh), *My Struggle*, (Cleveland: NEO Rubber Band, 1978);
Shelly's magazine, (Kent, Ohio, October, 1974);
Barbara Jo (Bobbie) Watson deposition taken on June 15, 1979 in the U.S. District Court Northern District of Ohio

Are We Not Men?

Eastern Division case between Robert Lewis, Plaintiff –vs-
Gerald V. Casale, et al, Defendants.

Chapter 10
INTERVIEWS:
Ed Barger, e-mail interview by Jade Dellinger, Dec. 4, 2001;
Ed Barger, e-mail interview by Jade Dellinger, Dec. 7, 2001;
Ed Barger, e-mail interview by Jade Dellinger, Dec. 8, 2001;
Ed Barger, e-mail interview by Jade Dellinger, Dec. 9, 2001;
Ed Barger, e-mail interview by Jade Dellinger, Dec. 18, 2001;
Jerry Casale, interview by Jeff Winner, March 11, 1993;
Jerry Casale, telephone interview by Jade Dellinger, June 11, 2001;
Gary Jackett, telephone interview by Jade Dellinger, Jan. 18, 2001;
Bob Lewis, e-mail interview by Jade Dellinger, Sept. 27, 2001;
Bob Lewis, e-mail interview by Jade Dellinger, Oct. 12, 2001;
Bob Lewis, e-mail interview by Jade Dellinger, Oct. 17, 2001;
Jennifer Licitri, telephone interview by Jade Dellinger, Oct. 18, 2001;
Bob Mothersbaugh, interview by Paul Provenza for checkout.com, 2001;
Mark Mothersbaugh, interview by Ampersand, Oct. 1981;
Mark Mothersbaugh, interview by Diana Fischer for icast.com, (date unknown);
Martin Reymann, telephone interview by Jade Dellinger, Nov. 7, 2001;
Bobbie Watson, e-mail interview by Jade Dellinger, Sept. 27, 2001;
Bobbie Watson, e-mail interview by Jade Dellinger, Sept. 28, 2001.
OTHER SOURCES:
Akron Beacon Journal files (Mark Mothersbaugh photo file);
Akron Beacon Journal, "Chris Meets Artist Max: Lesson Was Beyond His Wildest Hopes," Nov. 11, 1971;
Akron Beacon Journal, "Is Art Lost In Akron?" Aug. 27, 1973;
Akron Beacon Journal, "Artist Making His Stamp By Updating Past's Images, Feb. 2, 1975;
Akron city directory, 1975;
Bob Lewis, ca. 1974 letter to Ed Dorn;
Bob Lewis, Jan. 17, 1975 (postmark) letter to Ed and Jenny Dorn;
Robert Mothersbaugh, address to DEVOtional Fan Convention, Cleveland, 2001 (transcript);
Booji Boy (a.k.a. Mark Mothersbaugh), *My Struggle*, (Cleveland: NEO Rubber Band, 1978);
Shelly's magazine, (Kent, Ohio, April/May 1975).

Chapter 11
INTERVIEWS:
Ed Barger, e-mail interview by Jade Dellinger, Nov. 29, 2001;
Jerry Casale, interview by *New Musical Express*, March 18, 1978;
Jerry Casale, interview by Jim Infirmary for *New York Rocker*, July 1977 (published July/August 1978);
Jerry Casale, interview by Jeff Winner; March 11, 1993;
Jerry Casale, telephone interview by Jade Dellinger, June 11, 2001;
Patrick Cullie, e-mail interview by Jade Dellinger, April 8, 2002;
Patrick Cullie, e-mail interview by Jade Dellinger, April 10, 2002;
Peter Gregg, posted on the MSN Spudtalk newsgroup, Oct. 29, 2001;
Bruce Hensal, telephone interview by Jade Dellinger, June 18, 2001;
Gary Jackett, telephone interview by Jade Dellinger, Jan. 18, 2001;
Bob Lewis, e-mail interview by Jade Dellinger, Oct. 11, 2001;
Bob Lewis, e-mail interview by Jade Dellinger, Oct. 12, 2001;

Bob Lewis, e-mail interview by Jade Dellinger, April 1, 2002;
Mark Mothersbaugh, interview by *Search & Destroy #7*, 1978;
Mark Mothersbaugh, interview for IRC/Apple Computer, Inc. online chat at Sundance Film Festival, Jan. 25, 1996;
Mark Mothersbaugh, interview by Michael Pilmer (date unknown).
OTHER SOURCES: Robert Bertholf, deposition taken on June 14, 1979 in the U.S. District Court Northern District of Ohio Eastern Division case between Robert Lewis, Plaintiff –vs- Gerald V. Casale, et al, Defendants;
Bob Lewis, Jan. 17, 1975 letter to Ed and Jennifer Dorn;
Bob Lewis, undated letter (c.1975) to Ed Dorn.

Chapter 12
INTERVIEWS:
Ed Barger, e-mail interview by Jade Dellinger, Dec. 1, 2001;
Ed Barger, e-mail interview by Jade Dellinger, Dec. 13, 2001;
Stiv Bators, interview by Larry Wichman for *Velvet* Magazine (date unknown);
Jerry Casale, interview by *Search & Destroy (#2)*, 1977;
Jerry Casale, interview by *Trouser Press*, Sept. 1979;
Jerry Casale, telephone interview by Jade Dellinger; June 11, 2001;
Gary Jackett, telephone interview by Jade Dellinger, Jan. 18, 2001;
Gary Jackett, telephone interview by Jade Dellinger, Feb. 2, 2001;
Bob Lewis, e-mail interview by Jade Dellinger, Sept. 26, 2001;
Jennifer Licitri, telephone interview by Jade Dellinger, Oct. 18, 2001;
Susan Massaro Aylward, e-mail interview by Jade Dellinger, Sept. 28, 2001;
Jim Mothersbaugh, interview by David Giffels, Sept. 4, 2002;
Mark Mothersbaugh, interview by *Trouser Press*, Sept. 1979;
Mark Mothersbaugh, interview by Michael Shore of *OMNI*, 1982;
Mark Mothersbaugh, interview by Joe Garden for *The Onion*, July 10, 1997;
Mark Mothersbaugh, interview by *Seconds* Magazine, 2000;
Martin Reymann, telephone interview by Jade Dellinger, Nov. 7, 2001.
OTHER SOURCES:
Akron Beacon Journal, Feb. 25, 1976, "2 businesses hit by robbers;"
Akron Beacon Journal, April 17, 1976, "Coventry man indicted in Greenlese slaying;"
Akron Beacon Journal, May 10, 1976, "Evidence illegal, case halts;"
Akron Beacon Journal, March 1, 1978, Akron police hold suspects in N.M. robbery, slaying;"
Akron Beacon Journal, March 11, 1978, "Fistfight puts jail inmate in city hospital;"
Pascal Bussy, *Kraftwerk: Man, Machine and Music* (Wembley, Middx., England: SAF Publishing, Ltd., 1993);
Jerry Casale, liner notes for *DEVO Live: The Mongoloid Years* (compact disc), Rykodisc, 1992;
Charlotte Pressler, CLE magazine, No. 1; CLE magazine 3A;
DEVO Live: The Mongoloid Years (compact disc), Rykodisc, 1992;
Clinton Heylin, *From the Velvets to the Voidoids: A Pre-Punk History for a Post-Punk World* (NY: Penguin Books, 1993);
Susan Massaro (Aylward), deposition taken on June 15, 1979 in the U.S. District Court Northern District of Ohio Eastern Division case between Robert Lewis, Plaintiff –vs- Gerald V. Casale, et al, Defendants;
Jim Mothersbaugh, address to DEVOtional Fan Convention, Cleveland, 2001 (transcript).

Chapter 13
INTERVIEWS:
Jerry Casale, interview by Rock Video Magazine, June 1984;
Jerry Casale, interview by Sammy Larson, 1993;
Jerry Casale, telephone interview by Jade Dellinger, June 11, 2001;
Gary Jackett, telephone interview by Jade Dellinger, Jan. 18, 2001;
Bob Lewis, interview by Rob Warmowski, (c.1996, Posted online at http://www.geocities.com/SunsetStrip/8539/bobL.html);
Jennifer Licitri, telephone interview by Jade Dellinger, Oct. 18, 2001;
Susan Massaro Aylward, e-mail interview by Jade Dellinger, Sept. 17, 2001;
Susan Massaro Aylward, e-mail interview by Jade Dellinger, Sept. 20, 2001;
Susan Massaro Aylward, e-mail interview by Jade Dellinger, Sept. 21, 2001;
Susan Massaro Aylward via e-mail interview by Jade Dellinger, Sept. 24, 2001;
Jim Mothersbaugh, interview by Victoria Reynolds Harrow for Northern Ohio LIVE, March 2000;
Mark Mothersbaugh, interview by Tim Pedersen for Roland Users Group, 1997;
Mark Mothersbaugh, interview by Diana Fischer for icast.com;
Robert Mothersbaugh, Sr., telephone interview by Jade Dellinger, July 26, 2000;
Debbie Smith, telephone interview by Jade Dellinger, April 11, 2001;
Bobbie Watson, e-mail interview by Jade Dellinger, Sept. 26, 2001;
Bobbie Watson, e-mail interview by Jade Dellinger, Sept. 27, 2001.
OTHER SOURCES:
Devo, *Hardcore Volume 1: '74-'77* (compact disc), Rykodisc, 1990;
Bob Lewis, Apr. 9, 1976 (postmark) postcard to Ed and Jenny Dorn;
Susan Massaro (Aylward), deposition taken on June 15, 1979 in the U.S. District Court Northern District of Ohio Eastern Division case between Robert Lewis, Plaintiff –vs- Gerald V. Casale, et al, Defendants;
Reverend B.H. Shadduck, *Jocko-Homo Heavenbound* (Roger, OH: Jocko-Homo Pub. Co., 1924);
DEVO: The Complete Truth About De-Evolution, Voyager laserdisc, 1993;
Barbara Jo (Bobbie) Watson deposition taken on June 15, 1979 in the U.S. District Court Northern District of Ohio Eastern Division case between Robert Lewis, Plaintiff –vs- Gerald V. Casale, et al, Defendants.

Chapter 14
INTERVIEWS:
Ed Barger, e-mail interview by Jade Dellinger, Dec. 1, 2001;
Chris Butler, telephone interview by Jade Dellinger, April 10, 2001;
Ralph Carney, e-mail interview by Jade Dellinger, July 20, 2000;
Ralph Carney, e-mail interview by Jade Dellinger, July 24, 2000;
Ralph Carney, e-mail interview by Jade Dellinger, Jan. 26, 2001;
Jerry Casale, July 1977 interview by Jim Infirmary for *New York Rocker*, published July/August 1978;
Jerry Casale, Australian newspaper article, 1980 (clipping - specifics unknown);
Jerry Casale, telephone interview by Jade Dellinger, June 11, 2001;
Harvey Gold, interview by David Giffels, Sept. 3, 2002;

Bob Lewis, telephone interview by Jade Dellinger, Jan. 8, 2001;
Bob Lewis, e-mail interview by Jade Dellinger, Oct. 17, 2001;
Susan Massaro Aylward, e-mail interview by Jade Dellinger, Sept. 17, 2001;
Susan Massaro Aylward, e-mail interview by Jade Dellinger, Sept. 20, 2001;
Mark Mothersbaugh, Australian newspaper article, 1981 (clipping - specifics unknown);
Alan Myers, telephone interview by Jade Dellinger, Jan. 24, 2001.
OTHER SOURCES:
Headley Gritter, *Rock-n-Roll Asylum* (New York, N.Y.: Delilah Books, 1984);
Frank Zappa & The Mothers of Invention, *Freak Out!*, (1966, Verve LP).

Chapter 15
INTERVIEWS:
Ed Barger, e-mail interview by Jade Dellinger, Dec. 4, 2001;
Ed Barger, e-mail interview by Jade Dellinger, Dec. 6, 2001;
Rod Firestone (a.k.a. Ward Welch), e-mail interview by Jade Dellinger, Dec. 7, 2000;
Rod Firestone, interview by David Giffels, June 2001;
Susan Schmidt Horning, e-mail interview by Jade Dellinger, Nov. 9, 2001;
Gary Jackett, telephone interview by Jade Dellinger, Jan. 18, 2001;
Scott Krauss, interview by Colin McFrangos, (date unknown);
Susan Massaro Aylward, e-mail interview by Jade Dellinger, Sept. 28, 2001;
Mark Mothersbaugh, interview by Michael Pilmer, April 26, 2001;
Nick Nicholis, interview by David Giffels, June 1999;
David Thomas, e-mail interview by Jade Dellinger, July 4, 2002;
Bobbie Watson, e-mail interview by Jade Dellinger, Sept. 27, 2001.
OTHER SOURCES:
Jerry Casale, liner notes for *DEVO Live: The Mongoloid Years* (compact disc), Rykodisc, 1992;
Devo, *Hardcore Volume 1: '74-'77* (compact disc), Rykodisc, 1990;
Clinton Heylin, *From the Velvets to the Voidoids: A Pre-Punk History for a Post-Punk World* (NY: Penguin Books, 1993);
Scene magazine (Cleveland), Dec. 9th,1976; *Scene* magazine (Cleveland), Jan. 27, 1977;
Steve Love and David Giffels, *Wheels of Fortune: The Story of Rubber in Akron*, (Akron: University of Akron Press, 1998).

Chapter 16
INTERVIEWS:
Stiv Bators, interview by Search & Destroy #4, 1977;
Jerry Casale, July 1977 interview by Jim Infirmary for *New York Rocker*, published July/August 1978;
Jerry Casale, interview by Donna Kossy for *Puncture*, 1995;
Cheetah Chrome e-mail interview by Jade Dellinger, May 21, 2002;
DEVO (unidentified member) describes it to *Search & Destroy (#3)* in 1977;
Susan Schmidt Horning, e-mail interview by Jade Dellinger, Nov. 9, 2001;
Alan Horvath, e-mail interview by Jade Dellinger, Feb. 19, 2002;
Gary Jackett, telephone interview by Jade Dellinger, Feb. 2, 2001;
Bob Lewis, e-mail interview by Jade Dellinger, Sept. 26, 2001;
Bob Lewis, e-mail interview by Jade Dellinger, Feb. 19, 2002;

Are We Not Men?

Bob Lewis, undated interview by Jade Dellinger;
Jennifer Licitri, telephone interview by Jade Dellinger, Oct. 18, 2001;
Susan Massaro Aylward, e-mail interview by Jade Dellinger, Sept. 20, 2001;
Mark Mothersbaugh, interview by Michael Hurray for *Heavy Metal*, March 12, 1977;
Mark Mothersbaugh, interview by Joe Garden for *The Onion*, July 10, 1997;
Mark Mothersbaugh, interview by Tim Pedersen for Roland Users Group, 1997;
Mark Mothersbaugh, interview by *Seconds Magazine*, issue 5001, 2000;
Marty Reymann, telephone interview by Jade Dellinger, Nov. 7, 2001;
Debbie Smith, telephone interview by Jade Dellinger, April 11, 2001;
Bobbie Watson, e-mail interview by Jade Dellinger, Sept. 28, 2001.
OTHER SOURCES:
Booji Boy (a.k.a. Mark Mothersbaugh), *My Struggle*, (Cleveland: NEO Rubber Band, 1978);
DEVO Live: The Mongoloid Years (compact disc), Rykodisc, 1992;
Clinton Heylin, *From the Velvets to the Voidoids: A Pre-Punk History for a Post-Punk World* (NY: Penguin Books, 1993);
"rjs," March 2002 postcard;
"rjs," April 25, 2002 postcard;
Scene magazine files;
Scene magazine, April 14, 1977;
Barbara Jo (Bobbie) Watson deposition taken on June 15, 1979 in the U.S. District Court Northern District of Ohio Eastern Division case between Robert Lewis, Plaintiff –vs–Gerald V. Casale, et al, Defendants;
WKDD-Radio Rap Sheet, Dec. 1976.

Chapter 17
INTERVIEWS:
Jerry Casale, interview by INKnineteen, May 2000;
Jerry Casale, telephone interview by Jade Dellinger, June 11, 2001;
Devo (unidentified member), interview by *Search & Destroy* #2, 1977;
Cheetah Chrome, e-mail interview by Jade Dellinger, May 21, 2002;
Gary Jackett, telephone interview by Jade Dellinger, Feb. 2, 2001;
Susan Massaro Aylward, e-mail interview by Jade Dellinger, Sept. 17, 2001;
Mark Mothersbaugh, interview by *Search & Destroy* #7, 1978;
Mark Mothersbaugh, interview by Jere Chandler for *REWIND* (formerly *For the Record*), 1997;
Alan Myers, telephone interview by Jade Dellinger, Jan. 24, 2001.
OTHER SOURCES:
Debbie Harry and Chris Stein (ed. Victor Bockris), *Making Tracks: The Rise of Blondie* (London: Elm Tree Books, 1982);
New York Rocker, July/August, 1978.

Chapter 18
INTERVIEWS:
Ed Barger, e-mail interview by Jade Dellinger, Sept. 26, 2001;
Jerry Casale, interview by Paul Freeman for cnn.com, May 23, 2000;
Jerry Casale, telephone interview by Jade Dellinger, Feb. 19, 2001;
Gary Jackett, telephone interview by Jade Dellinger, Jan. 18,

2001;
Susan Massaro Aylward, e-mail interview by Jade Dellinger, Oct. 10, 2001;
Susan Massaro Aylward, e-mail interview by Jade Dellinger, Oct. 11, 2001;
Bob Mothersbaugh, interview by Paul Provenza for checkout.com, 2001;
Mark Mothersbaugh, July 1977 interview by Jim Infirmary for *New York Rocker*, published July/August 1978;
Mark Mothersbaugh, interview by Music World On-Line, (date unknown);
Sonny Vincent, e-mail interview by Jade Dellinger, Oct. 5, 2002;
Bobbie Watson, e-mail interview by Jade Dellinger, Oct. 1, 2001.
OTHER SOURCES:
DEVO Live: The Mongoloid Years (compact disc), Rykodisc, 1992.

Chapter 19
INTERVIEWS:
Ed Barger, e-mail interview by Jade Dellinger, Dec. 8, 2001;
Ed Barger, e-mail interview by Jade Dellinger, Dec. 9, 2001;
Ed Barger, e-mail interview by Jade Dellinger, Dec. 13, 2001;
Jerry Casale, July 1977 interview by Jim Infirmary for *New York Rocker*, published July/August 1978;
Jerry Casale, interview by INKnineteen, May 2000;
Jerry Casale, telephone interview by Jade Dellinger, June 11, 2001;
Bob Lewis, e-mail interview by Jade Dellinger, Sept. 26, 2001;
Bob Lewis, e-mail interview by Jade Dellinger, Sept. 28, 2001;
Susan Massaro Aylward, e-mail interview by Jade Dellinger, Oct. 11, 2001;
Mark Mothersbaugh, interview by Joe Gardner for *The Onion*, 1997;
Mark Mothersbaugh, interview by Jere Chandler for *REWIND* (formerly *For the Record*), 1997;
Mark Mothersbaugh, interview by Tim Pedersen for Roland Users Group, 1997;
Mark Mothersbaugh interview by Diana Fischer for icast.com, (date unknown);
Nick Nicholis, interview by David Giffels, June 1999.
OTHER SOURCES:
Robert Edward Casale, deposition taken on April 3, 1979 in the U.S. District Court Northern District of Ohio Eastern Division case between Robert Lewis, Plaintiff –vs- Gerald V. Casale, et al, Defendants and the U.S. District Court Central District of California case between Gerald Casale, Robert Casale, Robert Mothersbaugh, Mark Mothersbaugh, Alan Myers and Devo, Inc., a corporation, Plaintiffs – vs- Robert Lewis, Defendant;
Clinton Heylin, *From the Velvets to the Voidoids: A Pre-Punk History for a Post-Punk World* (NY: Penguin Books, 1993);
Hilly Krystal, CBGB's history on cbgb.com;
New York Rocker, July/August 1978; Patricia Romanowski and Holly George-Warren (eds.),
The New Rolling Stone Encyclopedia of Rock & Roll (NY: Fireside, 1995);
Barbara Jo (Bobbie) Watson deposition taken on June 15, 1979 in the U.S. District Court Northern District of Ohio Eastern Division case between Robert Lewis, Plaintiff –vs-Gerald V. Casale, et al, Defendants.

Chapter 20
INTERVIEWS:
Ed Barger, e-mail interview by Jade Dellinger, Dec. 4, 2001;
Ed Barger, e-mail interview by Jade Dellinger, Dec. 7, 2001;
Ed Barger, e-mail interview by Jade Dellinger, Dec. 8, 2001;
Ed Barger, e-mail interview by Jade Dellinger, Dec. 9, 2001;

Ed Barger, e-mail interview by Jade Dellinger, April 30, 2002;
Jerry Casale, telephone interview by Jade Dellinger, June 11, 2001;
Devo, uncredited transcript of ca. 1978 interview by "Puddie and Liz," found in the files of Festival East Concerts, Inc. in Buffalo;
Brian Eno, interview by Caroline Coon for *RITZ*, ca. 1977;
Brian Eno, interview by Roman Kozak for unknown publication (article titled "Math Qualities of Music Interest Eno"), ca.1978;
Brian Eno, interview by Stanley Mieses for unknown UK publication, (article titled "Eno, before and after"), ca.1977;
Gary Jackett telephone interview by Jade Dellinger, Feb. 2, 2001;
Bob Lewis, e-mail interview by Jade Dellinger, Sept. 28, 2001;
Susan Massaro Aylward, e-mail interview by Jade Dellinger, Oct. 10, 2001;
Susan Massaro Aylward, e-mail interview by Jade Dellinger, Oct. 11, 2001;
Mark Mothersbaugh, interview by Jere Chandler for *REWIND* (formerly *For the Record*), 1997;
Tim Story, e-mail interview by Jade Dellinger, Oct. 11, 2001;
Bobbie Watson, e-mail interview by Jade Dellinger, Sept. 27, 2001.
OTHER SOURCES:
David Bowman, *This Must Be the Place: The Adventures of Talking Heads in the 20th Century* (NY: HarperCollins, 2001);
Jimmy McDonough, *Shakey: Neil Young's Biography* (NY: Random House, 2002);
Scene magazine, Feb. 23, 1978;
James Stark, *PUNK '77 : An Inside Look at the San Francisco Rock n' Roll Scene, 1977* (San Francisco, CA: Stark Grafix, 1992);
Barbara Jo (Bobbie) Watson deposition taken on June 15, 1979 in the U.S. District Court Northern District of Ohio Eastern Division case between Robert Lewis, Plaintiff –vs- Gerald V. Casale, et al, Defendants.

Chapter 21
INTERVIEWS:
Bob Lewis, interview by Rob Warmowski, (c.1996, Posted online at http://www.geocities.com/SunsetStrip/8539/bobL.html);
Robert L. Mothersbaugh, Sr. telephone interview by Jade Dellinger, July 26, 2000;
Debbie Smith, telephone interview by Jade Dellinger, April 11, 2001;
Susan Massaro Aylward, e-mail interview by Jade Dellinger, Sept. 20, 2000;
Mark Mothersbaugh, interview by Michael Pilmer, April 26, 2001;
Bobbie Watson, e-mail interview by Jade Dellinger, Sept. 27, 2001.
OTHER SOURCES:
Akron Beacon Journal, "The story of the century," Dec. 31, 1999;
Canyon Cinema, Inc, marketing materials for "Mongoloid," 1978;
Jerry Casale, "Drooling For Dollars," from the laserdisc *DEVO: The Complete Truth About De-Evolution*, Voyager, 1993. New York Rocker, July/August 1978;
Photographed copy of Devo's chart comparing record deals.

Chapter 22
INTERVIEWS:
Ed Barger, e-mail interview by Jade Dellinger, Dec. 8, 2001;
Jerry Casale, interview by *Toast* Magazine, May 2, 2000;
Holger Czukay, e-mail interview by Jade Dellinger, Aug. 28, 2002;

Brian Eno, interview by Caroline Coon for *RITZ*, ca. 1977;
Brian Eno, interview by Roman Kozak for unknown publication (article titled "Math Qualities of Music Interest Eno"), ca.1978;
Brian Eno, interview by Stanley Mieses for unknown UK publication, (article titled "Eno, before and after"), ca.1977;
Brian Eno, interview by Andy Gill for *Mojo*, June 1995;
Bob Lewis, e-mail interview by Jade Dellinger, Sept. 28, 2001;
Jennifer Licitri, telephone interview by Jade Dellinger, Oct. 18, 2001;
Mark Mothersbaugh, interview by David Giffels, August, 1996;
Mark Mothersbaugh, interview by *The Onion*, July 10, 1997;
Mark Mothersbaugh, interview by Jere Chandler for *REWIND* (formerly *For the Record*), 1997;
Mark Mothersbaugh, interview by Adam Gnade for *Mean Street*, May 2000;
Mark Mothersbaugh, interview by Michael Pilmer, April 26, 2001;
Mark Mothersbaugh, interview by Music World On-Line, (date unknown).
OTHER SOURCES:
Jerry Casale, "Drooling For Dollars," from the laserdisc *DEVO: The Complete Truth About De-Evolution*, Voyager, 1993;
Devo's original notes for first three albums (Collection of Debbie Smith, Akron, Ohio);
Paul Krassner, *Pot Stories for the Soul*, (N.Y.: High Times, 1999);
Mark Mothersbaugh, address at the University of South Florida Contemporary Art Museum in conjunction with "Art in the News" (an art project for The Tampa Tribune, Curated by Jade Dellinger & Margaret Miller);
New York Rocker, July/August 1978.

Chapter 23
INTERVIEWS:
Jerry Casale, interview by *Melody Maker*, Nov. 25, 1978;
Rod Firestone, interview by David Giffels, June 2001;
Harvey Gold, interview by David Giffels, Sept. 3, 2002;
Mark Mothersbaugh, interview by David Giffels, August, 1996;
Mark Mothersbaugh, interview by "E.K." for RocknRollreporter.com, 1996;
Mark Mothersbaugh, interview by David Giffels, July 18, 1997;
Mark Mothersbaugh, interview by *Seconds Magazine*, Issue 5001, 2000;
Mark Mothersbaugh interview by Michael Pilmer, April 26, 2001;
Mark Mothersbaugh, uncredited 1978 interview in Devo Print Collection;
Nick Nicholis, interview by David Giffels, June 1999;
Bobbie Watson, e-mail interview by Jade Dellinger, Sept. 27, 2001.
OTHER SOURCES:
Jerry Casale, "Drooling For Dollars," from the laserdisc *DEVO: The Complete Truth About De-Evolution*, Voyager, 1993;
Robert Christgau, "A Real New Wave Rolls Out of Ohio," Village Voice, April 17, 1978;
Clinton Heylin, From *The Velvets to the Voidoids: A Pre-Punk History for a Post-Punk World* (NY: Penguin Books, 1993);
New York Rocker, July/August 1978.
Terry Southern, Terry Southern, Richard Branson, Simon Draper and Ken Berry, *Virgin: A History of Virgin Records*, (London, United Kingdom: Virgin Books, 1996).

Chapter 24
INTERVIEWS:
Ed Barger, e-mail interview by Jade Dellinger, April 4, 2002;
Jerry Casale, interview by *Melody Maker*, Nov. 25, 1978;

Are We Not Men?

Jerry Casale, telephone interview by Jade Dellinger, June 11, 2002;
Mark Mothersbaugh, interview by *Live 105 Modern Rock*, reprinted in *Spud Magazine*, 1988;
Dave Reymann, e-mail interview by Jade Dellinger, April 5, 2002;
Dave Reymann, e-mail interview by Jade Dellinger, April 6, 2002.

OTHER SOURCES:
David Downing, *Neil Young: The Man and his Music* (NY: Da Capo Press, 1994);
Human Highway (videotape), Shakey Pictures, 1982;
Jimmy McDonough, *SHAKEY: Neil Young's Biography* (NY: Random House, 2002);
Alexis Petridis, *Neil Young* (NY: Thunder's Mouth Press, 2000);
Rolling Stone, Feb. 8, 1979.

Chapter 25
INTERVIEWS:
Ed Barger, e-mail interview by Jade Dellinger, Dec. 9, 2001;
Richard Blocher, telephone interview by Jade Dellinger, Oct. 8, 2001;
Jerry Casale, interview by Melody Maker, Feb. 25, 1978;
Jerry Casale, interview by Melody Maker, Nov. 25, 1978;
Jerry Casale, interview by David Giffels, July 18, 1997;
Jerry Casale, interview by *On Tour* (PBS, Sunshine TV/KCET, Los Angeles), Aug. 1997;
Jerry Casale, address to PROMAX & BDA Conference in Chicago, 1997;
Devo, interview by *Search & Destroy No. 8*, 1978;
Bob Lewis, e-mail interview by Jade Dellinger, Sept. 28, 2001;
Susan Massaro Aylward, e-mail interview by Jade Dellinger, Sept. 17, 2001;
Susan Massaro Aylward, e-mail interview by Jade Dellinger, Sept. 21, 2001;
Susan Massaro Aylward, e-mail interview by Jade Dellinger, Sept. 28, 2001;
Susan Massaro Aylward, e-mail interview by Jade Dellinger, Oct. 10, 2001;
Mark Mothersbaugh, videotaped interview by Dan Bailey;
Debbie Smith, e-mail interview by Jade Dellinger, Oct. 7, 2001.

OTHER SOURCES:
Cincinnati Post, "Chi Chi grips it, whips it: Album cover a weird footnote," Sept. 5, 2002;
DEVO: The Complete Truth About De-Evolution (laserdisc), Voyager, 1993;
Michael Shore, *The Rolling Stone Book of Rock Video* (N.Y.: Rolling Stone Press, 1984).

Chapter 26
INTERVIEWS:
Ed Barger, e-mail interview by Jade Dellinger, Dec. 4, 2001;
Jerry Casale, interview by INKnineteen, May 2000;
Jerry Casale, interview by Wil Forbis of Acid Logic, 2000;
Jerry Casale, interview by the New Times of Palm Beach, (date unknown);
Bennett "Bud" Horowitz, e-mail interview by Jade Dellinger, May 8, 2002;
Bennett "Bud" Horowitz, e-mail interview by Jade Dellinger, May 10, 2002;
Bob Lewis, e-mail interview by Jade Dellinger, Sept. 30, 2001;
Bob Lewis, e-mail interview by Jade Dellinger, April 3, 2002;
Bob Mothersbaugh, interview by Paul Provenza for checkout.com, 2001;
Robert L. Mothersbaugh, Sr., telephone interview by Jade Dellinger, July 26, 2000;
Alan Myers, telephone interview by Jade Dellinger, Jan. 24, 2001.

OTHER SOURCES:
Creem Magazine, Dec. 1978;
Michael Shore, *The Rolling Stone Book of Rock Video* (N.Y.: Rolling Stone Press, 1984);
James Stark, *PUNK '77: An Inside Look at the San Francisco Rock n' Roll Scene, 1977* (San Francisco, CA: Stark Grafix, 1992);
Barbara Jo (Bobbie) Watson deposition taken on June 15, 1979 in the U.S. District Court Northern District of Ohio Eastern Division case between Robert Lewis, Plaintiff –vs– Gerald V. Casale, et al, Defendants.

Chapter 27
INTERVIEWS:
Ed Barger, e-mail interview by Jade Dellinger, Dec. 13, 2001;
Devo, uncredited transcript of ca. 1978 interview by "Puddie and Liz," found in the files of Festival East Concerts, Inc. in Buffalo; Bob Lewis, interview by Rob Warmowski, (c.1996, Posted online at http://www.geocities.com/SunsetStrip/8539/bobL.html);
Alan Mothersbaugh, interview by David Giffels, Oct. 14, 2002;
Jim Mothersbaugh, interview by David Giffels, Sept. 4, 2002;
Mark Mothersbaugh, interview by David Menconi for the Raleigh News & Observer, Sept. 3, 2002.

OTHER SOURCES:
Booji Boy (a.k.a. Mark Mothersbaugh), *My Struggle*, (Cleveland: NEO Rubber Band, 1978);
Creem Magazine, Dec. 1978;
Steve Love and David Giffels, *Wheels of Fortune: The Story of Rubber in Akron*, (Akron: University of Akron Press, 1998);
Jim Mothersbaugh, address to DEVOtional Fan Convention, Cleveland, 2001 (transcript);
DEVO: The Complete Truth About De-Evolution, (laserdisc), Voyager, 1993;
Rolling Stone, No. 279.

Chapter 28
INTERVIEWS:
Ed Barger, e-mail interview by Jade Dellinger, Dec. 1, 2001;
Ed Barger, e-mail interview by Jade Dellinger, Dec. 8, 2001;
Ed Barger, e-mail interview by Jade Dellinger, Dec. 9, 2001;
Ed Barger, e-mail interview by Jade Dellinger, May 17, 2002;
Bennett "Bud" Horowitz, e-mail interview by Jade Dellinger, May 8, 2002;
Billy Zoom, e-mail interview by Jade Dellinger, May 16, 2002.

OTHER SOURCES:
Akron Beacon Journal files;
Akron Compilation, (LP), Stiff Records, 1978;
Bowling Balls From Hell, (LP), Clone Records, 1980;
Bob Lewis, Dec. 1979 letter to Ed and Jenny Dorn;
Robert Mothersbaugh, Sr., address to DEVOtional Fan Convention, Cleveland, 2001 (transcript).

Chapter 29
INTERVIEWS:
David Allen, email interview, Oct. 2001;
Ed Barger, e-mail interview by Jade Dellinger, Dec. 1, 2001;
Ed Barger, e-mail interview by Jade Dellinger, Dec. 6, 2001;
Ed Barger, e-mail interview by Jade Dellinger, Dec. 8, 2001;
Beck, interview by *Vanity Fair*, Oct. 10, 2001;
Jerry Casale, interview by Sharisse Zeff for *Upbeat*, Aug., 1980;
Jerry Casale, interview by the *Boston Globe*, 1981;
Jerry Casale, online audio interview for the Experience Music Project's special exhibition "(Un)common Objects," 2002;
Susan Schmidt Horning, e-mail interview by Jade Dellinger, Nov. 9, 2001;
Gary Jackett, telephone interview by Jade Dellinger, Jan. 18, 2001;
Gary Jackett, telephone interview by Jade Dellinger, Feb. 2,

2001;
Dennis Keeley, e-mail interview by Jade Dellinger, Oct. 7, 2001;
Bob Lewis, e-mail interview by Jade Dellinger, Apr. 1, 2002;
Bob Mothersbaugh, interview by Paul Provenza for checkout.com, 2001;
Mark Mothersbaugh, interview by *Record Review*, Dec. 1980;
Mark Mothersbaugh, The Anti-Gravity Interview for The Sci-Fi Channel, Aug. 19, 1996;
Debbie Smith, e-mail interview by Jade Dellinger, Oct. 7, 2001;
Bobbie Watson, e-mail interview by Jade Dellinger, Sept. 27, 2001.
OTHER SOURCES:
Devo, *Freedom of Choice*, (LP) Warner Brothers, 1980;
Erich Fromm, *Escape From Freedom*, (NY: Holt, Rinehart And Winston, 1961. 22nd Printing);
Jim Mothersbaugh, address to DEVOtional Fan Convention, Cleveland, 2001 (transcript);
Mark Mothersbaugh, address on Dec. 19, 1999 at University of South Florida Contemporary Art Museum in conjunction with his "Art In The News" project (Curated by Jade Dellinger and Margaret Miller for The Tampa Tribune);
TONTO's Expanding Head Band: TONTO Rides Again CD (Viceroy Records, 1996);
Rolling Stone, No. 279.

Chapter 30
INTERVIEWS:
Ed Barger, e-mail interview by Jade Dellinger, Dec. 6, 2001;
Ralph Carney, e-mail interview by Jade Dellinger, July 20, 2000;
Jerry Casale, interview by the Daily Mirror (Sydney, Australia), 1980;
Jerry Casale, interview by Kristine McKenna for Musician Magazine, Feb. 1982;
Jerry Casale, interview by Thomas Wictor for *In Cold Sweat: Interviews with Really Scary Musicians* (New York, N.Y.: Limelight Editions, 2001);
Gary Jackett, telephone interview by Jade Dellinger, Feb. 2, 2001;
Bob Mothersbaugh, interview by Ernie Mejia and Chris Beyond for nofimagazine.com, 1999;
Bob Mothersbaugh, interview by Paul Provenza for checkout.com, 2001;
Jim Mothersbaugh, interview by David Giffels, Sept. 4, 2002;
Mark Mothersbaugh, interview by *Future Life Magazine* (Issue #23), Dec. 1980;
Mark Mothersbaugh, interview by Kristine McKenna for *Musician Magazine*, Feb. 1982;
Mark Mothersbaugh, interview by TalkCity.com, Aug. 26, 1998;
Mark Mothersbaugh, interview by Victoria Reynolds Harrow for Northern Ohio Live, March 2000;
Mark Mothersbaugh, videotaped interview by "go digital"/online, DATE;
Alan Myers, interview by *Future Life Magazine* (Issue #23), Dec. 1980;
Marty Reymann, telephone interview by Jade Dellinger, Nov. 7, 2001.
OTHER SOURCES:
Eric Boehlert, Salon.com, "Pay for play," March 14, 2001;
Eric Boehlert, Salon.com, "Radio's big bully," April 30, 2001;
Eric Boehlert, Salon.com, "Payola City," July 24, 2001;
Donald Clarke, *The Rise And Fall of Popular Music* (Toronto, ON, Canada McClelland & Stewart 1995);
Stan Cornyn, *Exploding: The Highs, Hits, Hype, Heroes, and Hustlers of the Warner Music Group* (NY: HarperEntertainment, 2002);

Clive Davis, *Clive: Inside the Record Business* (New York, N.Y.: William Morrow, 1975);
DEVO: The Complete Truth About De-Evolution (laserdisc), Voyager, 1993;
The Devo Movie, (13-page treatment), U.S. Copyright Office, Dec. 8, 1980;
David Marsh and James Bernard, *The New Book of Rock Lists: Greatest Songs About Masturbation*, (New York, N.Y.: Fireside/Simon & Schuster, 1994).

Chapter 31
INTERVIEWS:
Jerry Casale, interview by *Rock Video Magazine*, June 1984;
Patrick Cullie, e-mail interview by Jade Dellinger, April 8, 2002;
Bob Lewis, interview by Rob Warmowski, (c.1996, Posted online at http://www.geocities.com/SunsetStrip/8539/bobL.html);
Bob Lewis, e-mail interview by Jade Dellinger, Sept. 25, 2002;
Mark Mothersbaugh, interview by Michael Hurray, March 12, 1977;
Mark Mothersbaugh, interview by *The Sunday Telegraph* (Sydney, Australia), 1981;
Mark Mothersbaugh, interview by *Beautiful World*, Summer, 1985;
Mark Mothersbaugh, interview by TalkCity.com, Aug. 26, 1998;
Mark Mothersbaugh, interview by Victoria Reynolds Harrow for Northern Ohio LIVE, March 2000;
Rod Reisman, telephone interview by Jade Dellinger, Dec. 15, 2000.
OTHER SOURCES:
DEVO: The Complete Truth About De-Evolution (laserdisc), Voyager, 1993;
Devo, *New Traditionalists*, (LP) Warner Brothers., 1981;
Bob Lewis, Feb. 19, 1981 letter to Ed and Jenny Dorn.

Chapter 32
INTERVIEWS:
Jerry Casale, interview by Milt Petty for *Daily News*, Dec. 6, 1981;
Jerry Casale, interview by the *Austin Chronicle*, (clipping - date unknown);
Jerry Casale, uncredited May 20, 1995 videotaped interview;
Lance Hirsch, e-mail interview by Jade Dellinger, Nov. 10, 2001;
Fred Hollins, e-mail interview by Jade Dellinger, Nov. 9, 2001;
Brett Kruse, e-mail interview by Jade Dellinger, Nov. 2001;
Joe Machos, e-mail interview by Jade Dellinger, Aug. 3, 2001;
Mark Mothersbaugh, interview by *The Sunday Telegraph* (Sydney, Australia), 1981;
Mark Mothersbaugh, interview by "Mr. Bonzai" for *Mix Magazine*, Jan. 1995;
Mark Mothersbaugh, interview by Julene Snyder (1/9/01) for Yahoo.com (unedited version), Jan. 9, 2001;
Mark Mothersbaugh, videotaped interview by "go digital"/online;
Alan Myers, telephone interview by Jade Dellinger, Jan. 24, 2001;
Brian Schellenberger, e-mail interview by Jade Dellinger, Aug. 15, 2002.
OTHER SOURCES:
3-Devo concert, (videotape), Black Tie Entertainment, Oct. 31, 1982;
Beaumont Enterprise, Friday December 3, 1982;
William Burroughs, June 4, 1982 letter to Jerry Casale (including the poem "Pick Up Sticks");
DEVO: The Complete Truth About De-Evolution (laserdisc), Voyager, 1993;

Are We Not Men?

Devo, *Oh, No! It's Devo*, Warner Brothers, 1982;
Bob Lewis, Feb. 8, 1983 letter to Ed and Jennifer Dorn.

Chapter 33

INTERVIEWS:
Jerry Casale, interview by *Rock Video Magazine*, June 1984;
Jerry Casale, interview by Dan Bailey, Nov. 21, 1988;
Jerry Casale, interview by Harald Fette for Leeson (Das elektronische Fanzine Konstanz, Nr. 1), April 1995;
Jerry Casale, e-mail interview by Jade Dellinger, June 28, 2001;
Jerry Casale, interview by Thomas Wictor for *In Cold Sweat: Interviews with Really Scary Musicians* (New York, N.Y.: Limelight Editions, 2001);
Bob Lewis, e-mail interview by Jade Dellinger, April 1, 2002;
Bob Lewis, e-mail interview by Jade Dellinger, April 10, 2002;
Jim Mothersbaugh, interview by David Giffels, Sept. 4, 2002;
Alan Myers, telephone interview by Jade Dellinger, Jan. 24, 2001;
Frank Schubert, e-mail interview by Jade Dellinger, Jan. 27, 2001;
Frank Schubert, e-mail interview by Jade Dellinger, Feb. 6, 2001.
OTHER SOURCES:
DEVO: The Complete Truth About De-Evolution (laserdisc), Voyager, 1993;
Bob Lewis, Feb. 8, 1983 letter to Ed and Jennifer Dorn;
Jim McDonough, *SHAKEY: Neil Young's Biography* (NY: Random House, 2002);
Jim Mothersbaugh, address to DEVOtional Fan Convention, Cleveland, 2002;

Mark Mothersbaugh, address at the University of South Florida Contemporary Art Museum in conjunction with "Art in the News" (an art project for The Tampa Tribune, Curated by Jade Dellinger & Margaret Miller);
Robert L. Mothersbaugh, Sr. and Heather Miller, "Mothersbaugh/Miller songbook," U.S. Copyright Office, Washington, D.C., Aug. 10, 1983;
Rolling Stone No. 532.

Chapter 34

INTERVIEWS: Jerry Casale, interview by David Giffels, August, 1996;
Jerry Casale, interview by David Giffels, July 18, 1997;
Jim Mothersbaugh, interview by David Giffels, Sept. 4, 2002;
Mark Mothersbaugh, interview by David Giffels, August, 1996;
Mark Mothersbaugh, interview by David Giffels, July 18, 1997;
Mark Mothersbaugh, interview by Julene Snyder (1/9/01) for Yahoo.com (unedited version), Jan. 9, 2001.
OTHER SOURCES:
Chuck Crisafulli, *Los Angeles Times*, "Devo Evolved," Feb. 4, 1997;
Mark Dawidziak, *The (Cleveland) Plain Dealer*, "New Hats Fit Old-Time New-Wave Duo," July 26, 2002;
DEVO: The Complete Truth About De-Evolution (laserdisc), Voyager, 1993;
Chuck Klosterman, *Akron Beacon Journal*, "Oh, No, It's Not Devo," April 29, 2001;
Mark Mothersbaugh bio, Mutato Muzika;
Mark Mothersbaugh, postcard artworks exhibited at Psychedelic Solution Gallery in New York City, 1989.

Index

Symbols

3-D 11, 195
3-Devo 207

A

Ackroyd, Dan 163, 199
Adult Physiological Studies Center 40
Agora, The 115, 117, 128, 139
Akron 11
American Bandstand 185
Anderson, Ernie 17, 18
Attack of the 50 Foot Woman 18
Autobahn 81
A Hard Day's Night 24

B

Bangs, Lester 169
Barger, Ed 6, 22, 37, 38, 39, 67, 69, 74, 75,
     82, 92, 95, 107, 109, 110, 121, 123,
     125, 127, 128, 130, 133, 136, 143,
     155, 163, 168, 169, 170, 174, 175,
     179, 183, 197, 209, 210, 211, 212,
     213, 214, 215, 216, 217
Barry, Ken 149
Basil, Toni 129, 130, 139
Bates, Jules 4, 6, 180
Bators, Stiv 85, 108, 110, 212, 213
Beatles 9, 24, 26, 67, 89, 95, 120, 148, 164,
     169
Beck 11, 180, 216
Beefheart, Captain 28, 43, 99, 152
Beginning Was the End, The 122
Behemoth, Crocus 103, 105
Belushi, John 163
Bent, Rod 75, 104, 110, 125
Bertholf, Robert 6, 29, 50, 51, 52, 59, 60, 68,
     90, 112, 113, 121, 209, 211, 212
Betrock, Alan 17, 20, 21, 25, 55, 82, 96, 97,
     118, 119, 120, 162, 163, 169, 187
Bewlay Brothers 138
Blackwell, Chris 137, 140, 141
Black Tie Entertainment 196
Blanket Hill 33
Blondie 103, 114, 115, 116, 117, 121, 132,
     134, 158, 169, 214
Booji Boy 21, 37, 65, 74, 76, 78, 79, 81, 83,
     86, 89, 92, 93, 94, 95, 100, 111,
     112, 113, 119, 123, 126, 139, 153,
     154, 155, 156, 158, 161, 164, 184,
     190, 196, 198, 208, 209, 211, 212,

     214, 216
Bowie, David 114, 115, 116, 117, 128, 129,
     134, 135, 136, 138, 144, 148, 149,
     171
Branson, Richard 141, 142, 143, 147, 149,
     150, 215
Bubbi, Jim 43
Bucket Shop 96, 97
Burke, Clem 116
Burroughs, William 193, 194, 197, 217
Butler, Chris 6, 28, 31, 33, 36, 96, 99, 151,
     209, 210, 213
Buzzcocks 148

C

Can 70, 71, 144, 145, 211
Carney, Ralph 6, 98, 99, 176, 198, 213, 217
Casale, Bob *passim*
Casale, Jerry *passim*
Casale, Sherry 60, 121, 122, 123, 124
CBGB's 103, 107, 108
Chelsea Hotel 122, 134
Chinaman 74, 75, 76, 78, 83, 94, 112
Chi Pig 110, 117, 125, 140, 141, 152, 157,
     167, 176, 198
Chosen Few 110
Christgau, Robert 99, 151, 152, 215
Chrome, Cheetah 6, 108, 109, 110, 115, 116,
     119, 123, 213, 214
Clash, The 148
Clic, Buzz 6, 104
Cobra 103
Cobra, King 103, 104, 105, 107, 109
Cohen, Kip 111, 112, 117, 118, 128, 129,
     130, 131
Commuter's Cafeteria 13, 14, 28, 32, 34, 68
Cramps, The 19, 126
Crank It Back, A Play For The Country On Its
     Bicentennia 50
Creeley, Robert 51, 59, 60
Crypt, The 102, 104, 105, 106, 107, 108,
     109, 110, 114, 118, 121, 151, 170
Cullie, Patrick 6, 68, 69, 71, 77, 78, 79, 187,
     210, 211, 212, 217
Cuyahoga Falls 14, 23, 27
Czukay, Holger 144, 145, 215

D

Dada 20, 67
Davey Junior High 17

Are We Not Men?

Davey Tree Company 17
De-evolution 10
Dead Boys 85
DeFrange, Tim 16, 209
Destri, Jimmy 116
Devolution 41, 90
Diamond, Stan 138, 139, 147
Diary of a Nymph 40
Dorn, Edward 6, 29, 50, 51, 52, 59, 63, 67, 71, 72, 77, 78, 79, 90, 175, 186, 210, 211, 212, 213, 216, 217, 218
Dromette, Johnny 6, 125, 135
Drooling for Dollars 150, 151
Dylan, Bob 20, 21, 122, 194, 198, 201

E

Eagles, The 69, 77, 79, 85, 184, 187
Ellison, Harlan 52
Encyclopaedia Britannica 8
Eno, Brian 107, 126, 127, 134, 135, 136, 140, 143, 144, 145, 146, 147, 171, 174, 215
Eric's, Liverpool 148
Exploding Plastic Inevitable 9
Expressionism 20, 28

F

Fidler, Nancy Brown 26
Flossy Bobbit 38, 183
Freeman, Karen 92, 94, 214
Freemon, Peggy 35, 68
Fripp, Robert 126, 127, 134, 135

G

General Boy 23, 92, 94, 158, 163, 203
Ghoulardi 18, 19, 20, 64, 86, 126, 196, 209
Goodyear 20, 90, 102, 103, 104, 137
Gorj 42, 43, 44, 47, 48, 60, 74, 85, 86, 91, 180
Governance Chambers 59, 60, 90, 92, 94, 95
Gregg, Peter 6, 17, 20, 28, 29, 33, 36, 37, 52, 66, 67, 77, 78, 155, 162, 209, 210, 211, 212
Griffin, Dane 38, 39
Guru 144
Guru Guru 144

H

Hall, Cora 43, 44, 46, 72, 75
Harry, Debbie 6, 110, 115, 157, 167, 176, 213, 214, 215, 216, 217
Hendrix, Jimi 65, 122, 200, 201
Hensal, Bruce 6, 36, 68, 81, 210, 211, 212
Hinckley Jnr, John 12, 194, 204, 207
Hoffman, Abbey 52
Hopper, Dennis 154, 155

Horowitz, Bennet (Bud) 161, 216
Huey, Baby 16, 20,
Human Highway 152
Hurray, Michael 114, 186, 209, 214, 217
Hynde, Chrissie 26, 36, 176
Hynde, Terry 26, 36, 49, 176, 215

I

Interior, Lux 19, 126
In the Beginning was the End: The Truth About De-evolution 93
Island of Lost Souls 18
Island Records 6, 18, 20, 63, 64, 91, 137, 138, 140, 148, 203, 206, 211
"I Want to Hold Your Hand" 24

J

Jackett, General 6, 28, 29, 44, 46, 48, 72, 77, 86, 92, 94, 110, 119, 123, 127, 133, 135, 178, 183, 184, 197, 209, 210, 211, 212, 213, 214, 215, 216, 217
James Gang 31
Jarmusch, Jim 19
Jocko-Homo Heavenbound 8
Jones, Brian 13

K

Kent State University 6, 10, 13, 14, 15, 17, 19, 20, 26, 27, 28, 30, 31, 32, 34, 35, 38, 39, 43, 44, 45, 47, 48, 50, 51, 52, 53, 56, 58, 59, 60, 61, 63, 65, 66, 68, 70, 75, 79, 86, 89, 90, 96, 103, 109, 110, 112, 122, 132, 138, 141, 150, 151, 170, 173, 179, 193, 198, 208, 210, 211, 212
Kidney, Bob 48, 49, 50, 65
King Cobra 103
Kiss 10, 11, 16, 101, 122, 161, 174, 177, 211
Kiss Maerth, Oscar 10
Klosterman, Chuck 8, 10, 55, 56, 57, 58, 63, 95, 209, 211, 213, 218
Knebworth 160
Kraftwerk 81, 85, 122, 144, 212
Krause, Allison 10, 31, 34, 72
Krieger-Field studios 68, 69, 70, 107
Kristal, Hilly 107, 118, 126

L

Leary, Timothy 201
Lee Hooker, John 21
Lennon, John 10, 24, 27, 107, 126, 127
Lewis, Bob *passim*
Licitri, Jennifer 6, 40, 75, 86, 92, 112, 155, 157, 210, 212, 213, 214, 215
Lollapalooza 206

M

Macoska, Janet 158
Maglione, Tim 6, 49, 50, 210
Mailer, Norman 52
Mangels, Robert 186
Man Ray 119
Margouleff, Robert 177
Marina 76, 81, 92, 94, 115, 135
Massaro, Susan 6, 90, 94, 102, 114, 116, 134,
    152, 175, 186, 210, 212, 213, 214,
    215, 216
Max's Kansas City 108, 118, 119, 121, 123,
    126, 134
MC5 9
McCartney, Paul 10, 107
McGough, Dale 37, 39, 210
Measles 13, 30, 33, 53
Michener, James 34, 35, 150
MIDI 11, 197
Miller, Jeffrey 31, 33, 215, 217, 218
Mirwin, Cathy "Chatty" 75
Moby 11, 206
Mothersbaugh, Bob *passim*
Mothersbaugh, Jim *passim*
Mothersbaugh, Mark *passim*
Mottram, Eric 5, 28, 30, 44, 46, 210
Mr. Potato Head 21, 22
MTV 37, 114, 129, 189, 190, 191, 193, 199,
    207
Mutato Muzika 204
Myers, Alan 6, 11, 19, 79, 96, 97, 105, 106,
    110, 111, 117, 131, 162, 168, 170,
    183, 192, 194, 201, 213, 214, 216,
    217, 218
Myers, Kate 89, 111, 112, 113
Myers, Pete 18
My Struggle 21, 37

N

National Guard 33
Neu 144
Nicholis, Nick 6, 103, 125, 151, 152, 176,
    213, 214, 215
Nirvana 11, 206
Nixon, President Richard 31, 113, 159
Numbers Band, The 36, 48, 49, 50, 55, 65,
    66, 96, 97, 103, 151, 171, 176, 207

O

oblique strategies 136, 145
Ohio National Guardsmen 10

P

Pee-wee's Playhouse 202
Pere Ubu 19, 103, 104, 105, 106, 108, 110,
    111, 121, 151, 176, 185, 203, 207
Pink Flamingos 79
Plank, Conrad 144
Plastic Reality 9, 12
Poison Ivy 126
Pootman 43
Pop, Iggy 9, 108, 114, 115, 116, 117, 128,
    129, 130, 131, 134
Powell, Mike 38, 39, 85
Pretenders, The 26
Public Image 177

R

"Rainy Day Women #12 & 35" 21
Rage Against the Machine 11
Ramones, The 103, 121, 122, 169
Ratzer, Mary Margaret 23
Readers Vs. Breeders 44, 47, 48
Reisman, Rod 6, 16, 49, 52, 54, 56, 209, 210,
    211, 217
Reymann, Marty 6, 37, 38, 39, 56, 67, 69,
    73, 84, 109, 110, 133, 155, 197, 210,
    211, 212, 214, 216, 217
Richards, Keith 78, 126
Rivers, Johnny 8
Roberts, Elliot 156, 161, 162, 169, 170
Robinson, Dave 15, 137, 140
Rocket from the Tombs 103, 108, 113, 205
Rodriguez, Chi Chi 112, 159, 160, 165
Rolling Stones 20
Rollins, Henry 11, 206
Roosevelt High School 20
Rotten, Johnny 9, 142, 143, 153, 177
Rubber City Rebels 104, 176
Rugrats 204, 205
Rust Never Sleeps 153, 161

S

Sampedro, Frank (Poncho) 156
Satisfied Mind, The 21
Saturday Night Live 9, 162, 167, 170
Sat Sun Mat 26
Saul, Murray 83, 163
Scheuer, Sandra 33
School for Sex 40
Schroeder, William 33
Scott, Ken 171
Sextet Devo 53, 54, 55, 56, 57, 58, 59, 71,
    90, 100
Sex Pistols 9, 148
Shadduck, Dr B.H. 8, 57, 58, 209, 211, 213
Shelly's Book Bar 70, 71, 72, 86, 211, 212
Sigmond RJ 113
Sire Records 108, 116, 124, 151

Smith, Patti 103, 121, 169
Soundgarden 11, 205, 206
Southern, Terry 150
Springsteen, Bruce 82, 170, 201
St. Patrick's 16
Stark, James 131, 215, 216
Starwood, The 128, 129, 130, 132, 133, 151
Statler, Chuck 48, 89, 92, 93, 114, 156
Stein, Chris 115, 116, 151, 158, 214
Sternberg, Liam 152, 198
Stiff Records 60, 70, 126, 137, 139, 144, 146, 147, 152, 159, 176, 216
Stockwell, Dean 129, 132, 152, 154
Stringer, Sherry Lynn 10, 60, 62, 63, 65, 122, 177, 211
Suicide 38, 103, 126
Sullivan, Ed 9, 24, 26, 120, 148, 164
Sun Ra 81
Swanson, Charles 29, 35, 180

T

Talking Heads 116
Thomas, David 6, 19, 103, 105, 106, 111, 125, 176, 209, 210, 213, 217, 218
Tin Huey 28, 96, 99, 103, 105, 125, 151, 176, 198, 207
Topanga Canyon 77, 78

U

Ubu 19
U Got Me Bugged 24, 25

V

Valentine, Gary 115, 116, 117
Velvet Underground 152
Verlaine, Tom 103
Virgin Records 141, 142, 146, 147, 149, 150, 215

W

"Whip It" 11, 12
Waddington, Linda 93, 141, 142, 157
Waitresses, The 28, 96, 99, 151, 176, 198, 199
Wall of Voodoo 196
Walsh, Joe 13, 30, 31, 35, 36, 65, 68, 69, 77, 78, 80, 81, 187
Warhol, Andy 73, 113, 124, 149, 204
Warner Bros 99, 138, 140, 141, 143, 146, 147, 149, 150, 151, 156, 159, 160, 162, 167, 169, 170, 181, 182, 184, 187, 198, 201, 202
Waters, John 79
Watson, Bobbie 6, 14, 28, 35, 36, 43, 69, 75, 76, 92, 93, 94, 102, 123, 127, 152, 158, 175, 186, 197, 209, 210, 211, 212, 213, 214, 215, 216, 217
WEA 199
Webb, Bob 33
Weber, Fred 6, 33, 52, 53, 54, 56, 68, 71, 100, 210, 211
Weizyncki, Ronnie 24
Welch, Ward 75, 103, 104, 107, 213
Wells, H.G. 18, 63, 64
Whitaker, William 6, 150, 162, 186, 197
WHORE 32
Willard, Fred 9, 163, 164
Wonder Woman 41

Y

Yardbirds 17, 20, 28
Young, Neil 11, 132, 152, 153, 154, 155, 156, 161, 162, 171, 194, 216

Z

Zabrucky, John 48
Zappa, Frank 126, 187, 213

SAF, HELTER SKELTER and FIREFLY Books

Mail Order

All SAF, Helter Skelter and Firefly titles are available by mail order from the world-famous Helter Skelter bookshop.

Telephone: +44 (0)20 7836 1151
or Fax: +44 (0)20 7240 9880

Office hours: Mon-Fri 10:00am – 7:00pm,
Sat: 10:00am – 6:00pm, Sun: closed.

**Helter Skelter Bookshop, 4 Denmark Street, London,
WC2H 8LL, United Kingdom.**

If you are in London come and visit us and browse the titles in person.

Order Online

For the latest on SAF and Firefly titles, or to order books online,
check the SAF website.

You can also browse the full range of rock, pop, jazz and experimental music books we have available, as well as keeping up with our latest releases and special offers.

You can also contact us via email, and request a catalogue.

**info@safpublishing.com
www.safpublishing.com**

saf publishing

www.safpublishing.com